Movement
Training
for the
Stage and
Screen

Movement

THE ORGANIC

Training

CONNECTION

for the

BETWEEN MIND,

Stage and

SPIRIT, AND BODY

Screen

*Jean
Sabatine*

BACK STAGE BOOKS
An imprint of Watson-Guptill Publications, New York

All photographs taken and processed by Thomas Hoebbel.
Line drawings in the exercise chapter by Nan Cadorin.
The subject in Chapter 3 is Deidra Johnson.
The subjects in Chapter 5 are Brian Coughlin, Rob Harrison,
Angela Parks, and Deidra Johnson.

Quotations on pp. 17, 42, 43, 46, and 47 are taken from:
Webster's *New World Dictionary of the American Language.*
Second College Edition. Cleveland and New York: William Collins
and New World Publishing Company, Inc., 1972 and 1970.

Senior Editor: Paul Lukas
Associate Editor: Dale Ramsey
Designer: Areta Buk
Production Manager: Ellen Greene

First published in 1995 in the United States
by Back Stage Books,
an imprint of Watson-Guptill Publications,
a division of BPI Communications, Inc.,
1515 Broadway, New York, NY 10036

Library of Congress Cataloging-in-Publication Data

Sabatine, Jean.
    Movement training for the stage and screen : the organic
  connection between mind, spirit, and body / Jean Sabatine.
        p. cm.
    Includes bibliographical references and index.
    ISBN 0-8230-7712-8
    1. Movement (Acting) I. Title.
  PN2071.M6S22 1995
  792'.028—dc20   95-13387
                                                           CIP

Manufactured in the United States of America

1 2 3 4 5 / 99 98 97 96 95

To my students—with your talent, commitment, and creativity, I have discovered and perfected the tools that I use to help those who have come after you. Your collaboration with me would never have been possible, however, without the support and education provided by my parents, Frank and Jane Sabatine. To them I owe all the honor and dedication that I have received from you.

ACKNOWLEDGMENTS

I would like to thank God for his guidance and inspiration. I gratefully acknowledge the contributions of Keith Grant, David Hodge, Joe Dunham, Vinnie Mancarella, and, especially, Laura Sheehan, for her encouragement and belief in me and the concepts in this book, as well as her contributions and assistance in the preparation of the manuscript.

I also thank Deidra Johnson for her precise and beautiful work in the exercise sections. Brian Coughlin, Rob Harrison, Deidra Johnson, and Angela Parks all deserve thanks and praise for their creative essence work in Chapter 5.

Last, but not least, I want to thank my dear and loyal friend and companion, Champ, for all his patience and unconditional love.

Contents

Foreword

Movement Training for the Stage and Screen: The Organic Connection Between Mind, Spirit, and Body fills an aching void in actor training literature and movement writing in general. This book unites the three primary disciplines of acting—acting, voice, and movement.

Two essential and often elusive actor's tools are focus and energy. No artist can improve the quality of his or her craft if these basics are lacking. Prof. Sabatine provides a streamlined process whereby actors can improve their physical, mental, and spiritual concentration, which in turn breeds energy. There is a rationale to the system here devised, and the author skillfully guides the artist through each section of study. It is a pathway to clarity and energy. Once the route is learned, the actor need never be lost again on the journey to bettering his or her craft.

In Prof. Sabatine's successfully developed theory, an actor is provided with a step-by-step process for dealing with characterizations in a variety of theatrical images and character types. While many of the techniques described in this book will be familiar to the trained actor, its chief strength is that it builds upon the foundation of established theory and techniques in movement, incorporates fresh approaches, and presents the combined material in a logical and systematic manner.

The theory was developed during Prof. Sabatine's extensive experience as a teacher of movement and choreography. The resulting text is distinguished by a clarity of thought and precision of language that makes the work readable and accessible—even to the reader who is not dance-oriented. This new and expanded book includes some beautiful and pertinent work on the relationship of the mind, spirit, and body, including easy exercises to illustrate the way you can incorporate the Triadic Approach into your professional and personal life.

Prof. Sabatine is an expert at blazing a clear trail. She is well trained in presenting her material in a cogent, organized fashion. The text provides numerous photographs to aid in comprehension of the exercises and theory. Appendixes provide a course syllabus along with suggestions for planning individual classes and aid in selecting music to match the tempo of the exercises.

While *Movement Training for the Stage and Screen* will be an excellent workbook for teachers and students of movement, its appeal will go beyond that segment of the artistic world. For example, directors might use one exploration or series of explorations outlined in this book to suit their own specific cast situation. I have no doubt that Prof. Sabatine's book will be warmly welcomed. A generous and thoughtful gift she has given us—a work that will be hungrily consumed by academic and nonacademic theater/movement professionals everywhere—this book will nourish, satisfy, and delight its readers for years to come.

David Young
Graduate research professor
University of Florida

Preface

Since the initial publication of this book under the title *The Actor's Image,* my theory has evolved to include the element of the human spirit, the thread that completes the triad of the organic connection of mind, spirit, and body. These three translate into thought, emotion, and action, respectively. While most actors are aware of their emotional, spiritual selves, few cultivate their spirituality, or higher self, in developing their acting technique. And yet, the spirit is the cornerstone of our humanity. This revised and expanded edition, *Movement Training for the Stage and Screen,* includes exercises that involve the chakras, affirmations, and breathing techniques to utilize the human spirit.

Part of the purpose of this book is to impress on the theater audience at large the value and intricate nature of the area we loosely call "stage movement." More important, however, are the many techniques and concepts useful to a wide body of theater artists and valuable to anyone confronted with the problems of bringing a performance text alive—or, for that matter, of creating a performance text.

In many instances in this text, the title "director" could easily be substituted for my term "instructor"; and while I am specifically referring to *movement* instructors, *acting* teachers can just as easily use (and many have used) many of the techniques I describe. My interest is in maintaining a consistent focus. I feel the need to express the concepts within a *movement* framework. So, although actors, directors, and acting teachers may not be directly addressed in what follows, it is not because their interests or needs are not encouraged or met, but that there is a far greater need and interest that I mean to arouse.

Movement training for actors is very little understood, and I believe that as a discipline it is separate from any other. As an authority on both dance *and* stage movement, I find that while my classes in dance and stage movement benefit from my expertise in both, they remain separate disciplines and must always be treated as distinct from each other. This is why I ardently proclaim that training in mime, stage combat, or T'ai Chi is *not* movement training for the actor. They are all excellent and fascinating *supplementary* disciplines—as are ballet, modern dance, jazz dance, and the Alexander Technique. A student of acting or a stage movement teacher can only benefit from supplementary training in these areas, but a person trained solely in any of these is neither a teacher of movement training for actors nor an actor with adequate training in movement for the craft of acting.

Although I have studied and taught extensively in period dance and movement of various styles, this discipline is another entirely separate one which, although it may be extremely beneficial to the actor, fails to deal with many realities of the actor's task. My students in period movement classes benefit from being trained in my actors' movement theory, for actors then understand that the movement of a given period was natural and appropriate (that is, organic), because of people's dress, life-style and social expectations. But actors specifically and solely trained in period movement will be lacking in many other awarenesses that they will need in the modern theater, even if they only want to do "Shakespeare in the Park" for the rest of their lives.

Among the chapters that follow, Chapter 3, "Exercises," is especially important. It provides the reader with a physical warm-up, complete with illustrations necessary to understand each one, descriptions of what each is designed to do, how each relates to the whole warm-up process, and cautionary notes on how to know when an exercise is helpful or harmful to your body. Appendix 4 contains a list of musical selections that will help in the enjoyment of the exercise; it also provides a framework for judging the optimum tempo of each exercise.

Chapter 4, "Explorations," deals with a step-by-step process of exploration of various techniques for body awareness and movement that leads the reader to an understanding of the relationship of mind, spirit, and body. The value of each exploration is enhanced by its relative placement, the explanations of the lessons to be learned from each, and the detailed discussion of the elements involved.

Finally, in "Applications," Chapter 5, the reader gains a technique for using the explorations in a systematic approach to characterization. Although the worth of this work can be determined only by its practice, interested parties have an opportunity to observe how it is accomplished through photographs of actual applications.

The final chapter is contributed by practicing professionals. It concerns their use of the theory in three distinct theatrical experiences.

Thus, for the movement specialist and nonspecialist alike, this book provides a guide to a developmental approach of teaching movement *for actors*. For the actor and director, it provides many tools that can be used in the development of character, either independently or collaboratively. For all theater specialists, it provides a concise theory and philosophy that produces a conceptual and practical basis for analyzing what we see—and helping us all to see better.

¹ *Introduction*

Ideally, an actor should be thoroughly trained to deal effectively with the three areas essential to performance on the stage: acting, voice, and movement. Because of the practical improbability of finding a towering talent capable of mastering and teaching all three demanding disciplines, the current philosophy in theater today is to find specialists in each discipline and to weld them into a single effective team, a coherent unit that can provide instruction to developing talent in their separate, mutually supportive areas.

This is a wise and seemingly inescapable philosophy and one to which most theater artists willingly subscribe. Each of the three disciplines incorporates a wide body of material within it and requires the utmost care and many years of intense training and experience to produce a capable teacher. Common sense dictates the employment of three highly trained specialists who are aware of the requirements and basic application of the other areas involved to train professionals.

Practically speaking, however, many training situations fall short of this ideal, and in those cases certain ad hoc adjustments can be made to approach the conservatory ideal. A single theater generalist or specialist in one of the three primary areas may be asked to train actors in areas outside his or her specialization; when this happens, the only recourse is to fall back on the literature pertaining to those areas.

Although there are many lucid, well-written texts to aid one in the acting and voice areas, there are none to equal them in the movement field. This text is designed in part to fill that void. It deals with the practical problems of conditioning the mind, spirit and body of actors and uses a broad base of proven techniques. It is not a survey of various specialized approaches but a cohesive body of practical material focused and directed by easily comprehended theory.

There has been no generally accepted model of a course in basic movement for actors, though there are many exceptional movement specialists in theater today. This text is designed to provide the first (and, we hope, not the last) words specifically aimed at dealing effectively with the need for well-formulated goals, theory, and techniques. If at least some agreement can be made among a majority of specialists concerning the essentials of a basic movement course for actors, perhaps a more lucid body of literature will evolve to discuss the relevance, relationship, and application of the many movement specialties. When should an actor study the movement and dance of certain periods and styles? Are gymnastics, weight lifting, or circus skills important to an actor's development? How can aikido, karate, or T'ai Chi be helpful or harmful to an actor? How much should an actor know? How do we best approach the further physical development of an actor?

We cannot even begin to ask those questions until specialists in movement training agree on the desired nature of a basic course. This book aims to provide the essential framework of such a course, combined with a healthy body of material necessary to give it substance and coherence.

Before we begin to discuss movement for actors' training, we must address several questions. The first is: What disciplines are *not* movement for actors' training?

Mime, ballet, modern dance, jazz dance, T'ai Chi, karate, physical education, rolfing, fencing, stage combat, approaches like the Alexander technique and effort-shape, and so on—none of these disciplines is movement for actors' training in and of themselves. However, almost all the pioneers and teachers of movement for actors began as students of these disciplines because there were no programs targeted for actors; they had to find elements of training that they could adapt to the task. It is certainly beneficial for an actors' movement instructor to be exposed to as many of these disciplines as possible. But to think that any one of them in its pure form would be for the training of actors would be a mistake.

I investigated various approaches to movement training for actors years ago, on a research grant from Pennsylvania State University. I interviewed some of the leading pioneers in the field and discovered that almost all had begun teaching one of the aforementioned disciplines, only to realize that more was needed. For instance, Joseph Gifford, a movement teacher of many years who had been a student of Charles Weidman, Doris Humphrey, and José Limon, said, "I taught what I knew, dance technique; thank God, after the first year I turned around and looked at what I was doing and realized it was absolutely the wrong thing. I was tying them in knots. They weren't going to be dancers." Sophia Delza, author of *T'ai Chi Chuan* (New York: David McKay, 1961) pointed out that T'ai Chi has nothing to do with any performing art. One does T'ai Chi for one's self; it is a ritual art that can be experienced only by the performer.

Robert Moulton, a former student of Louis Horst, Martha Graham, and José Limon who took his early inspiration from Rudolf Laban noted, "At that time [the late 1950s and early '60s] it was thought by many in the theater that if an actor was really *feeling* inside, all the edges were supposed to take care of themselves. You would speak right, and move right." But he discovered that this didn't happen and concluded that the purely internal focus was not enough. He also discovered that though the Graham technique worked well for *Oedipus Rex,* it didn't work for contemporary drama. So he, like the others, had to modify his concepts and approach to the actor. Aileen Crow started as an actress and progressively studied dance, effort-shape, and Alexander technique. Although she has taught classes in each of these disciplines, her movement theory and practice consists of a blend of all three.

Of course, any of these disciplines may be a firm *foundation* for the training of the actor. Louis Campbell studied many disciplines, including Lecoq mime, and although he believes in that discipline as a learning base, he readily admits that mime has its own private gestural language that cannot fully cope with intention or character. It is, as he points out, an excellent discipline for "precise articulation of physical form" and offers a superb process for freeing an individual. However, he is eclectic, and he bonds the many separate philosophies and disciplines to his area of interest. Finally, Robert Benedetti, who is not really a movement specialist but rather a director, writer, and teacher, has authored an important book in the field. In *The Actor at Work* (Englewood Cliffs, N. J.: Prentice-Hall, 1970), his basis for total acting training is the belief that such training can come about only in an atmosphere that supplies study in voice and movement as well as in acting. I agree with Benedetti's philosophy; therefore, the best environment for training is a conservatory in which the acting, speech, and movement instructors function as a unit, working with a group of actors. They become a team of skilled and knowledgeable specialists who understand each other's task and orchestrate their individual efforts toward the common goal.

Once one agrees with this approach, it should become evident that if a movement teacher is unfamiliar with the common goal, then he or she is unprepared to teach movement for the actor. The movement teacher must be familiar with the disciplines of voice and acting in order to design a training program of maximum effectiveness.

That is the key to this discussion: The *design* is ultimately more important than the approach.

Again, there are any number of possible foundations to build on, but the ultimate end form must reflect the same concern, which is not to produce a dancer, mime, or gymnast, but an actor. And this requires more than just physically conditioning the actor.

This leads us to a second question: What *is* movement training for actors? It is simply a program divided into training sessions designed to provide actors with awareness and control of their physical, mental, and emotional instruments. Moreover, it should be designed so that actors acquire techniques to deal with their own alignment, tension, breathing, movement, and acting problems once the trainer is no longer there. In short, it is a program of instruction that guides talented, intelligent, and sensitive individuals to become versatile experts in their own stage movement. Ultimately, then, the goal of actors' movement training should be the integration of mind, spirit, and body. The whole organism must be in harmony with itself so that it is ready for interaction. Important lessons that the actor must learn are:

- Proper alignment
- Proper balance of tension and relaxation
- Proper breathing techniques

- Proper warm-up techniques
- An understanding of his or her own body
- An understanding of his or her personal mannerisms
- An understanding of basic movement elements (space, time, energy, and so on)
- An understanding of the mind-spirit-body connection (thought-feeling-action, so that movements are motivated)
- The ability to work with others
- The ability to work alone
- Independence from constant monitoring
- The ability to apply acting technique to movement problems
- The ability to apply movement technique to acting problems
- The art of centering
- Proper use of internal and external techniques

The basic requirements to become a specialist in movement training for actors are as follows:

- Sound acting training
- A thorough understanding of the body and body mechanics through anatomy and kinesiology courses
- Experience in verbal and nonverbal improvisation (that is, exploration) techniques
- Sound dance and movement training
- Experience in teaching acting and movement specialist courses
- An understanding of the voice

Other specialized techniques or disciplines are supplementary and of secondary importance.

Instructors in the field of movement for actors need, furthermore, to specify their personal theories or philosophies of movement. They need to set a goal for their actors' training. (What do I want actors to acquire from this?)

Finally, each instructor must develop a plan of action—a system that he or she will use to guide an actor's growth in understanding and ability. Of course, teachers in any field must have clear objectives and systems to guide both themselves and their students, yet all too often I have found it necessary to state this fact in regard to movement for actors. Such a plan of action is my main goal in this book, the product of years of research and practical experience with actors and directors in various professional training programs based on a conservatory approach—that is, the theory has evolved through lessons learned from the actors and their teachers in classes designed to teach movement for the stage *along with* acting and voice classes.

Generally speaking, the acting model I have used for the development of my approach to movement training is the Method, a realistic approach to acting in which the actor strives for close, personal identification with the role. The

Method is more dependent on the *inner* realities of the actor and the character than on the purely external manipulations of the voice and body. I call the *external* approach simply "technique," as it is defined by the dictionary:

> **technique** (tek nēk´), *n.* 1. the method of procedure (with reference to practical or formal details), or way of using basic skills, in rendering an artistic work or carrying out a scientific or mechanical operation. 2. the degree of expertness in following this (*a pianist with good technique but poor expression*) [my italics]

I believe that both approaches are valid. Indeed, no actor functions without his or her own particular blend of the Method and technique. Therefore, any movement training for the actor must appeal to both the internal and external aspects of acting in order to give each individual the opportunity to find this balance.

It was with this belief that I initially approached the task of creating a coherent and practical method of movement training for the actor. Having now worked in theater and dance for many years, I retain that belief. My training and experience have led me to the inescapable conclusion that the mind, spirit, and body are a single entity. Although this statement is hardly novel, I am constantly surprised by the number of people in theater and dance who overlook, ignore, and even scoff at this notion.

The evidence of a profound connection between the mind and body is overwhelming. Unless an individual willfully prohibits it, the body invariably reflects the emotions and intentions of the mind. When the body is strong or when it is tired, ill, or weak, the mind responds accordingly. The interaction of mind, spirit, and body is universally present in humankind. This is not to say that the connection among them is an invariable constant whereby we can eliminate all consideration of individuality. On the contrary, the interaction of mind, spirit, and body, though universal, is as different from person to person as are the potentialities of these elements.

Not every person will react in exactly the same manner to a given situation. When cornered, one person will cower in fear, another will turn in anger and fight, and another will merely stand dumbfounded. I do not propose that understanding even crudely the connection among mind, spirit, and body can help us to predict an individual's reaction to a given situation. Neither is prediction a desirable or important consideration. I do propose, however, that whatever the individual's reaction is mentally or emotionally, it will manifest itself physically.

The concept of having an initial thought (mind), then a feeling or emotion (spirit), and finally doing an action (body), is known as *the organic connection*. This is the single most important concept in my theory of stage movement. It is central to all the material contained in this book, and the guide by which I teach. From this single unifying concept come all the other guiding principles of my work.

One of these principles is individual development and choice. Because each of us as individuals possesses a unique set of strengths and weaknesses, I find it important to stress to my students that each person will progress at a different rate. One will find exercises that speak more profoundly to him or her than others and must choose to use what works for him, not worrying whether someone else is getting further ahead or dropping behind. Some will show excellent strength and endurance but poor coordination, others patience and elasticity but low energy and drive. The most important message here is that training or performing is not a competition. Unless a healthier attitude is encouraged, students tend to compare themselves, and actors are no exception. A competitive attitude may well be appropriate and desirable for track and field, but it is unsuitable and even destructive to the pursuit of self-awareness and self-development. Therefore, I stress that it is not success that is important (that is, a good-looking or flashy product) but personal commitment to developing self-awareness, understanding, and even compassion. It is important that each person realize that he or she is on a personal quest and that the exercises and explorations I provide are not tests but opportunities. Each actor must understand that there will be exercises that others can accomplish more easily, or that one lesson will seem to offer little while another will bestow a chance to soar—yet none of these potential occurrences is related to victory or defeat. They are the very essence of self-discovery—the first step toward development as an artist.

It is an ideal toward which we are working, not a product. This is a process of self-discovery directed toward grasping more completely the connection between mind, spirit, and body. This three-way connection is the key to organic acting, where the inner realities of the character are revealed through *actions*. The goal is always ahead of the actor. He (or she) should try to make maximum use of his body, intellect, experience, and sensitivity in creating and performing a role for the purpose of communicating the playwright's and/or director's idea. The actor must develop a certain discipline that will allow him the proper blend of control and freedom to help in the achievement of the ideal.

Many experienced actors are concerned with this ideal, and many, thoroughly dedicated to it, have evolved their own method of achieving that ideal. These fortunate few have found what works for them, and they continue to seek it when necessary, when the challenge is great enough. They must be admired for it. George C. Scott supposedly never had an acting or movement class in his life, and yet his characters consistently have a vibrant, believable, and understandable life. For the less fortunate, less experienced majority who have not found the necessary formula, a single startling exception such as Scott does not mean that all actors should abandon training entirely. On the contrary, a majority of professional actors repeatedly come back to the classroom in a continuing effort to perfect their craft.

Beginning as well as advanced actors must be aided in the continuing development of their own discipline. The system of movement training I have developed is not the panacea or *the* special formula that guarantees success in producing great actors, and ultimately the individual is responsible for creating his or her own method. But mine is a consistent and cohesive one that has guided me, my students, and other instructors in organizing the intellectual and kinetic development of the actor; it should provide actors with the discipline and tools with which to function in their craft.

The succeeding chapters present a system of movement exercises, explorations, and practical applications I call the *Triad*. It is designed to awaken actors to certain truths about themselves and their relationships to the world in order to maximize their potential as actors. The actor's job is to seek the blend of internal and external methods that she (or he) will use in working, to find the balance of mind, spirit, and body. The actor is responsible for her choices and must determine how she best functions, finding the keys that operate the many mechanisms within the self, which only the actor can know.

The instructor's job is to provide an atmosphere of trust, cooperation, direction, and focus to the group, and to be sensitive and responsive to the actors' needs. Discipline must be balanced with creative flexibility in order to allow maximum growth.

In the following program, the series of exercises are to be performed daily as part of a mind-spirit-body warm-up, combined with explorations of the body and other basic elements of stage movement (breathing, alignment, gesture, use of music, and numerous other elements). Because each group of actors is unique, alternate exercises and explorations have been suggested, and creative additions of individual instructors and the intelligent adjustment of class routine and the order of topics are encouraged. Although I have placed the exercises and explorations in the order I try to follow, I vary this orderly progression when it becomes necessary and sometimes find this extremely beneficial. However, I do advise reserving the Abstractions or Essence Theory until the indicated time period. It is an extremely difficult concept to communicate or assimilate, and if actors haven't been prepared by the necessary physical, spiritual, and mental conditioning, Essence Theory could prove to be useless (and even a great frustration) to them.

This is a complex and misunderstood field, one that is still just developing. Future trainers of actors will refine the work present experts have begun, so it is important that they receive as much support and the best and most thorough information on training techniques and theories that have been discovered to date.

² *The Program*

The program I have designed is a system of movement training that assures a
solid, broad starting point, maintains a developmental progression, and extends
actors' abilities in such a way that they can confidently expect to be effective
in a host of acting styles. Where beneficial I have drawn on certain of the special
approaches to movement (giving credit to those approaches or their originators
where possible and appropriate), but I have sought to maintain the sense of
a firm central technique, a nucleus of skills from which forays into peripheral
studies can be launched without the risk of losing one's place. This central
technique is guided by my philosophy of movement training—discussed in the
introductory chapter—which I will return to periodically throughout this text.
Because this is such an important concept, I shall restate it here.

The Organic Nature of Acting

I believe in the organic nature of the craft of acting. Put simply, this means
that the actors' only tools of expression are their voice and body guided by their
mental and emotional attributes. The relationship between the actor's physical,
mental, and emotional nature forms the organic entity. Therefore, any training
must seek to strengthen this organic entity. In this nuclear design, then, the
actor's experiences are allowed to grow in a controlled way. Awareness of, and
confidence in, his or her technique and organic development should similarly
grow. Finally, the actor's range of acting and movement accomplishments will
follow suit.

ASSUMPTIONS

There are certain assumptions underlying this program for movement study.

Movement Specialists. First, the instructor must be someone trained in both
acting and dance/movement, a movement specialist. A person whose training
lacks this combination—an acting coach in a crash workshop on modern dance,
a dance instructor invited in and handed some acting texts, or a fitness expert
who is cautioned, "No, not calisthenics exactly. . . ."—such a person is likely
to bring about some painful experiences for all concerned. No matter how
much dance, mime, fencing, or gymnastics one may have mastered, there is
no substitute for direct and deep training in acting and dance/movement.

A Foundation to Build Upon. Second, this program assumes that the goal for acting is an ability to perform in all kinds of theater styles: naturalistic, period, romantic, children's, nonverbal, everything from comedy of manners to Theater of Cruelty. This program is designed to establish a foundation. It cannot promise complete polish in any style, but the actor will be ready to pursue specific areas of study that directly relate to any specific theatrical mode that is interesting or compelling.

A Conservatory Situation. Third, this program was devised for a conservatory-type teaching situation, where stage movement study is integrated with the work of the acting and voice coach. It is assumed that frequently this program will be most effective in a series of in-class projects and productions that are the product of a three-way collaboration. Stage movement study has its well-marked dimensions, and the study succeeds best when students are pursuing separate but related voice and acting training.

One Year's Work. Last, the basic course will presumably fit about a one-year course of study (see the sample course syllabus in the Appendix).

The Three Stages of Training: The Triad

On these assumptions rests a three-stage developmental progression: exercises, explorations, and applications.

EXERCISES

In the initial phase, engaging in exercises, the actor is devoted to the fundamental tasks of aligning (internally as well as externally) and conditioning the body, making it strong, sensitive, and supple. Like any educational process, this work involves adding and subtracting: on the one hand, adding endurance, suppleness, awareness, economy, precision in moving, and related qualities, while, on the other hand, simultaneously stripping away physical quirks and customary bad movement habits, including awkward gestures, excess tension, a casual carriage, and, most basic, an inexpressive immobility.

In effect, the task of the movement specialist is to try to restore the actor's body to the natural grace and ease it was intended to have, before the body developed all the tics, slouches, slumps, and masks that social experience imposes on bone, tissue, and the emotions. The goal is a finely tuned instrument capable of expression and articulation of nuances clearly and effectively.

EXPLORATIONS

The second and more advanced exploration phase takes the actor further along the path toward a renovation. As he (or she) continues to condition himself through a daily discipline of a growing number and variety of exercises, he will be led to explore his inner nature and his relationship to the world—including other people. Through a series of studies on space, time, energy, gesture, and emotion, the actor learns what happens as he moves through space and how he orients himself to the world according to time. He discovers what people do as they *kinetically* relate to other people and the world.

In the exploration phase, the actor learns everything he can about how the body can be expressive and how the world looks when seen in terms of movement. He will be able to see how the physical environment affects his internal reality. Through experimentation he will learn that by adjusting his physical mechanism he can affect his inner being and, conversely, that through simple applications of the Method (sense-memory, emotional recall, and so forth) he can affect the way his body moves. This is the most exciting and valuable point in the development of an actor in stage movement training. At this point the actor begins to understand his organic nature—the connection between his mind, spirit, and body. The actor's knowledge of how the mind, spirit, and body mutually affect each other is the key to further development, and the ultimate goal of this phase of study. Then, with this knowledge, he can concentrate on applying his learning by adjusting inner and outer realities in order to effect a different persona—that is, a character.

APPLICATIONS

In the applications phase, I have tried to arrange a sequence of movement studies that will bring the actor to the doorstep of characterization. The actor must continue to acquire a range of movement experiences, building a large movement vocabulary to employ in the various applications he will bring to specific acting assignments. I try to give assignments of an increasingly specific nature, based on the student's accumulated expertise as it applies to characterization. For instance, at an early stage, I will ask students to find (through observation or intuition) the walk of a character they are familiar with or are working on, and the major intentions of their characters in a given scene. The aim here is to focus the student's mind, spirit, and body on the problem of applying a growing awareness and skills to a particular project. From the broad base of experimentation and exploration, he then moves into the more specific area of applications.

Collaboration with Acting Training

It is in the applications phase that the movement specialist may seem to run afoul of an acting coach or a director who feels that characterization falls solely into his or her province. In the acting coach's view, movement is primarily toning up the body, or fencing, and the like—harmless but useless space analysis. This is a political issue in the profession, and there is no sense in proposing a pat way to deal with the situation, which can be thorny.

I simply emphasize that just because I attempt to deal specifically with characterization does not mean that I believe movement classes *alone* can effectively eliminate the need for sound acting training. Nothing can! Rather, my endeavors reflect a belief that we should use every tool available to assist the actor in the development of his total mechanism. My goal in approaching characterization through movement is to provide another possible avenue of growth. I envision a collaborative and supportive effort designed to aid the acting coach. The point is not to engage in polemics, but to perceive the full spectrum of movement training, from subtracting physical deficits to physicalizing a stage character.

³ *Exercises*

Suppose you are an actor who desires to master the physical mechanism, your body. How do you approach this project? The key is the desire; all else follows from that. If you want to develop your own body fully, you must first envision its full potential, which is invariably greater than you may first imagine. You must aim toward an ideal version of yourself. Otherwise, all your early aches, strains, and awkwardness will lead you to believe that your old, familiar physical shell is intractable, hopeless stuff. Yet you must discover your own limitations, unique gifts, and liabilities. One person's body may be loose and limber and thus adept at stretches; another's may be tightly strung, giving it a compactness and a surer balance. Unless you (as each actor must) clearly understand that your body is unique, you may be led into a false security or despair by looking around and comparing apparent progress. Your work may become ineffective. You should think realistically, remain mindful of unalterable peculiarities in your physical makeup, and strive to become aware of all you can do to attain your ideal. Most importantly, you must maintain your desire and belief and expect that you can and will master your physical mechanism.

Fundamentals

The movement instructor can be particularly helpful in this regard. In some cases the instructor may have to devise special exercises for individuals to do to overcome certain blocks and to keep them in pace with the rest of the class. Later, exercises may be devised and adapted to specific acting projects. Most useful to the actor initially, however, is a reliable set of fundamental exercises and principles.

This chapter contains a set of exercises I have found effective, which are organized by a few principles I believe essential for movement training for the actor. The key idea to keep in mind in developing an exercise regimen—both in teaching it and in performing it—is to follow the proper developmental sequence. Basic principles must come before elaborate or complex movements and concepts; slow, easy work must come before the fast and arduous. Most important of all, do not try stretches in the early part of a day's work. Many dancers and fitness buffs go right onto the floor, first thing, and tug vigorously at their muscles to get themselves stretched out. Not only is this hazardous, it is foolish, because the opposite result, stiff and sore muscles, most frequently occurs. Preventing injury while stretching and strengthening the body depends on executing a proper sequence of exercises. So, for example, pliés should precede jumping and stretches. The other important aspects of this work are to continually encourage proper breath and energy flows, the economical use of force, and the proper blend of tension and relaxation.

I have exercises that deal with these concepts specifically, but because of their universal nature, the actor's attention should be focused on them repeatedly—especially on breathing. Proper breathing helps counteract excessive tension and encourages proper energy flow, which allows for a more economical application of force. On the other hand, improper breathing technique (such as holding the breath, or shallow chest breathing) *promotes* needless tension that inhibits energy flow and prevents economical application of force. Above all else, I continually remind actors to breathe.

The technique offered here is but a sample of the kind of basic and sequential work needed, and any instructor will need and wish to supply many more exercises. With assistance, the actor will find those exercises that are most helpful for specific problems. The basic objectives of this stage of training are to eliminate needless tension, achieve a functional balance between tension and relaxation, align the body (internal and external), condition the body for strength, flexibility, and endurance, and develop awareness of the body (that is, a kinesthetic sense). These objectives should provide the principles for selecting all further exercises.

Most of the following exercises can be done to music. I find that music aids my control of the exercises, freeing me from setting and maintaining a tempo, thus allowing me to aid the actors' efforts. It also gives them a certain guide by which to move. I have found that rock and commercial jazz are best to use because they provide a heavy bass beat. For each exercise that can be done to music I have suggested more than one piece of music (see Appendix 4) to indicate what I consider appropriate tempos once actors have learned the movements. In teaching any exercise, of course, it is best to work at a slow, easy tempo without music. The instructor may use a hand drum or simply call out the counts and movements.

Relaxation: The First Step

The first step in the developmental process is to awaken an awareness of the body's natural, relaxed condition. This is a difficult first step, given that tension is our society's bogeyman.

Tension is a neurological phenomenon that combines mental strain and taut muscles. Most tension is unnecessary. Anxiety is an incompetent way of coping with most feared eventualities, and overly tense muscles are useless even in physical emergencies. (Stanislavsky's often cited proof of the inefficiency of tension involved asking an actor to perform mental acts while under the strain of hefting a piano.)

Excess tension cripples our emotional, mental, and physical well-being, yet all movement, acts, and thoughts proceed from some amount of tension. The trick is to recover the capacity for relaxation while retaining the right amount of tension. This is the body's natural, relaxed condition.

To help the actor to an awareness of this state, the first step should be to provide the experience of utter and complete relaxation. Then the actor is ready to progress to the next level of kinesthetic awareness. In the following exercises this level of complete relaxation should be attained as a prelude to any exertions. This state should be returned to periodically between short periods during which the attention is focused on movement, in order to further reinforce the sensation of total relaxation. In these exercises the movement teacher should also try to bring a sense of calm to the actors' minds, so that this feeling of well-being will aid the relaxation process. The instructor's voice can be artfully directed to modulate the audible atmosphere with slow rhythms and a soft tone. Soft music and soft lighting also help.

ATTENTION FLOW

Lying flat on the floor with face up and eyes closed, follow these steps.

1. Place the arms, slightly bent, alongside the body and allow them to fall into a comfortable position. Extend the legs straight out along the floor away from your head and allow them to roll outward in a comfortable position.
2. Release all the joints in your body. Breathe gently in and out, in and out.
3. Feel your body sag into itself. Feel the gravity. It is a heavy, distinct force, but it is not oppressive.
4. Breathe gently in and out from the diaphragm: Take a deep breath in for your body. Exhale all the physical tension. Next, take a deep breath in for your mind. Exhale all the negativity from your mind. Take a deep breath in for your spirit. Exhale and feel your spirit rejuvenated and refreshed. Take a deep breath. Exhale and feel the integration of the mind, spirit, and body. Know that you are ready.

Once the actor assumes this position the instructor guides him (or her) into an utterly relaxed state by moving his attention over the entire body, part by part, successively directing awareness from one extremity to its opposite. Like a gentle wave or tide, the instructor's voice sweeps the actor's attention across his body, briefly pausing over minute portions of the body, in a regular and calming advance. At each brief pause the actor becomes specifically conscious of a muscle that he then loosens and drains of its tension. Continuing from the steps above, then:

5. Feel the muscle of your right calf. Feel how it rests lightly on the floor, where it touches the floor, and how the floor forces the top part of the muscle to bulge up and out. Feel the tension in your calf dissolve and drain slowly into the floor.

6. Now move your attention up the leg, through the stomach, chest, neck, face, to your forehead. Feel the tension in the muscles there. Release those muscles. Imagine your forehead broadening and opening. Let the eyebrows fall naturally into place and then the scalp. Feel the tension lift from your forehead as your entire head begins to feel that it is freely floating in space.

Special focus should be placed on the centers of tension: forehead, neck, and shoulders most commonly. Ideally, once the actor passes his attention through his body in this manner, he will discover how many parts of his body he never notices, in which he now feels absolutely limp. In practice it may require some concerted effort to break down an actor's resistance to relaxing. Panic in the face of this process of collapsing is uncommon, but it is not a strange anxiety either, and its effects may resemble the proverbial description of what it feels like to die a slow death. (One also thinks of Socrates narrating the progress of the hemlock in his body.) But anxiety should dissipate as the actor begins to savor the lively sensations of relaxation and the awareness of how much of his body he can actually feel. Most actors greatly enjoy the exercise. It is helpful to return frequently the actor's attention to his breathing, to fix his mind upon his breathing only. The routine should be done every day for several weeks, in much the same way every time, so that the actor can gain the ability to talk himself into this condition when alone. Mastering self-induced relaxation is the first step to mastering tension, but it is not an easy or quick process.

RELAXATION AND TENSION

Complete relaxation collapses the body into a sort of rag doll. Complete tension hardens the body to stone. To move at all and to move economically we must strike a balance. To reach the proper balance we must start with the limp body, so we can slowly escalate the degrees of tension we generate for precise tasks and movements and closely observe and remember the degrees of tension we are employing for each task. This is all the principle of economy of movement entails, avoiding the use of too much tension to perform a muscular task.

Tense and Relax. Begin this exercise lying on the floor in a completely relaxed position. Then, tense individual muscles one at a time and observe how each one is working. Next make combinations of tensed muscles, building up to a totally tensed body. Finally, return to a complete collapse. This process should be a dramatic one, and if the effects are not obvious enough or sufficiently gradual, repeat the exercise.

Tense and Relax Sequentially. This exercise is conducted exactly as the previous exercise, except that the tension/relaxation process is executed sequentially from the toes through the legs, buttocks, stomach, fingers, hands, arms, chest, neck, and head. Especially important in this version is that once a body part has been fully tensed and relaxed, no tension should be allowed to creep back into it— especially while the focus is on another body part.

1. Begin the process in the toes on one side of the body. Tense and relax only the toes on that side, then include the foot, then add the calf, then the thigh. When the entire leg is tensed, it should be lifted slightly (no more than an inch) from the floor. When it is relaxed, the leg should fall suddenly to the floor as all the tension rushes out of it. Feel the warm, tingling sensation—the complete weightlessness of the entire leg free from all tension. Feel the relief of complete relaxation of just this leg.

2. Repeat this entire process on the other side of your body, remembering to maintain the relaxation in the other leg. Move the tension/relaxation process through your toes, then the foot, the calf, and your entire leg. Once again, feel the sensations of complete relaxation now in both legs.

3. Tense just the buttocks and hold the tension while you ensure that the legs are still relaxed. Then relax your buttocks. You should be free from all tension from just below your waist down.

4. Continue with the stomach and then move to the fingers on one side of your body. Proceed with the tension/relaxation in your hand, forearm, then your full arm, raising it off the floor slightly. Then, let it collapse back to the floor. Repeat the process on the other arm.

5. Now just the chest muscles—no stomach or shoulder tension—then just the shoulders. Lift them off the floor, then push them up around the ears and back down. Now let your shoulders collapse, and take some time to feel the relaxation below your neck. Pass your attention through every part. You should feel as though you are floating slightly off the floor.

6. Proceed with this process to the neck, then to the facial mask. Work your face in many different ways. Open your mouth and eyes wide and raise your eyebrows—then move all the muscles in the other direction so that the eyes squint, teeth clamp, and lips stretch wide. (Be careful that tension is only in the face.) Now work your facial mask every way you can. Then relax. Concentrate on your breathing.

7. Finally, tense every muscle in your body and hold it several seconds while you tighten each muscle. Now collapse. Let all tension drain out of you into the floor. Feel it drain away as you fill yourself with warm fresh air, breathing in and out, in and out.

Minimum Effort Movement. Carefully employing the minimum amount of muscular tension needed, do the following steps:

1. Extend your arms and legs out to their natural limits and slowly return them to your sides.

2. Next, move from this supine position to a seated position.

3. Then move to a standing position through the same process.

4. Try a walk using only the tension or positive energy you need to walk around the room.

Throughout these and similar routines involving elementary movements, the actor will be surprised by how little tension is actually required to move the body about. He should also be pleased with his resisting the temptation to apply a sudden surge of tension to execute a simple movement. Simple movements are self-instructive, and it is only by the actor's observing and inwardly making kinetic notes that the lessons of tension and relaxation can take hold. Once he has a firm sense of controlling tension in simple moves, he should progress to more complicated and arduous feats. His pleasure should grow as he finds that he almost never needs a great amount of tension, even in apparently arduous tasks. This should promote confidence and, in the long run, inspire creativity.

Relaxation and tension work is most essential in the early part of training, when the actor is still not all that familiar with his body. I find it useful, however, to return to this work from time to time, especially when actors are experiencing stress and tension during, say, a difficult and challenging assignment. If, at a later stage in his training, an actor becomes nervous or frustrated about an exploration, and thus tense, this is the ideal time to return to relaxation work. Once again, the technique for discovering the minimum amount of tension needed is directed toward the actor's being able to work on himself at will and knowing when it is necessary to employ, such as in classic instances of stage fright. In the applications unit I will discuss a theory of characterization based on gradations of tension (see Chapter 5).

Posture and Alignment: The Second Step

My thinking and theory have evolved in this area to include the element of spirit as the thread or through-line in the organic connection of mind, spirit, and body. These elements translate into thought, emotion, and action. Therefore, I find it essential that we not only align our gross anatomy (our physiology or bodies) but our subtle anatomy, or *chakras,* so that we are aligned internally as well as externally, the whole organism in harmony with itself. I will go into depth on the process later in the text. It is a lengthy process, and I recommend waiting until the end of the exercise session to do it.

The term *posture* is frequently misread to imply a frozen, inert stance, a carriage somehow stilted and formal, as opposed to natural standing and walking. This is unfortunate, especially as it creates confusion between what is "natural" and what is habit. Perhaps the point is obvious, but it cannot be overstated. What typically happens to our bodies in growing up is that we acquire distorted and misshapen ways of holding ourselves. We slouch, sink, slump, shuffle, and laze awkwardly and inefficiently upon our frame, generally undermining the very purposes of our skeletal structure. Unless our attention is forcefully called to what is slovenly in our posture or carriage, we remain blissfully ignorant of our distortions. Often, too, we grow fond of our favorite distortions, thinking this little slump is "really me." It requires some tact to point out otherwise to the actor.

Frequently, it is these distortions of posture and alignment that thwart clean, expressive, and effective movement. For an actor, such problems spell professional disaster; she (or he) drags her misshapen image into every characterization, and unless her bad habits happen to be extraordinarily captivating, leading into a career as a popular single-type character actor, her professional opportunities are likely to be severely limited. One caveat, and it is the opposite danger: The actor who has so perfected her posture, alignment, and carriage that she has become enchanted with her new self may drag it beautifully into every characterization, making all roles resemble one off-duty ballet dancer. Stage movement works to recover the lost potential for natural development, an ideal posture, and a free carriage. So the goal is to leave our more glaring idiosyncrasies behind in the wings and, with this mastery, to recreate any other posture called for in a characterization. So let us start with the immobile body and readjust the frame, which all our muscles—the agents of movements—have shaped.

The logical point at which to begin, then, is the simple, natural erect stance. Metaphorically speaking, the body consists of layers of blocks that must be stacked directly on one another, in a state of equipoise, over one's center of gravity. If one block is out of line, the whole stack is distorted, balance weakens, and movement grows awkward. For example, slouched shoulders cause the pelvis to tilt, which in turn thrusts the buttocks out. The tiers of a body so arranged are precariously stacked and are ill-fitted to move well. Walking in such a posture produces a heavy amble and places undue stress on the heels.

There are several alignment problems that occur fairly frequently. Some of these are problems quite apart from the usual "cool slump" many teenagers and younger adults endeavor to affect. These are, in many cases, irreparable problems caused by the original construction of the spinal column in the individual, by an accident or illness, or by habitual and continual poor posture. In each case involving a problem with the spine, great care must be taken not to try to force it to do anything that may cause further problems. In every instance the person involved will either know beforehand or must be encouraged to seek medical assistance to discover the cause of any great discomfort involved in any exercise. A ruptured or herniated disc, scoliosis (lateral curvature of the spine), a fused spine or fused vertebrae, and a foreshortened spine are but a few of the many problems that may be present, or that may even be misrepresented or misunderstood by the sufferer. These are serious problems that only qualified medical specialists can deal with. Fortunately, pain is a fairly accurate measure and should be heeded in all cases.

Most problems, however, are not so severe. The most common problems arise when weight is placed either too far forward or too far back (Fig. 3-1); shoulders and head are slung forward (Fig. 3-2) or back (Fig. 3-3); shoulders are tensed up toward the ears (more common with men, Fig. 3-4); the pelvis tilts (more common with women, Fig. 3-5); or in some combination of these problems. In order to solve these problems, the major goal for both actors and teachers is to correct their self-image (the internal personal image of what is good posture) and corresponding kinetic feeling of proper posture.

NATURAL ALIGNMENT

Let us straighten out this crumbling structure, starting from the foundation.

1. First, position the feet about six to eight inches apart and parallel (or just slightly turned out if exact parallel is too difficult to manage). The weight of the body should plummet straight down, directly to the center of the space between the feet, a little in front of the ankles.
2. The knees should be released, not locked back or bent.

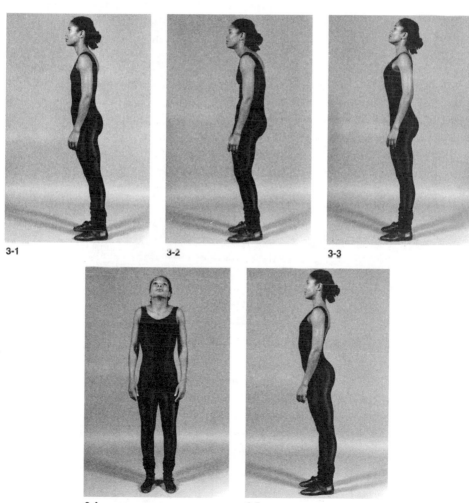

3-1   3-2   3-3

3-4   3-5

3. Lengthen the abdominal muscles by pulling across and up, as if you were trying to flatten your stomach. (The stomach muscles are designed to hold your internal organs in position. By pulling up vertically and laterally with your stomach muscles, you simultaneously lose the unnecessary bulge, align your spine, and place your internal organs in their proper position.) This will put the pelvis directly in line with the center of the body, rather than tipped back.

4. The rib cage must be in a neutral position (that is, not tilted forward, back, left or right) and the chest lifted, as though there were a string attached to the exact center of your sternum and someone were pulling evenly and gently at a 60-degree angle toward the ceiling. This will broaden and lengthen the back.

5. Shoulders are dropped and relaxed, neither pressed forward nor pulled back.

6. The back should be left open by not pinching the shoulders together.

7. The head is lifted and balanced squarely on top of the spine, and the neck is relaxed.

Now we have each level of the body properly stacked and aligned, with the center strongly built for all subsequent moving (Fig. 3-6 and 3-7). At first it may seem peculiar to try this alignment, but it is the natural alignment, and the balance, poise, and readiness it confers will soon seem very natural.

I have found this statement from the Alexander Technique to be most useful in aiding external alignment: "Let my neck be free to let my head go forward and up to let my back lengthen and widen." Actors should accompany this mental dialogue with mental images of the words actually having the effect they describe. For example, as they say, "Let my neck be free," they can imagine they have freed it, repeating this until they really feel the freedom in the neck. Similar visual images ca be used for each part of the statement. (Visual images are wonderful and powerful tools.)

Alignment Test 1. The correct aligned position (that is, natural alignment) must be tested. Here is a sample test:

1. From what you feel is the natural standing position, start with the head and slowly curve the spine down until the hands touch the floor. Your feet remain flat, and as you move into the final collapsed position, the back is smoothly curved, the legs are slightly bent, and the hands are grazing the floor (Figures 3-11, 3-10, 3-9, and 3-8, in that order).

2. To resume the standing posture, straighten the knees and slowly reassemble a lengthened back by successively straightening the spine to an erect line (Fig. 3-8 through 3-11).

If in the collapse and ascent you can hold your balance, the posture passes this test as "natural." If not, start over.

3-6

3-7

3-8

3-9

3-10

3-11

Alignment Test 2. This is the best method I know for determining whether you are aligned properly. It may be added to the end of Alignment Test 1 or it may be done independently. I use it at vital transition points during the exercises and explorations.

1. From a natural standing position press up through your feet onto your toes (by "press up," I mean to apply a steady, even flow of energy so that you rise up slowly, rather than pop up quickly) (Fig. 3-12).
2. Now come back down slowly through your feet until you are again in your natural standing position.

3-12

If you had to shift your weight forward or back to press up onto your toes, your alignment is off. If you had to shift your weight forward to rise, you probably stand with your weight too far back on your heels (and you are not prepared to move). If you had to shift your weight back, you are probably either bent forward at the waist or you are leaning too far forward with your weight too much on your toes (and you have little capability for anything but forward movement).

There are other tests one can apply, but the main stress is on learning to assume proper alignment at will until it becomes second nature.

Breathing: The Foundation

Breathing is the foundation of our organic nature. The breath brings us life-sustaining oxygen and carries away the carbon dioxide produced by our bodies. Breathing provides fuel for the mind and body. A secondary function of breathing is to provide the vocal cords with the means for operation. Fortunately, the same rules that govern the efficient production of vocal expression also govern the efficient production of all other muscular efforts. These rules include the proper blend of tension and relaxation, proper alignment, and harmonizing of breath patterns with patterns of movement.

This does not mean that I wish to eliminate the need for the speech or voice teacher. On the contrary, my work in breath control is designed to help establish positive habit patterns in this collaborative process of actor training, in an area where our responsibilities happily overlap. I say "happily" because one cannot overestimate the benefit of good breath control for the actor. And the more positive reinforcement an actor has, the more likely she (or he) will quickly establish good habits and proper control through consistent attention to correct technique.

Going back to the beginning, the guiding principle involved in my methodology is the development of the actor as an organic entity. This first involves developing his organic awareness of himself. Each step so far has led in this direction, but breathing provides the best key and most obvious example of the organic connections among the mind, spirit, and body.

Breathing is largely an automatic function which the novice actor takes for granted, but it can also be consciously controlled. In approaching the breathing mechanism, then, we are subtly exploring the rudiments, or more accurately, the basics of the organic connections of the mind, spirit, and body. The act of breathing unites them in a natural, free-flowing process. It is a process taken for granted and performed without any conscious awareness. Because breathing is the foundation of our being, it is an excellent starting point in our study of movement training. This exercise combines a simple physiological act with mental and spiritual images, resulting in an organic connection.

BREATHING TO CLEANSE THE SYSTEM

Ideally, this exercise should be done as part of the warm-up and then incorporated into the daily routine. For maximum effect, it should be done three times a day— once in the morning, once at midday, and once before going to sleep. In a classroom situation, this exercise should be done after constructive rest (p. 72), while the actors are still lying in a neutral, supine position. It can be included, however, at any point that actors need to cleanse their physical, mental, and spiritual selves.

At first, the exercise will focus solely on the physical act of breathing. Once this technique is mastered, you will include vocal "affirmations."

1. Assume a neutral position on the floor. Clear the mind of all clutter and the body of all tension.
2. Breathe gently in and out from the diaphragm. Take a deep breath in for your body. Exhale all the physical tension.

   Take a deep breath in for your mind. Exhale all the negativity from your mind.

   Take a deep breath in for your spirit. Exhale and feel your spirit rejuvenated and refreshed.

Take a deep breath. Exhale and feel the integration of the mind, spirit, and body. Know that you are ready. (From here on we will refer back to this exercise.)

3. Begin by inhaling deeply from the diaphragm as you count to 2. Hold this breath for eight counts and exhale for four. As you exhale, feel the toxic substances washing out of your system.

Repeat this process for a total of ten breaths. Once the actors have mastered the process and are breathing without strain, build the ratio up to a 4-16-8 count. When this is accomplished, add the following affirmations:

1. Inhale to a count of 4, breathing in "Energy." Hold this thought and breathe for a count of 16, exhaling all "Lethargy" for a count of 8.
2. Inhale four counts of "Sunshine." Let this image permeate your being for a count of 16. Exhale all your "Negativity" for a count of 8.
3. Breathe in four counts of "Enthusiasm." Hold for a count of 16, letting go of "Boredom and Dreariness" for a count of 8.
4. Inhale four counts of "Love." Feel love radiate from your heart through your being for a count of 16. Rid yourself of all "Hate" by exhaling for a count of 8.
5. Inhale for four counts, breathing in "Faith." Believe in yourself and the universe for a count of 16, and exhale all "Doubt" for a count of 8.
6. On four counts, breathe in "Hope." Hold this idea for 16 breaths and exhale "Despair" for 8.
7. Breathe in "Courage" for 4 counts. Hold this idea for a count of 16, exhaling all "Fear" for a count of 8.
8. Inhale "Light" for four counts, holding this breath for 16, ridding yourself of "Darkness" for 8.
9. For four counts, breathe in "Dreams" and feel them flow through your being for 16. Then flush out "Nightmares" for 8.
10. Affirm your "Self" by breathing in for four counts and sensing your personal power. Hold this for 16 and let go of any negative residue for 8.
11. Finally, breathe in and say, "I am getting better and better in every way, in all parts of my being—mind, spirit, and body)." Exhale and feel harmony with your being.

These are some examples of affirmations to be used with this exercise. As the instructor leads actors through this exercise, he or she is free to create other affirmations in accordance with their needs.

In some exercises approached for the first time, it is beneficial to focus the attention on the principles before beginning. Breathing is one area in which it is not beneficial to forewarn the actors that they will be focusing attention on this aspect of themselves because a self-conscious conceptualizing behavior will interfere with autonomic functioning. So in the first approach to breathing it is wise to use a misdirection technique, so that the actors will find themselves observing their unconscious breathing, and then move slowly into control without being self-conscious.

Walk, Run, Walk, Lie Down. Any number of misdirection ploys will do. Here's one that is very effective.

1. Walk in a leisurely manner around the room. Just relax and enjoy yourself.
2. Now pick up the pace as though you had somewhere to go. Walk faster and faster. Observe how this affects you.
3. Now you're in a hurry. Take it into a jog; then into a run. Take your time at each level to feel what this does to you.
4. Run as fast as you safely can. Notice how this affects you.
5. Slow quickly back to a walk.
6. Slow the walk until you stop.
7. Now gently lie down on your back and get your breath back. Notice how you feel. Close your eyes.
8. Feel the difference of this position. Feel the air rushing in and out of your body.
9. Relax. Continue to get your breath.
10. Relax down into the floor, as if it were a big feather bed. Feel how comfortable this is. You should be breathing naturally now, easily and slowly, in and out, in and out.
11. Feel how pleasant it is just to relax, just breathing slowly, naturally, in and out.
12. Move your attention, keeping your eyes closed, just allowing your mind to focus on your breathing. Feel how your diaphragm expands as you breathe in and how your chest lifts slightly at the very end of the breath. Breathe in and out, in and out.
13. Feel how your chest and diaphragm collapse gently and easily as you breathe out.
14. This is your natural breath rhythm. This is how you were meant to breathe.
15. Try not to change or control your breath pattern as you observe the mechanics of how you breathe naturally. (This will force the actors to apply will power and control their breathing, which is part of the lesson. Although they won't know it, they are now on the threshold between subconscious and conscious control, which is the point I have been working toward. The attempt not to engage in conscious control while consciously observing the phenomenon is a vital and intricate organic movement.)
16. Although it is difficult not to affect your breath pattern as you focus on it, try to relax.
17. Try to continue breathing naturally, keeping your breath pattern even, smooth, and uninterrupted as you rise to a standing position. Find the easiest, most economical way to get to your feet, and once you've started, keep going, so that you don't interrupt your breath pattern.

18. Once you're up, try to feel the same relaxed sensation of your breathing on the floor, with your diaphragm expanding and collapsing as the air comes in and out, in and out.
19. Now find your alignment.
20. Open your eyes, press up through your feet.
21. Relax. Shake out the tension.
22. Let's talk about it.

When the actors get to step 21 in this exercise and are told to relax and shake out the tension (signaling an end to the exercise), generally there is a huge intake of breath and a long sigh as they all release conscious control of their breathing apparatus. Usually, someone will point out that it became very difficult to continue abstaining from conscious control of breathing once the attention was focused on it, and that controlling breathing in an effort to keep it natural was even more difficult.

This is normal. When an actor is told "focus your attention on your breathing, but don't interfere with it," for the first time, it is like saying, "don't think about yawning," or "don't think about alligators." Eventually this will be an easy exercise. It should become almost automatic; that is, the actor should be able to find a natural breathing pattern as a means to eliminate tension and provide proper breath support for speaking and movement. This ability should become as effortless as finding one's balance on a bicycle, and just as with bicycle-riding skill, the actor will never need to relearn it once the skill is truly mastered.

The Mechanics of Motion. Let us observe breathing mechanics and their relation to movement.

1. First lie on your back on the floor, arms at your sides, and relax.
2. Inhale and note the tension as the filling lungs lift first the diaphragm, and then the chest, outward.
3. Now exhale and feel the relaxing muscles as the torso collapses.
4. Repeat the process several times and exaggerate slightly the tension and relaxation, inhaling more deeply and exhaling more fully.
5. Next, experiment in breathing in a variety of tempos: quick, irregular, at long intervals, and so on.
6. Try mating tempos with simple movements done in the same tempo. (For instance, lift the arms slowly over the head as you inhale in a matching tempo. Bring the arms down sharply as you exhale in a rush of air.)
7. Now stand and, starting at step 2, go through each step until you are mating movement with breath. Note the similarities and the differences in the effort needed to achieve the proper breathing technique at each stage of the process between the standing and lying positions.

This second exercise can be repeated intermittently rather than daily. On each return to it, the actors should move more freely and adventurously as their breath control, muscular coordination, and strength improve. This exercise reveals that, to a greater or lesser extent, all exercises are breathing exercises, since one should always seek to mate breathing with movement. So, especially in the early training process, continual reinforcement of proper breathing with movement is essential.

Once again, this kind of experimenting is aimed at learning to phrase inhalation and exhalation rhythms to a sequence of exertions. This is an area of constant concern for me as a movement teacher, and I return repeatedly to this thesis while leading all other exercises, because proper breath control is essential to all the actor's endeavors. As you can see, this is an area where the voice and movement specialists must have overlapping responsibility because the actor needs to master breathing more efficiently. Basically, the actor needs to work on deep breathing, opening the lungs to their full capacity. Mere gulps of air, our ordinary skimpy intake, do not admit a sufficient amount of oxygen into our system for a smooth and flowing performance in the strenuous work ahead.

Spine Studies

As a special way to heighten awareness of the actor's natural posture and the importance of the skeletal frame, especially regarding breathing, let us briefly examine the spine. The spine is a part of the body that most people never think about until they injure it. Actors cannot afford that luxury.

The spine is that linked column of vertebrae that keeps us erect and permits us to move. To get the feel of how the spine works, divide it into three separate parts: the upper back (that series of vertebrae from the head to just below the shoulder blades), the middle back (that series of vertebrae from the shoulder blades to the waist), and the lower back (that series of remaining vertebrae from the waist to the coccyx at the base of the spine). Gently experiment with bending. Try to feel how each section bends. Notice that each section slightly overlaps the next (since totally isolated movement of one vertebra is impossible).

It is usually a pleasant surprise to discover that one can actually bend one's middle spine. Just knowing that the poor, neglected, non-sensitive (except when it's scratched, and then it can be ecstatically sensitive) back has a life of its own, with parts to be moved and observed, should prove stimulating for the actor in working toward a more expressive body.

SEQUENTIAL RELAXATION

Here is an exercise for warming up the spine.

1. Assume an aligned stance with feet parallel (no wider than your hips), knees "soft"—that is, relaxed, not locked or rigid—and arms hung naturally at your sides (Fig. 3-7).

2. Drop the head forward and around and relax the upper back. Just relax and hang into the muscles, feeling the weight for a count of 8. Then very gently relax the upper back eight times in the same 8-count tempo. (Let the arms hang naturally throughout this exercise.) At this point the hands should hang about mid-thigh (Fig. 3-11).
3. Now add the middle back and hang for a count of 8 (Fig. 3-10). Then relax both sections as one piece for another 8. Do not raise the shoulders; keep them relaxed. Hands should hang about knee height.
4. Now add the lower back and hang and relax (Fig. 3-9). Do not release the pelvis. The hands should hang about midway between the knees and ankles.
5. Now release the pelvis and allow gravity to pull your body headfirst toward the floor directly in front of and between your feet. With your arms hanging naturally, let your hands touch the floor (Fig. 3-8). Keep the knees soft. Repeat the relax and hang (let gravity take over and let the spine stretch itself naturally).
6. Let the spine relax (release the neck and head). Again let gravity take over, stretching your spine naturally. Breathe deeply in and out, and as you exhale feel the body relax deeper and stretch further. Do this twice more, each time allowing the body to stretch on the exhalation of the breath. (Remember, the stretching comes in the exhalation. Do not force the stretch, just let it happen.)
7. Now slowly and sequentially, stage by stage, bring the body back up to the initial erect, naturally aligned stance. Take a count of 8 to come up. The pelvis rotates forward (as the torso lifts up) and comes under as the lower back rotates up into place. Then the middle back comes vertebra by vertebra into place. Finally, the upper back comes up sequentially. The head should continue to hang forward, because the neck should be totally relaxed until the last moment when that portion of the upper back slides back into place.
8. Once back to a standing position, and aligned and centered, press up through the feet onto tiptoes (I find this to be a helpful image for the actor).
    Hereafter I will sometimes refer to this as a *relevé* motion, or I may alternate *relevé* with the direction to "press up through the feet." Test your balance (Fig. 3-12). Slowly come down through the feet. If any shifting of weight was needed to relevé, your center is not precisely located.
9. Repeat the exercise (steps 1 to 7) again for a count of 8 at each stage. If prepared, repeat again in four counts per stage.

The next exercise is also for the spine, but it helps with breath control and alignment as well. Each of the exercises in this spine series should also develop awareness of, and greater flexibility in, the spine.

BREATHING IN
As in the last exercise, start from a relaxed position (knees soft, upper body relaxed over the knees, as in Fig. 3-8).

1. Bend over and relax. Inhale for a count of 8. Then exhale for another 8. Now, inhaling for a count of 8, sequentially bring yourself up, through your spine, to a standing position with legs straight, knees soft, pelvis tucked, and with lower, middle, and upper body in place, shoulders down, neck in line with the spine, and head on top of the neck.

2. Gradually release your breath, exhaling for a count of 8, as you slowly and sequentially return to the position at the start. In the beginning of the exercise always inhale and exhale one to three times to relax the spine before you begin to straighten it.

3. If both raising and lowering is fully sequential and the breathing timed with it, move on to repeat the exercise for four counts—then, when ready, in two counts. *Caution:* Always keep the movement in control, and always stay centered.

SWING AND UP

Now let's try a variation—a slightly more vigorous exercise that is good for the circulation and utilizes a different approach to the spine.

1. Start in the same position as in the last exercise, that is, over and relaxed, with knees bent (Fig. 3-13). Gently pulse the head up and down, four times.

2. Swing the head and neck from side to side, right and left. Repeat. Be sure the neck stays relaxed. Let the body breathe naturally with the movement.

3. Now add the shoulders, arms, and torso into the swinging, right (Fig. 3-14) and left (Fig. 3-15). Swing right again, but let the swing carry you erect (Fig. 3-16) at the peak, as your arms reach toward the ceiling. Then let gravity drop you down toward the floor on the left back (Fig. 3-17) through the original position. Repeat in the reverse direction. Repeat on both sides.

4. Then, after the fourth swing, stop applying force and allow gravity to bring the body gradually to a halt. With the body returned to the opening position, slowly come up through the spine, as in the first two exercises, straightening the legs, bringing the pelvis under, rotating up through the lower, middle, and upper back to a natural alignment.

5. Test your alignment. Relevé, come up and slowly down through the feet.

These exercises for the spine are important for a variety of reasons. Probably the most important reason is that the musculature involved is more specifically and directly concerned with the breathing mechanisms than with any other body part. The spine provides the primary structural support for the entire upper body and is assisted in this function by the musculature of the back, chest, and abdomen. It is vital that this musculature be strong and flexible—and that it be warmed up early in the exercise session so that the spine is protected from possible injury.

Also, although for the sake of convenience I have titled this section spine studies, it must be pointed out that a more significant principle is actually at work here. It is called the principle of *centering*.

3-13

3-14

3-15

3-16

3-17

Centering: Finding the Source of All Movement

The guiding principle in our discussion thus far has been to encourage organic awareness and development. One of the prime tools I use to do this is the concept of centering. Centering is merely the process of finding one's center. This is difficult for most people, only because most people have never thought they had a "center." For the movement instructor, as well as for the actor, this is an essential concept that is both useful and operative on many levels.

Let us start with the dictionary definitions of the term and then discuss them as they apply to movement. According to Webster's *New World Dictionary of the American Language* (Second College Edition, 1972):

> center *n* 1: a point equally distant from all points on the circumference of a circle or surface of a sphere. 2: the point around which anything revolves; pivot. 3: a place at which an activity or complex of activities is carried on (a shopping center), from which ideas, influences, etc., emanate (Paris, the fashion center), or to which many people are attracted (a center of interest). 4: the approximate middle point, place, or part of anything. 5: a group of nerve cells regulating a particular function (the vasomotor centers). *v.t.* 1: to place in, at, or near the center. 2: to gather to one place; gather to a point. 3: to furnish with a center.

It is obvious that none of the above definitions specifically deals with the human body or being, but the concepts provided can be used to aid us in our task as artists and teachers.

Generally, the torso, from the pelvis to the neck, can be thought of as "as the point around which anything revolves; pivot. . . ," for the arms, legs, and neck are all attached to it. The spine, the rib cage, and the surrounding musculature can be construed as "a place at which an activity or complex of activities is carried on. . . ," the site of major organs and bodily functions.

It must be noted that, for a variety of reasons, each individual's center is different from another's even when both have attained their ideal postures. Looking at the general case, however, we see that there is a correlation between the center of the torso and the definitions of the center as "a point equally distant from all points on the circumference of a circle or surface of a sphere." A lateral cross section of the chest cavity, viewed from the vertical, reveals an elliptical or oval shape (see illustration) whose center is equidistant from the corresponding sides of the ellipse. Vertical cross sections of the torso when viewed from the lateral reveal two ovals whose centers are displaced by volume toward the larger end of the shapes. These three reference points roughly correspond to a fist-sized spherical shape that is located at the bottom of the sternum in line with the vertical spine, midway between the ribs on either side, and also midway between the front and back of the chest cavity.

It is no accident that this reference point exists. Human beings are bipedal creatures and so they depend on a symmetrical shape. Also, since they stand erect, with most of their weight in the upper body, they must have a high center of gravity. Specifically, however, I believe the center is "a place . . . from which ideas, influences, etc., emanate," because all movement should have its origin in the torso—that is, the center. This is a difficult concept to prove, but it is useful to explore the hypothesis.

**LATERAL CROSS SECTION
(CHEST CAVITY)**

**VERTICAL CROSS SECTION
(TORSO)**

**VERTICAL CROSS SECTION
(TORSO)**

THE PHYSICAL CENTER

The muscles of any major body part, being connected to the muscles of the torso (and dependent on the oxygen borne by the blood circulated from the lungs by the muscles of the heart, which lies in or near the center), must be alerted to begin preparing to execute the contemplated movement, or the movement will be poorly executed and appear disjointed as a result of poor organic commitment. This thesis is borne out by the inference from the definitions of the center as "a group of nerve cells regulating a particular function . . . ," and also by the awareness that the decision to move does not originate in the muscle itself, but in the brain, from which the impulse is carried, through chemically stimulated electrical impulses, down the spinal cord through the torso to each muscle group involved.

We know that this action is initiated by the brain, and following this reasoning we are led to believe that the origin of all movement is the brain. But is it not true that the constant interaction of the body (continually receiving and transmitting information to the brain) and the brain (constantly measuring and evaluating the incoming data and sending back different information) forms a unity, an inseparable and mutual dependency of reception and response?

Therefore, when I speak of the center I am referring to that point or area at which the constantly flowing impulses gather to one place as they pass on their way to various destinations, so that I can provide the actor with a conceptual tool to focus further effort.

THE MENTAL CENTER

Mentally, the center, especially for an actor, is an extension of her (or his) physical center, since all ideas and designs are fed through the physical center to the body. The actor must do this because she is working in a communicative art form and depends on her body to actualize concepts. A mathematician could conceivably solve a problem in theoretical calculus without needing to so much as raise an eyebrow, but the actor's problems demand that she use her physical instrument almost constantly to solve a problem—or at least to test a solution.

Also, the mathematician subliminally alters physically while focusing on a problem. This means that the degree and type of mental activity occurring in a human is (regardless of profession or race or sex) ultimately linked through some sort of organic balancing, measuring, and monitoring system designed to produce the ideal physical state for that activity. This system is a function of centering.

THE EMOTIONAL CENTER

What of the emotions? How do they relate to this concept of the center? First let us examine what we call emotion. The dictionary's definition of emotion is:

emotion *n* 1: a. a strong feeling; excitement. b. the state or capability of having the feelings aroused to the point of awareness. 2: any specific feeling; any of various complex reactions with both neutral and physical manifestations, as love, hate, fear, anger, etc.

It is emotion that provides the key to understanding the concept of center and that unites the seemingly isolated mental and physical aspects of humanity. Any emotion seems to begin as a physical sensation in the area of the torso near the heart and spreads outward to the extremities. Observe athletes in their reactions to winning or losing a contest and you will be able to mark the progress of the impetus to scream in pain or leap in joy at sudden changes of fortune. You can see their bodies begin to crumble and sag from the center as the certainty of defeat begins to dawn upon them, or begin to swell outward from the center as they realize the nearness of victory.

Athletes serve so well for this, because their focus is so keen on the competition at hand that they lose self-consciousness about their emotions. They are spontaneously reacting with their entire being to the events transpiring around them.

Small children are also excellent to study in this regard because they too are uninhibited about showing their emotions. If you observe a child who is dramatically surprised by, say, a door slamming or a sudden bump on the head, you can actually watch as his face changes from normal concentration to total surprise, as his eyes and hands fly open and his entire body lifts from the center to an effort to gather enough outside data. Then, while he is still in that position, his attention focuses inward to gather still more information from his body. Then, as he comes to understand the situation, his chest will begin to collapse from pain or hurt, or inflate with pleasure or joy.

When I speak of the center, I am referring to the area in the mid-chest where all action originates, where all reaction first manifests itself, that small area of the upper torso we must position in relationship to the rest of the erect body so that it provides the proper balance of forces to effect natural balance and the conceptual focus for the actor's development of organic unity.

The center provides a conceptual focus for the actor's various endeavors in training. Through the concept of center the actor will develop an understanding of himself as an organic unity of mind, spirit, and body, and not as a series of unrelated parts. Thus by the mere mention of the word "center" in the right contexts, the actor will begin to form a definition of the term that will accommodate the various uses to which I put it. As he forms this definition, he will be unconsciously using his physical sensations, emotional reactions, and intellectual powers. He will, in other words, be forming an organic understanding of the term, while taking the first steps in finding his center. This process, *centering*, forms the basis for the organic entity's development.

I have placed this preliminary discussion of the term here in order to provide a link between the first exercises and the others to follow. Since all movement comes from the center and depends on proper breathing techniques, the quality of the movements and their execution is linked not only to the developmental process described earlier (wherein slow, easy work precedes complicated or physically demanding exercises), but also to the necessity for total body awareness and commitment to tension-free execution of seemingly isolated movements.

Spirit: The Unifying Force

We now understand the importance of centering, be it mental, physical, or emotional. But what use are these elements taken separately? The truly organic actor instinctively knows that these three elements are connected by the human spirit. The term "spirit," in and of itself, is a difficult one to define and even more difficult to comprehend. To be truly organic (on stage or in life) one must develop the spiritual self much as one would a muscle of the body. The verbal definition of spirit is:

> **spirit** *n* 1. the life principle, especially in man, originally regarded as inherent in the breath, or as infused by a deity. 2. the thinking, motivating, feeling part of man often distinguished from the body.

Spirit, as the force unifying the elements of the triad of thought, emotion, and action, cannot be located in either the mind, the body, or the emotions, but is instead the invisible through-line connecting all three. Most actors can easily recognize and utilize their emotions. With development of the spiritual self, however, the pool of emotions becomes greater on-stage. Thoughts and actions occur spontaneously. The life of the play and player are organically rooted in the moment.

How then does one develop the spirit? First and most important is simply the acknowledgment of its existence. Beyond that, each person must find a personal path to spiritual development. Whether it be the balancing of the chakras, meditation, prayer, a walk in nature, listening to music—something must be done each and every day not only to exercise the mind and body but the spirit as well. This is the only way to achieve the true organic connection.

ISOLATION EXERCISES

The unique movement properties of all parts of the body should be rediscovered. The principle at work here is isolating each part to analyze its movement independently. Isolation is the single most important path to a supple and expressive body.

The neck, for example, is seldom thought of in terms of its movement. Moving the neck forward, sideways, and backwards, actors should find an amazing flexibility. With concentration and discipline, they can uncover a similar elasticity in the shoulders, rib cage, and pelvis. These parts are normally somewhat immobile, compared to one's hands, arms, and legs, but if actors can learn to rotate the rib cage, they will rethink the possibilities of motion inherent in more dynamic parts of the body. Through repeating carefully controlled isolation exercises, they can discover how supple the human body can and should be. By simply unlocking those muscles they can acquire a sense of fluidity, grace, and precision of movement.

Head Rotation. This exercise helps to relax the muscles of the neck. Put the feet in parallel position and properly align the body. Do the following steps:

1. Drop the head forward and down; slowly rotate the head to the right, to the back, to the left, and then forward in eight counts. Allow your jaw to relax and fall open as your head rotates toward the back, and close the jaw as it comes forward again. It helps one to obtain more fluidity by inhaling on the first four counts (as your head moves toward the back) and exhaling on the last four counts (as your head moves toward the front).
2. Let your head hang naturally as if it were a weight suspended from a short elastic band—don't push it forward, back, or to either side—just apply the force laterally and let the head do the rest naturally. Keep the flow of energy even.
3. Repeat the same exercise rotating your head to the left. Once you have mastered the movement in eight counts, do it in four counts.

Percussive Head Rotation. This is done with energy that is not sustained but pulsating (this is more fully explained in Chapter 4). Begin with your feet parallel and your body aligned (knees soft).

1. Drop the head forward on the first count.
2. On the third count, bring the head center to the original position.
3. On the fifth count, drop the head back, to the limit of the neck's ability, until you are looking at the ceiling. Do not throw your chest out or you'll be off-center.
4. On the seventh count, bring the head back to the center.
5. Repeat steps 1 through 4 taking two counts for each movement.
6. After you have completed the entire (forward, center, back, center) pattern twice, tilt the head to the right side in two counts without changing the angle of your face to the front wall (that is, you should still be looking at yourself in the mirror, with your head tilted to the side. See Fig. 3-22).
7. Bring the head back to center on two counts (Fig. 3-21).
8. Then, on the next two counts, tilt the head to the left (in the same manner as you did to the right).

3-18

3-19

3-20

3-21

3-22

9. Bring the head center again on the next two counts.
10. Repeat the right-left sequence again using two counts for each movement.

Once the group as a whole has conquered the basic movements, I ask them to try the entire exercise using one count for each movement. Some groups require several weeks to reach this point; others are ready to try it in one week. When they have mastered it both ways, they can do the entire exercise organically, without deliberation or hesitation, using either two counts or one count for each movement and without following someone's guidance. Next I move to a greater level of complexity by adding an arm pattern to the head movement. In the following steps, which continue the exercise, each arm movement receives two counts.

11. As you tilt your head gently forward, bring the lower arms up to the shoulders (by simply bending at the elbows), with the palms of the hands facing the body and the fingers pointing toward the ceiling (Fig. 3-18).
12. As you bring your head back to center, raise both arms to a 60-degree angle toward the ceiling, making certain that the shoulders do not rise—keep excess tension from the shoulders. Palms face each other, arms are straight (Fig. 3-19).
13. Now, as you drop your head back, bring your arms out and down to form oblique angles from the plane of your body, so that they are parallel to the floor just slightly below shoulder height. Arms are straight, palms are face up (Fig. 3-20).
14. As the head comes to center again, bend the elbows and rotate the arms inward; your palms should come to your chest with the arms still parallel to the floor just below the shoulders (Fig. 3-21).
15. Repeat positions 11 through 16 with the arms as you repeat the head pattern (forward, center, back, center).
16. With the arms in the ending position (see position 4 preceding), as you move your head to the right (see position 6 preceding) open your arms until the palms face forward (Fig. 3-22).
17. As you bring your head to center, bring the arms back to their closed position (palms to chest, arms parallel to the floor).
18. Keep the arms in that position as the head tilts left.
19. Open the arms until the palms face front again as the head comes to center.
20. Keep the arms open as the head tilts right.
21. Close the arms as the head comes center.
22. Keep the arms closed as the head tilts left.
23. Open the arms as the head comes center.

Notice that the arms only open and close (once the forward, center, back, center pattern is completed) when the head centers, except for the first initial movement to the side. This is a simple pattern to teach, and it is simple in theory, but the coordination of the head movement with the arm pattern (especially the side-to-side movement) is very difficult to master. So actor and instructor alike will want to take time with the initial learning stages.

Once this has been mastered, however, the actor will have passed a barrier in kinesthetic awareness and muscular dexterity. She (or he) will also have opened another door to organic movement, because she will have been forced to use her mind more than her muscles and make it a part of her. Moreover, this exercise forces a new level of centering ability, for the entire body is united in this single purpose. The legs support the breathing-balanced torso while the other extremities move (simultaneously or separately) and the mind monitors and responds to the various stimuli.

It is really far simpler for the actor than it sounds, and she may not realize the importance of this accomplishment, but once she learns to coordinate breathing with movements, she will have made a significant step forward toward developing as an organic entity.

The next exercise is more subtle and in many ways more difficult for a non-dancer than any we have looked at so far. But it is the next logical step in the organic warm-up because it develops flexibility in the torso.

Rib Cage Exercise. For flexibility of the torso, work on the following steps.

1. Move the rib cage directly to your right side on the count of 1 (Fig. 3-23).
2. Bring the rib cage back to center on the count of 2 (Fig. 3-24).
3. On the count of 3 move the rib cage to the left (Fig. 3-25).
4. And on the count of 4 come back to center.
5. Repeat steps 1 through 4 three times. Try to match your breathing with your movement. As you move to the side, inhale, and as you return to center, exhale. (Note: The tendency is to tilt the leading shoulder up and allow the trailing shoulder to fall. This should not happen when the exercise is performed correctly. Try to keep the shoulders in a straight line parallel to the floor. Another tendency is for tension to creep into the shoulders, forcing them up toward the ears. Concentration on breathing and relaxing them should help.)
6. Now begin again at center and move the chest forward on the first count (Fig. 3-26).
7. Center on the second count (Fig. 3-27).
8. Back on the count of 3 (Fig. 3-28).
9. Center on the count of 4.
10. Repeat steps 6 through 9 three times.

A good image to use for this exercise is to imagine that you have strings attached to your sternum in front, to a corresponding vertebra in the back, and to a rib on either side; the strings go at a 60-degree angle to the ceiling at each of the four points, and there is an equal amount of tension on each string, holding you on center. To move toward the right, imagine a person taking the string on your right

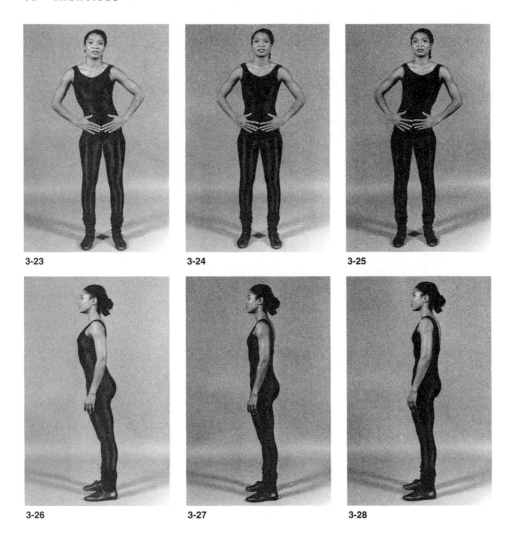

3-23　　　　　3-24　　　　　3-25

3-26　　　　　3-27　　　　　3-28

side and pulling up and away from you to the right. To come back to center, imagine that person releasing the string. To move front use the same imagery of the person in front pulling up and away from you, then releasing, and so on for the left and back. This image will keep you from slumping into the intended direction of travel and keep the shoulders relaxed and in a horizontal position, because the focus of attention (and the impetus for movement) is below the shoulders, at the center of the body.

Also note that it is essential to have the rib cage area relaxed to allow for freedom of movement. If there is tension in the body, it is from the waist down.

When you have grasped the above, you are ready to continue, following these steps.

11. Move the rib cage directly to the right side, to the front, to the left side, and to the back (using only one count for each movement). Then reverse and go to the left, front, right, and back. Repeat. Remember to keep the hips stationary so that you are not weaving and movement is happening in the torso area only.
12. Once you have mastered the above, add on the use of an arm pattern. As you take the rib cage to the right, place the left hand on the head and keep the right hand on your waist. Then, as you move the rib cage to the left, place the right hand on your head and return your left hand to your waist. Repeat.
13. Now raise both arms slightly in front of your shoulders, pointed on a 45-degree angle toward the ceiling. Move the torso, and hold on in the pelvic area, as you rotate right and left. When extending the arms toward the ceiling in front of you, be careful not to lift the shoulders.

Sustained Pelvis Circling. Place the feet parallel, with knees bent and arms down at the sides of the body (Fig. 3-29). Move the pelvis slowly in a circle to the right (Fig. 3-30), front (Fig. 3-31), left (Fig. 3-32), and back (Fig. 3-33). The movement should be with a sustained, even flow of energy. Now move left, front, right, and back. Repeat to both sides taking eight counts to complete each circle.

Percussive Pelvic Circling. Again, the difference is in the way the energy is applied to the movement. Instead of an even flow of energy, the movement is sudden and sharp. You hit the position and hold it a moment (example: right and hold, and front and hold, and so on.). Your starting position is the same as that of the preceding exercise. Rotate the pelvis in a circular but punctuated pattern. Push the hip right as you count 1, front on 3, left on 5, back on 7, then left, front, right and back.

Shoulder Roll. Place the feet in parallel position with the body aligned. Follow these steps:

1. Lift the shoulders up and down several times to ease out the tension and relax the shoulders.
2. Lift the right shoulder up on the count of 1 and drop it forward on 2. Then lift it up on 3 and drop it back to its natural placement on 4. Use the same process with the left shoulder, then repeat the series.
3. Now lift both shoulders up and drop them forward, then lift them up and return them back to the natural position. Do this four times.
4. Lift both shoulders, twist the right forward and the left back beyond the natural position (but not straining), then lift and return them to the natural position. Repeat this time twisting the left shoulder front and the right shoulder back.

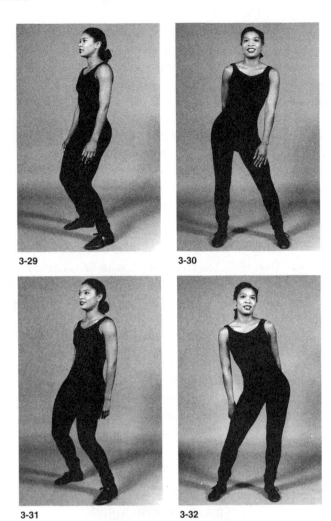

3-29

3-30

3-31

3-32

3-33

YOGA BREATHING EXERCISE

Do this exercise once or twice throughout the warm-up, as it helps to energize the body.

1. Stand with your feet hip-width apart and keep your knees soft. Keep your body erect. Place your arms down along the sides of the body. Place the thumb and first two fingers together.
2. As you inhale, feel the chest expand. Lift your arms to the sides of your body, shoulder height. Feel the lift in the chest. Your head should be lifted, your body open (Fig. 3-34).
3. As you exhale, slowly round the back and bend your knees. Let the arms come forward, keeping your hands relaxed. Let your spine relax, arms and hands hanging weightless at the sides of the body and resting on the sides of the legs. Repeat this three or four times (Fig. 3-35).

3-34

3-35

BACK ROLLS

You can repeat this exercise periodically throughout the warm-up.

1. Stand with your feet shoulder-width apart, knees bent. Lean slightly forward, releasing your hips, and place your hands on your thighs to support your weight. Keep your abdominal muscles pulled in and your back flat (Fig. 3-36).
2. Inhale and contract your abdominal muscles further. Roll your back up while tucking in your pelvis (Fig. 3-37). As you exhale, release the back to the starting position (Fig. 3-36).
3. Remember to breathe in as you contract, release when you exhale. Do the back roll four to eight times.

3-36   3-37

Principles of Proper Exercise and Warm-up

The human body is as fragile as it is supple. That is why I have emphasized avoiding strain. It is crucial that early conditioning work be performed at an easy, relaxed pace, slowly building strength, balance, endurance, and a sensitivity to the body. The practical goal is for actors to become alert monitors of their own organic machinery. They should not be tempted into careless, violent, wrenching exercises, but must patiently develop a conscious awareness of the body's capacities, gently leading the body forward, not shoving it beyond its present limits. Remember, since each person's body is different, progress can't be monitored by comparisons. Each person will excel at different exercises and will therefore progress in a manner unrelated to anyone else's. What each person needs to develop is a calm and thoughtful extension of skills rather than a need to succeed quickly.

However integrated, and whatever the other exercises supplied by instructor or actor, it will help to keep an eye on the following principles.

- The whole body should be warmed up. One part may receive special focus, but everything has to be ready to move.
- Preparatory work should *always* precede strenuous work.
- Any exercise can be varied or modified for the sake of variety or to focus on a special project or problem.
- The mechanics of every exercise should be taken apart, studied, and understood. Blind imitation eliminates any chance for internal observation or for the actor to do the exercise effectively at home. This is a basic tenet of my philosophy and is the starting point for developing mind/spirit/body awareness. The actor must understand the purpose and function—and remember the sequence—of each exercise; otherwise, he or she is capable only of a monkey-like imitation, which limits the growth of any kinesthetic awareness.

In these principles and in the sample program thus far offered, there is a solid basis for all the additional work that may be necessary or desirable.

Standing Exercises

The previous exercises have served specialized purposes. They were listed in an order that follows the principles of a proper warm-up and of a program of progressive skills acquisition. Also, in general, these exercises are listed in the same order I use in my daily warm-up (see Sample Structures, Appendix 2).

The next logical step is to provide basic exercises for a general toning of the total body. To fill this need I offer a series of exercises which are done in a standing position. Following these is a series of on-the-floor exercises.

STRETCH AND SWING

The following are steps for a gentle vertical stretching and relaxation exercise.

1. With feet parallel, lift the right arm straight above the head, alongside the ear, and stretch the right side of the torso up with it, for two counts (Fig. 3-38).
2. Lower the arm as you come to center for two counts.
3. Repeat the move with your left arm and torso; reach and stretch for two counts (Fig. 3-39).
4. Lower the arm and come to center for two counts.
5. Repeat the sequence for the right and left.
6. Bring both arms up together, reach, and stretch for two counts (Fig. 3-40).
7. Now, with both arms still above the head, begin to swing your arms and torso forward and down as you bend both knees. Releasing the pelvis, allow your body to swing down with the arms continuing down and back until you are in a semi-squat. Your head should be relaxed and between the knees, with the arms naturally extended behind you (as though you were preparing to dive off the starting block at the beginning of a swimming race.) This all happens in two counts (Fig. 3-41).
8. Swing back up into a flat-back position in two counts (Fig. 3-42). In the flat-back position the torso is parallel to the floor, forming a 90-degree angle with the legs, which are straight but with the knees relaxed. This is sometimes called the tabletop position, because the back is straight from pelvis to head, and the table legs are straight. The face points toward the floor to relieve tension in the neck and shoulder—that is, the neck is in line with the rest of the spine. Especially important is that the small of the back not be rounded, if possible (not all people can achieve this, and it should not be forced.) Maximum stretch is achieved the closer you can come to the ideal of a flat back and a 90-degree angle with the legs. Be gentle with this position, and hold it as you gently stretch the muscles in the back of your thighs and small of the back. Apply force gently by pulsing in an up and down motion with the entire torso, the hands and arms extending beside your ears and parallel to the floor. Pulse for four counts.
9. Swing down as you did in step 7, for two counts.
10. Swing up all the way to a standing position with both arms above the head as you did in step 6. (Use your arms' momentum to help swing you up, in two counts).

3-38   3-39   3-40

3-41   3-42

11. Lower both arms using two counts until you are back at the original position.

12. Repeat the entire exercise.

When you have learned to do the exercise as it is described above, try doing it without always bringing your arms back to neutral after you've stretched. Just leave out steps 2, 4, and 11. Once you've raised an arm and stretched it, keep it aloft (Fig. 3-35). Relax it a bit also, as you raise and stretch the other. This way, the exercise will flow more smoothly.

STRETCH TO THE SIDE

For a lateral stretching exercise, do the following:

1. Begin in the naturally aligned position.

2. On the count of 1, start to tilt the torso to the right while extending the right arm to the side. Keep your head facing straight forward but allow it to tilt to the right. Reach toward the wall on your right as if trying to touch it. Use two counts to stretch out the torso in this direction. The stretch should be felt along the left side of the torso, hip, and leg (Fig. 3-43).

3. Then use two counts to return to center.
4. Repeat the steps tilting to the left (the stretch will be felt along the right side) for two counts (Fig. 3-44).
5. Use two counts to return to center.
6. Repeat the steps for the right and left.
7. Move into a flat-back position, using a count of 4 to reach the final position, with arms extended slightly in front of the body and parallel to the floor. Your head should be in line with the spine, your face and eyes looking at the floor. Gently pulse in this position to stretch muscles in the lower back and the backs of the thighs (Fig. 3-45).
8. Slowly lift the back, making it rounded, and allow the head and arms to relax downward and hang naturally for four counts. Shoulders, neck, and back should be relaxed, knees straight but soft. Bounce for four counts.
9. Sequentially rise into the naturally aligned position and relevé to test your balance.
10. Repeat the entire exercise several times.

Once you have learned the exercise, eliminate steps 3 and 5 so that there is a better flow of movement and breath.

3-43

3-44

3-45

PLIÉ SEQUENCES

The term *plié*, which derives from the French word *plier*, means "to bend." When used in its original context, *plié* refers to a movement in which begins with the feet and legs in one of the six classical ballet positions, with the feet and legs turned out to their limit from the hips and the knees slowly bent so that knees and feet form the same angle with respect to the floor (see the description of classical pliés below). The back is held straight and centered.

In modern dance or jazz dance, the same general principles apply, except that the feet and legs are parallel to each other.

How does the concept apply in a movement for an actor's warm-up? The plié, in the classical (turned outward) position, works to strengthen the muscles on the inside of the thigh. In the parallel position, the plié works to strengthen the quadriceps or the top of the thighs. To exercise the leg muscles fully (as part of a full-body warm-up), both the turned-out and parallel positions should be used.

Parallel Pliés or Knee Bends. This exercise is good for balance and control, and for strengthening the legs.

1. Put your feet in a parallel position, eight to ten inches apart, with your weight centered.
2. Bend the knees directly over the feet, which point straight forward, in a smooth motion until the heels or the feet are forced to rise. Stop the downward motion just before the heels rise from the floor. This is called *demi-plié*, or small plié. Use two counts for this movement. Bring the hands up six inches from the shoulders, palms facing the shoulders (upper arms remain in position) as you plié (Fig. 3-46).
3. On two counts, rise back to the original position by simply straightening the knees (steps 2 and 3 comprise the demi-plié). At the same time raise the arms in a 60-degree angle toward the ceiling, palms facing each other (Fig. 3-47).
4. Relevé through both feet on two counts as you open your arms at right angles to your body (parallel to the floor), palms facing the ceiling (Fig. 3-48).
5. Bring the palms to the chest (arms still parallel to the floor) as you lower your heels to the floor in two counts (Fig. 3-49). (Steps 2 through 5 comprise the demi-plié sequence.)
6. Repeat the demi-plié sequence, making certain the knees go directly over the feet; think of sitting straight down; do not lift the heels or release the pelvis so that your torso tilts forward or buttocks jut out. Keep your back erect and your buttocks under you.
7. Now do the *grand-plié*, or full plié. Bend the knees in the same manner as before, except that this time, instead of stopping just before the heels come off the floor, continue the downward movement by bending the knees. Allow the heels to rise off the floor, using four counts from start to finish (Fig. 3-50). The arms repeat the same movements this time, following the longer counts to go with the larger movements of the legs.

8. Come back up to the original position by straightening the knees, forcing the heels down as soon as your legs will allow (that is, don't straighten the knees all the way and then drop down onto your heels). Use another count of 4 for this.

9. Repeat the grand-plié sequence, making sure you neither break the line of the torso forward or backward, nor release the pelvis. The lowest point in the downward momentum should occur just before the calf muscles touch the back of the thigh.

Note: The arm pattern should be added only after the mechanics and the sequence are thoroughly understood. Also note that this arm pattern is similar to that used in percussive head movements, discussed earlier in this chapter.

3-46

3-47

3-48

3-49

3-50

Classical Pliés. Once you have learned the entire exercise, you should learn the following sequence of exercises, which are explained below.

1. First position (two demi-pliés, count to 2 for each movement).
2. First position (two grand-pliés, count to 4 for each movement).
3. Transition to second position (count to 8).
4. Second position (two demi-pliés, count to 2 for each movement).
5. Second position (two grand-pliés, count to 4 for each movement).
6. Transition to first position (count to 8).
7. Repeat 1 through 6 with transition on other leg.
8. Add relevé to sequence.

1. Start with the *first position demi-plié* (Fig. 3-52 for demi-plié with arm pattern; see "Arm Patterns," below):
   a. Start with the feet in first position—heels together, feet turned out forming a right angle, and weight centered (Fig. 3-51).
   b. Take two counts to bend the knees. Force the knees wide open, knees directly over the feet. As in parallel demi-plié, go down to the point just before the heels are forced off the floor.
   c. Then use two counts to straighten the legs to the original position. (Remember, you are now working the muscles on the inside of the thighs as well as the buttocks).
   d. Repeat the demi-plié, making certain the knees go out directly over the feet.

2. The *first position grand-plié* is shown frontally beginning with Fig. 3-55 and from the side in 3-56. (Again, see "Arm Patterns," below.)
   a. Start this position after the second demi-plié when you have returned to the starting position.

3-51

b. Once again, bend the knees as before, but this time continue your downward motion through the point where the heels are lifted off the floor, stopping before you feel your control of your balance slipping or before your thighs touch your calf muscles. (This will be at a slightly different height for each person.) Use four counts for this.

c. Now rise smoothly back to the starting position by reversing the process, putting the heels down as quickly as possible; complete the rise by straightening the knees.

d. Repeat the grand-plié (steps b and c above), making certain that the back remains erect and does not tilt forward or back, and that the pelvis does not release backward or forward.

3. The *transition to second position* is as follows:
   a. You are now back in the starting position.
   b. Shift your weight onto the left leg and extend the right toe along the floor and directly to the side of the body, making certain both legs stay straight. You want to find the limit of the right leg's ability to keep the toe on the floor with the weight on the left leg. Count to 4 for this movement.
   c. Shift your weight so that it is now equally balanced between the two feet. Do this to the count of 4. The heels should be six to eight inches apart, with the weight centered between them. Feet and legs are turned out. You are now in *second position*.

4. The *second position demi-plié* (see Fig. 3-57 for demi-plié, with arm pattern):
   a. You are now in second position (end of step c in transition above).
   b. Bend the knees as you did in first position demi-plié with a count of 2.
   c. Straighten the knees as you did in first position demi-plié with a count of 2.
   d. Repeat, ending back at second position.
   Note: Since the heels never leave the floor in second position—in neither demi- nor grand-plié should the heels lift from the floor—the second position demi-plié is an estimation of half the distance from standing and grand-plié in second position.

5. The *second position grand-plié* (Fig. 3-58 for second position grand-plié with arm pattern):
   a. You begin from second position.
   b. Bend the knees again as you did for grand-plié in first position—deepening the position, but not lifting the heels—to the count of 4.
   c. Straighten the legs, lifting yourself back to standing second position, to the count of 4.
   d. Repeat, ending at second position.

3-52

3-53

3-54

3-55

3-56

3-57

3-58

6. *Transition to first position:*
    a. You are now back in second position.
    b. Shift your weight onto your left leg, allowing your right heel to lift from the floor—keeping your right toe on the floor—using a count of 4.
    c. Bring the right foot back to first position and shift the weight onto both feet, using a count of 4.

7. Repeat steps 1 through 6, but in the transitions, shift weight onto the right leg and extend the left foot along the floor.

Adding Relevé. After each plié, you can add a relevé to further strengthen the legs: Merely rise up on the toes in two counts from the demi-plié position, and four counts from the grand-plié position, and come down in the same number of counts.

Arm Patterns. There are various arm patterns that can be added once the basics of this exercise are conquered, and as with the parallel plié, the arm pattern will aid in coordination and control as well as strengthen the upper body. One pattern is to raise the arms in front of the body in plié (Fig. 3-52), 60 degrees over the head as you straighten (Fig. 3-53), to the side as you relevé (Fig. 3-54), and back to your sides as you come back to a starting position (Fig. 3-51). The arm pattern will keep the hands out of the way of the action of the legs and add a measure of grace to the movement.

SIDE STRETCHES FOR THE TORSO AND HAMSTRINGS

Begin standing in a moderate stride position, feet parallel, knees soft, twelve inches apart. This exercise is done to a count of 8.

1. On the count of 1, move arms out to the side, weight centered.
2. On the count of 2, reach your left arm up and over the head, and stretch the entire torso to the right. Keep the legs straight, the knees soft, and the weight centered.
3. Stretch for the remaining six counts in a very gentle pulsing movement toward the floor on the right. Be sure you are not jamming the muscles by trying to use maximum force in the stretch and pulse. (You are elongating the muscles, not jerking them.) Keep the stretch continuous.
4. Repeat on the left side, reaching your right arm over the head to the left.
5. Now do the steps using a count of 4.

LEG EXTENSIONS

There are three patterns in this exercise for strength, coordination, and balance. This exercise involves the *passé,* a movement of one leg in front of or behind another. Start with your feet in parallel position, arms extended out to the side in an airplane pose (use a barre, if available, at first).

1. Using two counts, bring the right leg up to a turned-in passé, with foot pointed (see Fig. 3-59 and 3-60 for front and side views).
2. Using two counts, extend the lower leg until the entire leg is straight and extended away from the body along the line of the thigh in the passé (Fig. 3-61), and flex the foot to the front
3. Bring the leg back to passé with two counts.
4. Bring the leg down with two counts.
5. Repeat with the left leg.

Now turn the feet out, into first position, and continue as follows:

6. Move the right leg into a turned-out passé (Fig. 3-62).
7. Extend the leg out to the side and flex the foot with two counts. Make sure the leg is slightly in front of the side position (Fig. 3-63).
8. Bring the leg back to a passé with two counts.
9. Place the leg down with two counts.
10. Repeat with the left leg.

Starting with feet parallel, do the third pattern:

11. Lift the right leg up to a turned-in passé with two counts.
12. Extend the right leg directly to the back, with the foot flexed, and make sure the leg stays turned in (Fig. 3-64).
13. Bring the leg back to a turned-in passé, with the foot pointed.
14. Place the leg down.
15. Repeat with the left.

Note: Make sure your weight is shifted to the supporting leg in all three patterns, and that you are pulled upright through the supporting side (don't slump or lean to that side to counterbalance your weight). The torso should remain directly over the hips throughout.

Variations on this exercise include adding the plié: As you extend the leg, you plié the supporting leg and, as you bring the leg back to passé, straighten the supporting leg. Or add the relevé: After the leg is extended, relevé through the supporting leg (Fig. 3-65).

BRUSHES (TENDU)

This exercise for strengthening legs, balance, and coordination and the following one are adapted from Matt Mattox, a noted jazz-dance teacher, actor, and dancer.

Tendu is another term borrowed from ballet, but since its specific definition is inadequate to my purpose, it is used here as a reference or orientation point for the informed actor. Generally, the movements represented by this term are correct for an actor's movement training in that they provide some principles on which our exercise is based. As in ballet's tendu, the weight is shifted onto the

3-59

3-60

3-61

3-62

3-63

3-64

3-65

supporting leg while the other leg is extended with the toes brushed along the floor. The alignment remains centered over the supporting leg.

But the difference is that here the feet are parallel, rather than turned out, as in ballet. The direction of the foot is straight and front-wise, rather than on the diagonal as in ballet, and the focus is on the toe leading, rather than on the heel as in ballet). The following form of tendu promotes more naturalistic movement patterns for today's theater.

1. Stand with the feet in parallel position, eight to ten inches apart, and arms at the side. Brush the right foot forward, extending the right foot and ankle completely, while keeping the toe in contact with the floor (Fig. 3-66). Bring the foot back, keeping contact with floor and not bending the knee or bending at the hips. Hips remain squarely positioned to the front. Repeat three more times on the right; then do the same four times with the left foot.

2. Repeat the exercise, again four times on each side, but this time allow the foot to continue forward until the toe leaves the floor six to eight inches. Lift the leg slightly, keeping both supporting and lifting legs straight, and do not lock the knees (Fig. 3-67).

3. Lift the right leg to your hip height or higher, but avoid buckling in the torso (Fig. 3-69). Count to 4 up, and again down. Repeat three more times on the right, then do the same four times on the left (Fig. 3-68).

4. Reverse the process, working from step 3 back to step 1.

Brushes should be done slowly at first, using four counts to raise and lower the leg. Later this timing can be reduced to two counts and finally to one count.

EIGHT-COUNT STRETCH

This exercise is meant to slowly warm up the spine and body. Use a very sustained and even flow of energy. *Keep the legs straight but the knees soft throughout.*

1. Place the feet in a parallel position, arms down. Your weight is centered. On a count of 8, slowly lift your arms up toward the ceiling, alongside the ears, and keep the shoulders down. (Fig. 3-70).

2. Now on a count of 8, slowly move into a flat-back position, arms in the same relationship with the body, but pointed now at the forward wall. Keep the head aligned with the spine (Fig. 3-71).

3. Again on a count of 8, take the body down to the floor, and let the palms of the hands touch the floor (Fig. 3-72). If you cannot, don't force it.

4. Bring the body straight up, arms back at the sides. Keep your weight centered. Do not snap back up in a whip-like movement but bring the torso and head up as a unit, slowly.

5. Repeat steps 1 through 4 three times, first using counts of 8, then counts of 4, and finally counts of 2. Maintain the straight leg throughout.

3-66

3-67

3-68

3-69

3-70

3-71

3-72

STRETCH SIDE, FLAT, SIDE, BACK

Begin this exercise for lateral and back stretch in the position in which you ended the preceding eight-count stretch.

1. Using a count of 8, lift the left arm over the head as you lean your body toward the right, and reach toward the right side with both hands. Keep the face forward.
2. Move into the flat-back position with arms out in the airplane-wings position. Elongate the body, breathe, and feel the energy going out through your finger tips and connecting with the universal energy.
3. Now lift your body up and tilt to the left with your right arm over the head. Using a count of 8, reach with both arms to the left side of the body.
4. Now make your body erect, bend your knees, and bring your arms down to both sides of your body. Keeping your back straight, tilt your head backward to its limit and look at the ceiling. Using a count of 8, just "hang" in this position.
5. Repeat the entire exercise using four counts for each movement.
6. Repeat the entire exercise using two counts for each movement.
7. Repeat finally using one count for each movement.

LAYOUTS FOR BALANCE, STRENGTH, AND COORDINATION

The layout is a very advanced exercise which, especially in the early learning periods, calls for some means of support. The actor should hold onto a chair back, another actor's arm, or a ballet barre. After becoming able to perform the exercise using proper breathing (that is, without holding the breath, or grunting), the actor should be permitted to try it without the support.

1. Begin with feet parallel and arms out to the side. On a count of 2, bring the right leg into a parallel or turned-in passé, with the foot pointed toward the floor. (Fig. 3-73).
2. Extend the leg directly forward and flex the foot toward the ceiling, using two counts (Fig. 3-74).
3. Move the leg around directly to the side—but not back—using two counts (Fig. 3-75).
4. Bend directly forward from the hips into a flat-back position, keeping your leg directly to the side, using two counts (Fig. 3-76).
5. Reverse step 4 by coming up to a standing position, with your leg still out to the side, using a count of 2. Keep the foot flexed and pointed toward the ceiling. (You have to rotate the hip under you to move toward this neutral position).
6. Bring the right leg into a turned-out passé, using two counts.
7. Bring the knee around in front of you, and place the foot down parallel and even with the other, using two counts.
8. Repeat the exercise on the left side. Throughout, be sure that the supporting leg is pulled up but that the knee is not locked.

3-73

3-74

3-75

3-76

Floor Exercises

UP·OVER·THE·BACK SHOULDER STAND PRESS

Here is an exercise designed for relaxing the spine. Begin by lying on your back, arms at your sides, with the small of your back as close to being flat on the floor as you can comfortably make it. Put your legs together parallel.

1. Lift legs, then hips, and extend your legs straight toward the ceiling, with your toes pointed. With your elbows on the floor, put your hands under your hips and hold the position for a moment (Fig. 3-77).
2. Now allow the feet and legs to continue in an arc over the head, finally touching the toes on the floor above the head, with the legs kept straight (Fig. 3-78).

3. Bend the knees and bring them to the ears (Fig. 3-79). Hang in this position and breathe deeply.
4. Then straighten your legs, extending the toes along the floor, and lift the legs over your head and hips, and hold once again in the vertical position, with the hands under the hips. Do not hold your breath, but allow it to flow in and out.
5. Slowly move the body back down through the spine—that is, making sure to bring each part of the spine to the floor (Fig. 3-80)—and lower the legs (Fig. 3-81). Breathe.
6. Repeat.

A variation would be to start with the legs in second position. When they are vertical, you can experiment with your balance by moving your legs forward and back and to the side independently from each other. Continue to breathe easily.

Note: The "yoga plow" can compress discs in your neck area. An alternate exercise for people with neck or back problems is the Fold-Up Stretch, a Middle Eastern prayer position (see Fig. 3-120).

CONSTRUCTIVE REST

This exercise is valuable as an aid to relaxation and breathing technique and as a help in eliminating pelvic tilt, which is so prevalent among women. Do this one in your own time.

Before you begin, do this deep-breathing exercise:

1. Take a deep breath to cleanse the body. Inhale, and as you exhale let go of all tension and stress in the body.
2. Take another deep breath to cleanse your mind. Inhale and take yourself to that special place that lets your mind be quiet and calm. Exhale and let go of all the negative thoughts in your mind.
3. Take another deep breath. Inhale for the spirit, and as you exhale feel your spirit renewed. Feel the connection of your mind, spirit, and body.

You might also want to do the deep breathe–affirmation exercise on p. 36.

Constructive rest is a position many dancers assume to give them maximum rest in the shortest time possible. I have heard dancers claim that in the twenty minutes between dance rehearsals they have gathered what feels like an hour's rest by using constructive rest. It is a useful passive exercise.

1. Begin by lying on your back, knees bent toward the ceiling and feet flat on the floor six to ten inches apart. Place your arms across the chest as you breathe easily, eyes closed. Feel the small of the back resting on the floor (Fig. 3-82). Lie in this position for at least thirty seconds to one minute before moving to the next step.

3-77

3-78

3-79

3-80

3-81

2. Gently slide the feet away from your body, trying to keep the small of your back on the floor by using your abdominal muscles. Maintain your breathing.

3. When you have extended your legs all the way to the floor, draw them back up to the starting position, and repeat twice more.

Some women, to achieve the desired goal of resting the small of the back on the floor, may have to draw their knees to their chest and hold them there easily with their hands (Fig. 3-83). This is because of the natural shape of the female body and of the tendency in this society for women to stand with the pelvis tilted back. This tilt can be part of an interesting character choice, but the actress should do it by choice. So she should eliminate it as her habitual quirk of alignment.

3-82

3-83

UP OVER EACH OTHER'S BACK

This exercise takes two people to perform. It gives a stretch to the lower back and the inner thigh. It is important that both people stay relaxed, breathe properly and do not bounce or push during the stretch. Movement should be relaxed and organic.

1. Pair up with someone of a similar body type and weight. Sit on the floor back to back.

2. Person A places the soles of the feet together and links arms with Person B, whose feet are flat on the floor.

3. Person A pulls B up over her (or his) back, as B pushes herself with her feet into the final stretch position.

4. In a forward stretch position, A is relaxed, breathing easily, feeling the stretch created in the lower back and insides of the thighs, which is caused by B lying on her back. B's back should conform to the shape of A's back—they should be head to head, shoulder to shoulder. B's hips should be resting on A's back.

5. After thirty seconds or so of a relaxed stretch, A should rise up into a sitting position; B cooperates with a simultaneous return to a sitting position.

6. The pair reverse roles, with Person A going up over B's back. A's feet are flat on the floor, while B has the soles of the feet together, legs relaxed out to the side.

7. Each person does each part two times.

SEQUENTIAL SITTING UP

This exercise increases abdominal strength and spine flexibility. You do not want to bounce. Stretching should be gradual and relaxed, never forced.

1. Lie on the back, face up, with the small of your back on the floor, arms at your sides, and feet extended.

2. To the count of 8, sequentially sit up, leading with the head and neck, then the upper, middle, and lower back, until you are hanging over your feet.

3. Flex the feet and hang (relax into the position) for another eight counts. Then stretch for eight counts. (Think of stretching from the back, not the shoulders. Lengthen the muscles, and don't tighten them. Relax and feel the energy flow.)

4. To the count of 8, bring your body back down, making sure each part of the spine touches the floor. Extend the feet on the way down.

5. Repeat the steps. Then cut the counts in half, to four counts for each part. Then halve those counts to two.

HEAD AND SPINE STRETCH

This exercise releases tension in the back and the neck.

1. Sit with the soles of the feet together; push the small of the back so that you sit up in a straight line, perpendicular to the floor (Fig. 3-84).

2. To the count of 8, rotate the head slowly to the right, back, left, and front. As you rotate the head, breathe in for four counts and exhale for four counts.

3. Repeat the movements to the left in eight counts.

4. Slowly relax the spine, which will round out the back, for four counts (Fig. 3-85).

5. Hang in this position for four counts.

6. Shake out all the tension in the shoulders and neck for four counts.

3-84

3-85

3-86

3-87

3-88

3-89

3-90

7. To the count of 4, reach forward from the small of the back, arms out from the body in an upward angle, shoulders down, and head in line with the spine. Think of stretching from the small of the back and of lengthening the body (Fig. 3-86).

8. To the count of 4, reach forward and up with the arms and arch the back. Then let the arms glide down alongside the body, and place your palms on the floor (Fig. 3-87).

9. Push upward through the pelvis toward the ceiling, and let the head lower into a relaxed position, using four counts (Fig. 3-88).

10. Return to position 8 using four counts.

11. Lift the arms from the floor and contract your abdomen using four counts.

12. Pushing from the small of the back, sit up straight (Fig. 3-84) using four counts.

13. Place the hands on the ankles and the elbows on the knees (rounding the back naturally), as you press the knees down to the floor. To the count of 4, exhale (always stretch on the exhale) (Fig. 3-89 and 3-90). Then release, for four counts. Repeat.

14. Repeat the entire exercise.

TORSO AND BODY STRETCH

1. Sit up straight and extend your left leg out in front of you. Cross the right leg over the left. Wrap your left arm around the right leg and place the right arm down along the side of the body (in line with the shoulder), placing the palm of the hand flat on the floor behind your back (Fig. 3-91).

2. As you twist the torso pull the knee toward your chest. Look over your right shoulder and exhale while pressing the right half of your buttocks on the floor (Fig. 3-92).

3. Breathe in as you sit up straight. Twist the torso and exhale.
4. Do this three more times, then do the same with your legs reversed, left leg over right.

3-91

3-92

Healthy Stretching. Stretching promotes flexibility and makes the body feel good. It provides the body with the ability to use muscles and joints through their full range of motion. According to *The Wellness Encyclopedia* (University of California, 1993), there are three basic types of stretching: ballistic, static, and contract-relax. The one to avoid is ballistic. In this type of stretching you stretch to your limit and perform quick percussive, repetitive, bouncing movements. This type of movement may do more harm than good. It may add to the risk of muscle soreness and/or injury.

In contrast to this type of stretching are static and contract-relax stretching. They are slower and gentler and use sustained amounts of energy instead of the percussive energy used by the ballistic style. Follow these rules for all the stretching exercises in the text:

1. Use a sustained amount of energy.
2. Remember that breathing is extremely important in stretching. On the exhale, you should assume the farthest point of your stretch. Think of elongating the body part as it is breathing.

3. Hold in your maximum stretch position for eight to thirty seconds. Relax and inhale. On the exhale, go a little farther into the stretch, never pushing or bouncing, but elongating. Hold and repeat several times.

Flexibility varies with each individual. Much of our flexibility depends on genetics. We can all improve our flexibility by stretching. You should only stretch *after* the body is warmed up. Stretching "cold" muscles may cause injury. It is better to do the following stretching exercises after warming up with the six previous floor exercises.

LEG UP AND STRETCH

For knee and ankle flexion, do the following:

1. Lie on your back with the small of your back on the floor, legs parallel, and feet pointed.
2. Bring the right knee up toward the chest, with both hands holding the leg. The other leg is bent with the foot on the floor (Fig. 3-93). Take the knee only as high as you can, and bring the lower leg to meet it
3. Extend the lower part of the leg upward, foot pointed, and gently pull back on it stretching and lengthening. Breathe in and out three times. On the exhale, pull the leg closer to your chest (Fig. 3-94).
4. Flex the foot and bend the knee slightly (Fig. 3-95), then extend the foot and straighten the leg (Fig. 3-94).

3-93

3-94

3-95

5. Using a count of 8, bring the leg down slowly, leading with the toe, which is extended.
6. Repeat the process with the left leg. Then repeat with each leg.
7. Then repeat the exercise with both legs simultaneously, but use a count of 16 in lowering the leg. To keep the small of the back down, press down in the abdominal area. Keep tension out of the neck and shoulders.

When stretching, assume your maximum stretch on the exhale, holding and elongating. Do not push—think of your legs as breathing, too.

KNEES INTO THE CHEST

Before doing this exercise, you might start off with a simple version:

1. Bring your knee up to your chest and inhale on the count of 1.
2. Hold your breath and hold your arms out to your sides.
3. Relax the spine as you exhale.

Once this is grasped, try the following exercise:

1. Begin this exercise seated, with the back straight and the knees drawn up to the chest, arms linked around the knees. Keep your feet flat on the floor (Fig. 3-96).
2. Place the arms out to the sides of the body, parallel to the floor, and lift the feet off the floor, extending the legs at a 45-degree angle to the floor with the feet together and pointed. Keep the back straight, but allow it to assume a 45-degree angle to the floor. You are now balanced in a V, with only your buttocks on the floor (Fig. 3-97).
3. Flex the right foot toward you. Both knees stay straight.
4. Point the right foot.
5. Flex the left foot toward you.
6. Point the left foot.
7. Repeat steps 3–6.
8. Flex both feet, keeping the knees bent (Fig. 3-98).
9. Point both feet.
10. Keeping the back straight and the toes pointed, bend both knees slightly so that the lower leg is parallel to the floor (Fig. 3-99).
11. Relax.
12. Now repeat steps 1–11 three times. Try to smile and breathe at the same time!

Note to the Instructor. To teach this exercise, you may allow the actors' arms to be not extended to the side but used instead to prop up the back. The fingers of both hands are placed on the floor behind the actor, adding a third point of contact to hands and buttocks. Actors should not be rushed to get to the point at which they can balance without their hands. The object is to work the stomach and back muscles, not to perform a trick.

3-96

3-97

3-98

3-99

FLEX AND EXTEND

For stretching the ankles and knees, do the following:

1. In a sitting position, extend your legs six inches apart and parallel. Keep your back straight and arms at the sides (Fig. 3-100).
2. To the count of 2, flex the right foot and bend the knee at the same time (Fig. 3-101). Don't slide the heel on the floor. Now, to the count of 2, extend the leg and the foot. Think of extending all through the leg and out through the toes.
3. Repeat the same sequence with the left foot. Then do it again for the right and the left.
4. Repeat the sequence with both feet, flexing and extending, four times.

5. Now gently take the body over the feet and hang for eight counts (Fig. 3-102).

6. Stretch toward the feet for eight counts, reaching from the back (Fig. 3-103). Stretching should be felt in the back of the thighs. Following the stretching principle on page 78, inhale for eight counts, and exhale for eight counts. Then assume your maximum stretch point. Next inhale for four counts, exhale for four counts and stretch more deeply. (Do not lock the knees; keep them soft.)

7. To the count of 4, reach forward with the arms (Fig. 3-104), reach out, and reach up (Fig. 3-105), arching the back (Fig. 3-106). Bring them down in a smooth circle, resting the weight on the elbows.

8. Slowly lift the right leg up for four counts, with foot extended and leg turned in (Fig. 3- 107). Flex the foot (Fig. 3-108) and slowly bring the leg down for four counts, keeping it turned in. (Inhale as you lift the leg, and exhale as you lower it. Follow this breathing for the remainder of this exercise.)

9. Repeat the same process for the left side.

10. Repeat for your right side, and then left side again, but when the leg is up, hold the leg at the ankle and stretch to the count of 4 (Fig. 3-109). Think of the leg as breathing.

3-100

3-101

3-102

3-103

3-104

3-105

3-106

3-107

3-108

3-109

SECOND POSITION FLEX AND EXTEND

This exercise is also designed to help you in stretching the legs and feet.

1. With your legs in second position, sit squarely on the buttocks with the torso directly above, with feet extended and knees pointing to the ceiling (not rolling in). Place the right arm in front of the pelvis, and the left behind the buttocks, to help hold the position (Fig. 3-110).

2. Flex the right foot and bend the knee for two counts (Fig. 3-111), and then extend through the foot and leg for another two counts. Don't let the heel slide along the floor; keep it stationary.

3. Repeat with the left leg, then repeat the right and the left again.

4. Do both legs at the same time, four times (Fig. 3-112).

5. To the count of 16, hang directly over both legs (Fig. 3-113), relaxing, not stretching. Then swing the body over to the right side and hang over the leg for sixteen counts. Repeat to the left. Next, inhale for eight counts, and exhale for eight counts in each position. (This helps you to relax the body before stretching.)

6. Now relax again forward, breathing in and out three times. On your final exhalation, gently stretch forward and down from the back. Keep the thigh muscles relaxed. Think of elongating the body as you exhale to your maximum stretch. Think of the energy flowing out through the body.

7. Now stretch the right leg using the same breathing technique. As you are reaching to the right side, your left arm should be reaching directly over your head (Fig. 3-114). Hold the stretch for a count of 16. Continue to lengthen the stretch. Do not bounce. Inhale and exhale. Go deeper and hold for eight counts.

8. Repeat to the left.

9. Now turn and face your right leg, hands on either side of it (Fig. 3-115). Breathing three times, relax and go deeper into the stretch each time you exhale (Fig. 3-116). On the third breath, reach over the leg with your torso, round your back, and stretch down over your right leg. Hold for a count of 16. Breathe in for eight counts. Hold for another eight counts (Fig. 3-117).

10. Repeat to the left side.

11. Once more, go directly over both legs. Breathe in and out three times. Hang for eight counts (Fig. 3-118) and assume your maximum stretch. Hold as you count to 16. Again think of elongating, not pushing. Breathe and hold for thirty seconds (Fig. 3-119).

3-110

3-111

3-112

3-113

3-114

3-115

3-116

3-117

3-118

3-119

BREATHING IN ON HANDS AND KNEES

To relax and increase the elasticity of the back, and for breathing technique, do the following:

1. On your hands and knees, form a flat back. Your face is looking at the floor, your hands and knees are on the floor, and your arms are extended straight out.
2. Breathe in to the count of 8 as you arch your back up toward the ceiling, moving sequentially from the small of the back to the base of the head. Think of filling the back with air.
3. Exhale to the count of 8 while sinking the spine sequentially toward the floor, going again from the small of the back to the base of the head. (The face will look forward briefly as the neck begins to sink toward the floor, and then the face in its turn will sink toward the floor.)
4. Repeat in eight counts up and breathing in, then eight counts down and breathing out.
5. Repeat in four counts breathing in; four counts breathing out.
6. Repeat in two counts breathing in; two counts breathing out.

STRETCH, SIT, PUSH THROUGH, AND SIT

To stretch the back and stomach muscles, this exercise begins in the classic Middle Eastern prayer position, the Fold-Up Stretch. *Caution:* Steps 2 and 3, for various reasons, may be difficult for some people. If so, just do Step 1.

1. Begin with the knees, face, and arms on the floor (Fig. 3-120).
2. Breathe in to the count of 4 as you come to a kneeling position, sitting on your lower legs with your arms at your sides (Fig. 3-121).
3. Breathe out to the count of 4 as you put your hands on the floor behind you and then push forward and up as far as you can with your pelvis (Fig. 3-122).
4. Breathe in as you return to the sitting position, to the count of 4.
5. Breathe out as you return to original position, to the count of 4.
6. Repeat, using four counts for each movement.
7. Repeat twice, using two counts for each movement.

BASIC CHEST PUSH-UP

This exercise is familiar, and a good one. You should do as many as you can without feeling a strain in the lower back.

1. Assume the standard push-up position either on your feet (Fig. 3-123) or on your knees (Fig. 3-124). Place your hands on the floor slightly farther apart than your shoulder width. Keep your body flat and your head in line with your spine. Tuck in your buttocks and your abdominal muscles.
2. Slowly lower your chest to the floor, bending your elbows as you inhale. Keep both legs straight and knees soft, maintaining the flat body (Fig. 3-125).
3. As you exhale, slowly straighten your arms and push back up. Avoid locking the elbows when you push up.

3-120

3-121

3-122

3-123

3-124

3-125

SIT-UPS

For strengthening the abdominal muscles, here is another well-known exercise. Yet it is one that requires some caution: you should not put pressure on the neck with your hands. All of the lifting is done with the abdominals. Also keep your lower back in contact with the floor throughout the entire exercise.

1. Lie on your back with your knees bent and feet flat on the floor. Place your hands gently behind the head, elbows out to the side (Fig. 3-126).
2. Lift your upper body off the floor using the abdominal muscles. Focus on the ceiling, keeping your neck in a neutral position. (Imagine holding an orange between your chin and neck.)
3. Contract your abdominal muscles and press the lower back into the floor while you're lifting the shoulder blades off the floor (Fig. 3-127). Exhale as you lift and hold.
4. Now lower the body, or roll back down and inhale.

HIP AND BACK STRETCH I

This is a good sequence to do after the push-ups and sit-ups.

1. Begin lying on your back with your knees pulled into your chest. Relax your head, neck, and spine (Fig. 3-128). You can also wrap your arms underneath your legs.
2. Take four slow deep breaths, ridding the body of all tension from head to toe. (Use the breathing technique on page 35.)

3-126

3-127

3-128

HIP AND BACK STRETCH II

1. Lie on your back with the knees bent, feet flat on the floor, arms out to the side of the body.
2. Now slowly contract the abdominals and lower your knees to the right side of the floor as far as you can comfortably go. Let both arms go to your left side. Hold. Breathe deeply feeling the stretch (Fig. 3-129).
3. Repeat, lowering your knees to the left side and your arms to the right side.

3-129

SIT, PUSH, SIT, ROLL

This is an exercise to improve upper body strength. Be careful as you decrease the count from 4 to 1 for each movement; keep the movement fluid and not jerky, maintaining your follow-through.

1. Lie face down on the floor with hands under the shoulders and elbows poking up (Fig. 3-130).
2. Breathe in as you roll to your right, keeping the right hand on the floor but lifting the left hand. Come up into a sitting position, with the right leg straight, the left bent toward the ceiling, and the left foot flat on floor six to eight inches from the right leg (Fig. 3-131).
3. To the count of 4, breathe out as you push your entire body off the floor and reach toward the ceiling with your left hand. Thrust your pelvis up as far as possible with your right arm straight. Your right hand, left foot (with bent left leg), and right foot (with straight leg) provide three points of contact with the floor (Fig. 3-132).
4. Breathe in for four counts as you sit back down.
5. Breathe out for four counts as you roll back to the starting position, with hands under shoulders.
6. Now repeat the sequence for the left side, using a count of 4 for each movement. This time the left leg stays straight, the left hand remains on the floor, the right hand lifts and extends, and the right leg lifts over the left and bends so that the right foot is flat on the floor.
7. Repeat the entire exercise four times, using only one count for each movement.

3-130

3-131

3-132

ARCH AND A EXERCISE

For upper body strength, do this exercise, being careful again to keep the movement fluid and not jerky, maintaining your follow-through.

1. Lie face down on the floor with hands under the shoulders and elbows poking up (Fig. 3-130). Take a deep breath and exhale.
2. To the count of 4, extend the arms straight out to their limit while you breathe in, and arch the back. Lift the face toward the ceiling. (Fig. 3-133).
3. Lift the pelvis off the floor, keeping the legs straight, and lift the pelvis as high as you can so that the body forms an A Position—while you breathe out in four counts (Fig. 3-134).
4. As you breathe to the count of 4, lift the left foot off the floor and the left leg over the right leg as you pivot your body on your right hand and foot. Your left hand will come off the floor. Bend your left leg as you lift it up and over the right leg (Fig. 3-135); this way you can stop your rolling momentum by placing your left foot on the floor as you turn body and face toward the ceiling.
5. To the count of 4, breathe out as you sit (Fig. 3-136).
6. To the count of 4, breathe in as you lift your pelvis toward the ceiling as far as you can, and reach your left hand toward the ceiling (Fig. 3-132).
7. Again breathe out for four counts as you sit, bringing your left arm down (Fig. 3-136).
8. Breathe in for four counts as you lift your pelvis off the floor, kicking your left leg up.
9. Pivot the torso with your weight on your right leg and hand, and catch yourself with your left hand as your body pivots toward your original position (Fig. 3-137).

10. To the count of 4, breathe out as you lower your left leg and torso back into the original position.
11. Repeat the movements for the left side, lifting your right leg and hand and maintaining your breathing technique.
12. Repeat, right and left, using two counts for each movement and matching your breath to the movement.
13. Repeat right and left again, using one count per movement.

Note to the Instructor. As you can see, this is a very advanced exercise and should not be taught when actors are first learning technique and building their strength. But after some prior conditioning, both men and women can gain much from this exercise.

3-133

3-134

3-135

3-136

3-137

PULSE, PULSE AND UP

This exercise is for strengthening the hamstrings. *Caution:* Don't force things.

1. To find the start position, stand and place the feet in the parallel plié position, do a deep plié, then place the palms of your hands on the floor in front and outside of the toes, Keep your head up. This is the starting position (Fig. 3-138).

2. Do two slow pulses (gentle bounces), followed by two quick pulses. Then slowly straighten the legs, keeping the knees soft, the hands on the floor (or as close as you can keep them), and the chest close to the knees (Fig. 3-139).

3. Once you have straightened the legs, repeat three more times. On the last repetition, grasp the ankles and, on a count of 4, gently stretch your chest toward your straightened legs (Fig. 3-140). Then breathe deeply. As you exhale, feel the spine stretch and the body go closer to the floor and ankles, Hold the stretch for a count of 16, or as many as 30. Do this three times.

4. Next, walk only with the hands (Fig. 3-141), keeping your feet flat on the floor. Walk with the feet to bring them up to meet the hands (Fig. 3-142). Grasp the ankles with both hands again and stretch your chest toward your legs for four more counts (Fig. 3-140). Slowly come up through the spine to a standing position.

Ending the Warm-up

FOOT FLEXIBILITY I

These exercises are for foot articulation and prepare the actor for jumps and leaps. Rather like running the engine of a rocket while the rocket is tied down, they teach the proper mechanics of jumping. In this case, your feet and legs are working as they would for a jump (only separately and not together as they will eventually need to), and your body is the rocket. In both cases the engine is warmed up and tested before using it to lift.

1. Assume first position as in classical ballet, with feet turned out and arms curved out at the side.

2. Lift just the right heel and press the ball of the foot into the floor (Fig. 3-143). Lower yourself, then repeat the lift and lower three more times. Then do the same with the left foot.

3. Now lift the foot in three stages: heel (Fig. 3-143), ball (Fig. 3-144), toe (Fig. 3-145), and bring the foot back down onto the floor, toe, ball, heel. Do this four times on each foot.

4. Now keep the three stages in rapid lifts—heel, ball, toe—and drops—toe, ball, heel—one count to come up, another to come down. Think of pushing the foot off the floor. Do not lift the hip.

3-138

3-139

3-140

3-141

3-142

3-143

3-144

3-145

FOOT FLEXIBILITY II

I call this a "lunge-feet" exercise. At first, do the exercise slowly. Once it becomes easier, do each move in one count.

1. Assume the starting position: feet turned out in the first position of classical ballet (Fig. 3-146).
2. Lift the right leg slightly off the floor, arms out to the side, in second position (Fig. 3-147).
3. Place your right leg (leg is turned out from hip) down with a small lunge in front of the body (leg is bent) (Fig. 3-148). Your left leg is straight.
4. Push the weight on the back of the left leg and straighten it. Lift the right and place it back to classical first position (Fig. 3-146).
5. Now do the same thing toward the side of the body. Assume first position. At the same time lift your arms in second position out to the side of the body. Lift the right leg sideways (Fig. 3-149).
6. Place the right leg down in a small lunge. Your leg is bent, the back left leg is straight—you are in a lunge position (Fig. 3-150).
7. Now place your weight on the back left leg and lift the right leg, placing it back at the original starting position.
8. Repeat the same steps using the left side; move to the front and to the side.

After the exercise is fully grasped you can add on the work of the feet, which would come after the lunge with both feet back.

9. Assume the front lunge position. Make sure the weight is centered and the foot turned out. Now go up through the foot, all the way through the point. Repeat six times.
10. Then shift the weight onto the back leg, extend the front leg, and return to the first position.
11. Do the same sequence with the feet to the side. Then do front, right, side, right, and then front, left, side, left with the left foot.

JUMPS

This exercise for strengthening and conditioning of the legs begins from the end position of the last exercise (in first position).

1. As a preparation, do four demi-pliés with a relevé between each plié, using one count for each movement (that is, plié down and straighten, relevé up and down). Keep the flow of energy smooth and even; the movement mustn't be jerky. The muscles of the feet and legs must work continually.
2. Instead of rising into relevé, on the last two counts use a burst of energy so that your feet rise off the floor in a small jump.

3-146

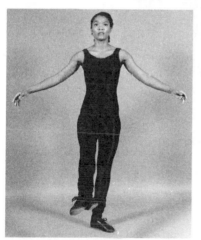

3-147

3-148

3-149

3-150

3. Continue these small jumps until you have done eight jumps in first position. On the last jump, move both legs into second and continue jumping in second position.
4. Then do four more jumps in first position, and four more in second.

Make certain that you begin each jump in plié, and that you land in plié, or you will give yourself shin splints. Also make certain you extend your feet in the air so that your toes point toward the floor as you land. Then you will land in succession: toe of the foot, ball of the foot, and finally the heel. Avoid making a loud thud when you land; otherwise you will hurt your foot. These are *small* jumps. Invariably someone in my early classes has taken this exercise to mean "Let's see how high you can jump!" This is not what's intended; I discourage it, for heroic efforts are out of place in any warm-up. Serious dedication to mastering the essentials of centering, strength and stretch is all that is required.

One more note: Do not buckle in the waist, or lift in the shoulders—the feet and legs do all the work! After the jump do some stretches for the calves, hamstrings, and quadriceps.

Remember to *hold each stretch for a period of fifteen to thirty seconds* to get the full benefit.

FRUSTRATION JUMPS
This will aid you in relaxation and easing mental strain.

1. Begin in a low squat, legs turned out, hands on the floor between the legs.
2. Leap as high in the air as you can, raising your arms up, flailing the legs and shouting out all your frustration!
3. Do three jumps in a row, allowing your body to collapse onto the floor at the end of the last jump. Then relax.

Instructors can use this to end an exercise session with a note of frivolity. It erases tension better than any other single technique I know of when combined with the following exercise.

BREATH RHYTHM
This exercise is usually done at the end of a warm-up, after vigorous exercise. It helps return one to a relaxed state.

1. Take a supine position, feet parallel, arms loose at your sides, and the small of the back on the floor. If the back will not lie flat, don't strain; just bend the knees and put the soles of your feet on the floor.
2. Talk or think yourself through the tension-draining process, or shake your tension out.

3. Once in a neutral state, concentrate on your breathing and try to find its rhythm. You will know when you have it.

4. With your breathing rhythm established, slowly rise to a standing position. Find the easiest way up so that you don't change or lose the rhythm. Rise in a fluid motion.

5. Once up, check on your alignment. Is your weight centered? Are your legs pulled up? Knees relaxed? Muscles pulled across? Shoulders down? Back open? Neck and face relaxed? Test your alignment by pressing up through your feet and down.

The Chakras

Just as we align our physical anatomy, the external self that houses mind and spirit, we must also align our subtler inner anatomy. We do this by balancing the *chakras*. This exercise, derived from ancient yogic practices, helps us to attain an inner balance which complements the alignment of the physical body.

Chakra is a Sanskrit word meaning "wheel," and a chakra is a spinning vortex of energy within us. Through these wheels of energy we receive, transmit, and process energy. There are seven major chakras; when these seven vortices are aligned, optimum energy as well as harmony is the result. Each chakra corresponds to one of the seven colors of the rainbow, to musical sound vibrations, and to the various glands of the endocrine system. As energy centers, they form a network through which the mind, spirit, and body are integrated into a holistic system.

Working with an understanding of the chakra system helps to create wholeness and integration within ourselves. We can use the system as a road map for journeying through our mind, spirit, and body to create harmony within ourselves and the universe.

As always, relaxation and breathing are an important part of the exercise. Begin with the following steps:

1. Lie down or sit in a relaxed, aligned position such as you would when meditating.

2. Relax, let go of your tensions and negative thoughts, and trust yourself to just *be*. Breathe deeply through the diaphragm, in and out. Feel new energy rushing into the body and stale energy flushing out all tensions. Feel the constant flow of energy flowing through you. Feel yourself grow light, gentle, airy—as if you were floating on a cloud. Continue to breathe deeply, in and out. Keep your mind, spirit, and body open and relaxed.

3. Take a deep breath for the entire body. Inhale, and as you exhale, let go of all tension and stress in the body.

4. Take another breath for the mind. Inhale, and take yourself to that special place that lets your mind be quiet and calm. Exhale, and let go of all the cobwebs and negative thoughts in your mind.

5. Take another deep breath for the spirit, and as you exhale feel your spirit renewed. Feel the connection of your mind, spirit, and body. Relax, let go.

Once the group is relaxed, begin the process to balance the chakras.

BALANCE AND ALIGNMENT OF CHAKRAS

1. Concentrate your energy and attention in the base of your spine. This is the base root chakra—the energy center which roots you to the earth. It is the force which gives vitality to the physical body. Its color is *red,* a deep, lush, vibrant red. It correlates in the body to the spine and kidneys; its element is the earth; it resonates to the note of C. It is the chakra through which you experience "fear of flight" and your instinct for survival. It deals with the mastery of the physical body, grounding, security, stability, and courage.

Now tune in to the universal energy we are all part of. Feel the vitality.

Its affirmation is "I have," "I am rooted in myself," "I have courage," "I am stable," and so on.

Breathe deeply through this chakra and envision the red permeating your spine. Exhale any problems in this area. Feel the richness of the earth and its energy flowing into your being.

2. Move to the next chakra, located in the lower abdomen—the spleen and the sexual and reproductive organs. The color is orange, like a wonderful sunrise or luscious orange. Its element is water—giving, receiving, cleansing, replenishing. It resonates to the note of D. It deals with sexuality, sensuality, relationships, and creativity.

Breathe deeply through this chakra and let the orange color cleanse and replenish your creativity and sensuality. To deal with any problems you might be having in the area of the spleen and reproductive organs, breathe deeply in and out through this chakra. Let go of all desire to control; instead, let yourself be very open and receptive to your creative will.

The affirmation is "I feel." "I feel myself creatively flowing through my being (mind, spirit, body)."

3. Move next to the third chakra, whose location is the center of the body, the solar plexus. The color is yellow; the element is fire; it resonates to the note of E. In the body, this chakra deals with the pancreas, digestive system, stomach, gall bladder, intestines, and nervous system. It is the clearinghouse of your emotions and the seat of your personal power and free will.

This is the chakra which allows for awakenings and transformations through positive use of your emotions. Breathe deeply through this chakra, relax and let go, feel your personal power, and affirm that you have access to that power. Think of your emotions as clouds—look at them and allow them to float by. Do not hold onto negative emotions; find them, deal with them, and allow them to pass. Let go.

The affirmation is "I can." "My personal power is growing stronger every day."

4. Move to the next chakra. This is the heart, which connects the lower chakras (the Chinese "yang," which is masculine) to the higher (the "yin," which is feminine). The color is a cool, lush, emerald green; its element is air; it resonates to the note of F. This is the chakra of love, the one by which we fall in love. In the body it governs the heart, the blood, and the circulatory, immune, and endocrine systems.

Now experience divine, unconditional love. Send love to the higher power—to God, the Universal Energy, however you perceive this power. Send love to yourself and your loved ones, to your enemies, to the universe. Forgive yourself and others. Open yourself up to feel peace and harmony. Accept yourself for who you are. Accept love and peace for yourself and offer it to others. Throw your heart over the barriers or obstacles in your life and the rest of you will follow.

The affirmation is "I love." "I put my love into everything I do."

Love can conquer all in its pure form. Feel your heart and its vibration through your entire being and outward to the universe, sending love and healing to all it meets.

5. Move up to the throat. Here the chakra color is blue; the element is ether. This chakra resonates to the note of G. Within the body, it deals with the throat, the thyroid gland, the lungs, and the vocal cords. It is the chakra of communication, expression, and judgment.

Envision the color blue permeating this chakra. Breathe deeply through it. Open up your center of communication. Don't be afraid to express yourself. This is where thinking and feeling connect. Express yourself in a positive, loving manner, even when dealing with a negative subject or feeling.

The affirmation is "I speak." "I express myself freely and easily."

Be nonjudgmental of yourself and others. Think: "Today, I will judge nothing that occurs. Everyone exists with me to be loved, not judged."

Know that everyone and everything is just where it needs to be at this point in time. The universe is as it is on purpose.

6. Move up to the center of the forehead to the brow chakra, the "third eye." The color is indigo, a mixture of red and blue. The element is light vision. This chakra resonates to the note of A. It correlates in the body to the pituitary gland. It governs the nervous system and the lower brain (the cerebellum).

This is where you experience your future, your dreams, your higher self, and your psychic abilities. See yourself as a spiritual being having a human experience. Tune into your intuition, insight, and imagination.

The affirmation is "I see." "I move toward my vision with purpose."

If you can believe it, you will see it. If you can visualize it, it will materialize. The universe is with you. Follow the light, dare to dream. Breathe deeply through your third eye and follow the light to your vision of the future.

7. The seventh chakra is the crown. The color is violet; the note is B. It governs the pineal gland. This is the most powerful chakra. The element is thought and will. It is here that we feel our oneness with the infinite, God, the higher power, the Universal Energy—however you perceive the source. This is the integration beyond space, time, and energy, beyond reality into divine wisdom. It connects you with all time (past, present, and future).

Its affirmation is "I know." "All the answers are within me."

Feel this chakra spiraling into infinity. The base root chakra grounds you to the earth; all other chakras spin up along your spine, connecting you to the universe. Know how special and unique you are. There is, and never will be, anyone like you. Also know that you are part of a greater whole, a member of the family of the universe.

When all the chakras are aligned, action and understanding become one. We feel a sense of harmony, peace, well-being. Feel both the external and internal parts of yourself as one. Know yourself, your destiny. Let go, and just *be*.

Feel all the chakras spiraling up the spine, the base root chakra rooted to the earth, and the crown chakra spiraling up to infinity. All of the energy connects and all the colors form the white light. Be in harmony with yourself and the universe. Open yourself up to new ideas. Ask and you shall receive, seek and you shall find. Knock and the universe shall open up to you and your needs. Follow the light and love of your heart and being. Keep your mind clear of negative thoughts. Keep your spirit strong and your body whole and healthy. Believe in your higher self, in your knowing. Journey through the light, always move towards the light.

Now tune into your breathing and breath rhythm so that you can balance the body that houses your thoughts (your mind, spirit, and soul).

Some Final Suggestions

To these suggested general exercises you will probably wish to add a good many more of your own choosing—more stretches, bounces, jumps, and certain calisthenics. To include all the exercises I use over a several-month period would have tripled the length of this section. Moreover, everyone has personal needs, preferences, and special circumstances, and therefore I invite the actor and the instructor to improvise and adapt as the situation warrants.

Remember, however, to keep in mind these basic rules:

1. It is important to maintain proper breathing.
2. Warm up the entire being (mind, spirit, and body).
3. Understand the purpose and mechanics of each exercise.
4. Start simply and easily before any strenuous work.
5. Use your exercises to focus the day's work.

Also, keep one more thing in mind: This is movement for actors—not for a dance class.

A given exercise should be kept simple, and the technique should be consistent and demand as little superfluous movement as possible. Sophisticated movements that demand a high degree of technical proficiency will close off actors from movement training sessions, instructors, and their own bodies. Exercises can encourage unwanted competition and tension and thus decrease spontaneity and cooperation. The longer a session meets, the more proficient the actors will become with the simple movements and the more readily will they respond as a group to additions like complicated arm patterns and more difficult exercises.

4 *Explorations*

Exploration has always been the first step toward exploitation. This is no less true of stage movement study. Until actors are aware of the full range and depth of their resources, how can they be expected to use them? I have detailed in this area of study many of the most useful tools I have found for this exploration and organized them in such a way as to provide the same type of progressive acquisition of skills as was detailed in "Exercises." Beginning with the most elementary (and necessary) explorations of the body, the actor is led through several series of explorations that demand and hence reveal progressively deeper levels of intellectual and emotional awareness. The program's seemingly random arrangement of the exploration series only appears rational once one understands the need to place the actor in a situation that is at once familiar and reassuring and in which he (or she) feels capable and responsible for increasing comprehension. This is why many of the explorations have the same starting sequence of instructions, and it is the reason for this particular sequence of explorations. It is also the key to providing a relaxed and positive atmosphere free of competition. Keep in mind that for all explorations, discussion must *follow,* not precede, the action. Too much information and answers to too many questions provide false road maps to uncharted areas. In other words, too much prior discussion destroys the very process we are trying to stimulate. I don't let actors ask, "how, what, why, or from where?" They will be able to tell me once they have returned. If one or two go off on a tangent and learn something other than what I intended—so what? And if one or two feel as though they have learned nothing, it is not unusual or alarming—many times the puzzle looks like a pile of pieces until it is assembled. Effort in one day may not be rewarded with brilliant success, and it is not daily reward actors should be led to expect. Rather, it is over a period of time, after much serious study, that awareness of progress can be detected. This is the attitude that must be encouraged. This is why it is important that past and future efforts be organized and related as continually as possible, and why some of the material in this book may seem repetitious. Nothing encourages future effort more than success at past effort, and if we can ensure success (that is, reward) at one level, we can guarantee future effort at another.

The material contained in this chapter is the heart of my stage movement training because it awakens the actor to the many levels and manners of the mind-spirit-body connection. It is frivolous and irresponsible to propose (as some do) that an actor need only condition and sensitize the body. That is physical education, not stage movement training. Stage movement training should awaken the actor to the world of movement: pure movement, abstract movement, and human movement and motivations especially. It should help the actor understand how emotions affect the body; how physical states affect the mental processes; how imagery, memories, and suggestions affect the body through the unconscious mind. Actors are generally more sensitive to spatial relationships, time compression, and states of energy in themselves and those around them than are most people. Stage movement training seeks to awaken actors to their own sensitivity, to make them more aware and confident about the things they may subconsciously already know, so that they can exploit that knowledge more fully. Also, it serves to awaken in them new ways of seeing and experiencing, to help them know more than they were capable of knowing before.

There is an odd fact associated with movement: While all movement is essentially nonverbal physicalization, it is also, paradoxically, invisible. Except when we watch some athletes, artists, and dancers, we are unaccustomed to seeing the movement we are looking at. Ordinarily we just do not consciously observe what we see, whether in our own movement or the movement in the world around us. Like the untutored witness to the crime who knows that someone shot someone else but is unable to say for certain which hand held the weapon, how many shots were fired, how long it took, or even whether a man or a woman did the deed—many times we are unable to "see" the movement of the world around us because we are so busy trying to understand it. Our explorations help to materialize and make visible for study this world of movement. It is interesting to note that seeing the world more clearly may help the actor to better understand it. explorations also help supply the guides with which we can chart this vast basically undiscovered world of movement.

The most useful guides are the basic concepts of all movement: space, time, and energy. All movement occurs in and occupies space; it is measured by time; and it requires energy to begin and complete itself. Space, time, and energy, then, provide the major frames for viewing this world. Throughout the explorations these three frames focus the study. The stress falls on the interplay between the actor's intellectual grasp of the concepts and a growing visceral awareness of the body. Again, while the order in which the explorations are presented has been consciously conceived for the most efficient learning, the order is not canonical; some revision, selection, and improvisation within the general framework, and a good many additions, are heartily recommended once the basic design is understood.

Explorations of the Body in Eight Phases

ISOLATION OF THE PARTS

This isolation work adds an awareness of motion to the already acquired discovery of segments of the anatomy.

Explore each area and limb and the structure of the body for its movement potential. Start with the head; rotate it, move it forward and back, side to side, vibrate with it, sway it, bounce it, get it moving every way you can imagine. (Always begin cautiously.)

Continue to discover all the movements you can with your arms, legs, feet, pelvis, torso, chest, even your elbow. Don't forget about all the muscles in your face.

Now build combinations. Add shoulder to arm, or add a hand, too, and a side of the torso.

Try isolated and combined explorations while stationary, while walking or ambling about, in different levels, prone, sitting, or standing. Stay relaxed, open, and loose. Acquire the feel of all these movements.

SELF-CONTACT AND SENSATIONS

Assuming a supine position on the floor, bring yourself to a neutral state by sapping the body of all its tension. You are going to be touching your body with three kinds of contact: slapping, tapping, and rubbing. (You may invent other kinds of touching on your own, preferably after you have explored these three.)

Once in a neutral state, you can move into any position that assists with the contact. But the progress of the contact should begin at the top of your head and move sequentially to your feet. The best way is to begin with one kind of touch and go over the whole body, starting by slapping head, ears, back of the neck, shoulders, all the way down to your ankles. Then run through with tapping, and so on. Try different intensities with a single touch—firm, light, sudden, slow, and so forth. Then mix up the three touches on a single area of the body: slap, tap, and scratch the thigh and mix up the intensities.

When the class is emotionally prepared, this exploration can be performed by two actors. This exploration is also good for warming up the actor and developing relaxation techniques.

JOURNEY THROUGH THE BODY

This exploration enables the actor to get to know his instrument and its many wonders and capabilities—to introduce the actor to his body. Approach this as if it were the first time you took such a trip.

1. Lie down and relax. Do the breathing exercise on page 35 to help clear and relax you.

2. Without moving, take a journey through your body. Sense what it feels like to stand, walk, run, jump, lift your arm, wink, and so on, without actually performing the physical task.

3. Now from the supine position on the floor gradually begin your trip, or discovery, of the body through movement. Begin to discover your body— isolating parts one at a time. Be as specific as you can. Notice all the detail of each part and its strengths and weaknesses.

4. As you begin to move from a supine position to a standing one, notice the difference in the physical mobility of this position. Each level in space and stance of the body offers new and different ranges of movement.

5. Explore the isolated parts as well as the total body and all the combinations of parts working separately and together. The possibilities are unlimited.

6. Just be free and spontaneous with your body and allow it to explore itself and discover its wonders.

The instructor can give direction or just allow the actors to explore without any verbal cues; each group in training is different. A combination of guidance and freedom usually works best.

MOVEMENT INITIATION

This exploration studies how a movement begins in one part of the body and is extended by follow-through into other physical segments.

Start with a simple hip rotation, moving only the hips. Then allow more and more of your body to follow the circular movement of the hips—with the hip rotation still clearly your focus—so your total body is moving from a single source, the hips.

Stop and renew simple hip rotation, but add movement of the thigh, then the whole leg, knee, calf, and foot. This is a succession of movement, and you should move the focus of the movement down the leg as you gradually extend and enlarge the movement.

Once you grasp the principles, experiment with other parts of the body. The hip is easiest, but the head and the shoulders also work well. Then explore how movement can originate in the center of the body, around the solar plexus, rib cage, and pelvis. Take head or limbs out from the center.

MOTION EXPLORING

This exploration employs some of the basic locomotor movements: walking, skipping, running, jumping, hopping, sliding, galloping, and so on. First, simply test and play with each of these locomotor styles, either in a random manner around the room or, for clearer observation, in lines of four actors moving abreast in waves across the floor. Then build combinations, such as skip-jump-slide, run-gallop-run-walk, or hop-slide-hop-slide. All this playing around is to develop a sense of freedom in moving about—freedom especially from the fear of moving, a fear developed from our loss of variety of locomotor styles somewhere around early adolescence. This type of movement is distinct from dance combinations that require specific, exacting "technique" that can inhibit rather than free an untrained actor's ability to feel and observe her (or his) body in motion.

MIRROR STUDY

The actors should pair off and face each other as though each were looking in a mirror. Initially, one should be designated as the originator, the other as the imitator. The two should be working to maintain the illusion that they are looking into a mirror. The action is imitation, and roles of originator and imitator should be exchanged. The originator should begin with an assortment of simple moves, gestures, twinges, twitches, and so on, avoiding movements that would force the imitator to turn his back to the originator. The imitator should try to become very quick and sure (and stay relaxed) with copying, closing the time gap as much as possible. This exploration can take five to ten minutes for each originator the first time through. The technique can be returned to frequently over a year's study in order to reinforce observation, concentration, and sensitivity. Eventually, the assignment of originator-imitator roles should no longer be necessary as the actors learn to trust and understand each other; they will both be originating and imitating simultaneously, and thus are spontaneously creating together. Actors skilled in this activity can remain focused and usefully involved for half an hour or more before tiring.

Viola Spolin is usually credited with conceiving mirror exercises. See her book *Improvisation for the Theatre* (Evanston, Ill.: Northwestern University Press, 1963).

An advanced variation is the question-and-answer technique. Instead of copying single movements, the point is to build an exchange, a set of signals and responses. The simple mirror work is needed to develop sensitivity to another's moves, as a prelude to answering. Make conversations: tell how you feel, what you are thinking about, what you are, what you want to do. But avoid close mime, code gesturing, or charade language. Trust yourself to express the essence of what you are trying to say directly. This is very difficult work initially, but it does help to get to know one another.

BLOSSOMING AND WITHERING

This exploration is derived from Jerzy Grotowski, author of *Towards a Poor Theatre* (New York: Simon & Schuster, 1968). Here, you explore the body by trying on the analogy of a body being born, coming to life, rising, developing, extending, discovering powers, maturing, peaking, until fully "blossomed." Start prone and slowly escalate your energy level as you go into whatever blossoming activity seems called for. Remain at the peak until it is fully explored. Then begin "withering." You slowly lose energy, and the body slowly collapses. Don't rush this exploration.

The most important benefit of this process is the finding of the peak, feeling what it is like to be so vibrant and alive. The study also reinforces tension and relaxation exercises and heightens a general body awareness while stimulating the imagination.

FACIAL MASKS

Assume any posture or position you wish, one that reflects some kind of attitude, personality, or emotion. Now find a face that goes with the body's attitude. Know who you are, what you want, where you are going—all to sharpen your grasp of the attitude you are forming with your body. Move around in this posture, sharpening your sense of the reality of this attitude. Starting with an external form, a coolly selected state of being, and by moving around in it, wearing the appropriate physical mask, you should begin to gain an internal sense of the attitude—the emotions and specific sensations of such an external bearing.

Once you have the feel of one attitude, select another, but this time start with a mask, a facial attitude, and then find the body to match the face. Now try to locate the "gut," the sensations of this attitude. Move around in this mind-body frame until you feel comfortable with it and it begins to soak through you.

Once all the actors feel secure in their selected identity, the group should attempt some rudimentary mingling, with individuals seeking to relate to one another from within identities. The directions cannot be explicit and predictive. The goal is a give-and-take openness to all the physical stimuli in mingling.

If the relating seems to be going smoothly, the whole group should come to a sudden freeze, one that crystallizes the identities. Each actor should study the nearest person, then slowly move in transition from her (or his) own posture and attitude into the other person's: first the obvious physical configuration, the mask, and then unfreezing, moving around, and trying to pick up the inner feel. After another freeze the process should be extended.

Now the process is reversed. Begin with fixing upon or creating an inner attitude. First, prone on the floor, regain a neutral state, drain out the tension, and clear the head of the previous masks. Lying there, think about all kinds of identities, characters, moods, and personalities, and select one to work with. Begin to take in or develop the feelings and thoughts of this identity, asking the same basic questions about it (that is, Who am I? What do I want? Where am I going?) Then assume this identity. You are still on the floor, but within you is "the psyche," the gut, of this identity. Now, arise, reborn into another identity and discover the facial mask, the appropriate body, the revealing movements.

This work involves primitive characterization. The study explores getting inside alien identities through two routes—starting from the outside, an external, technical route, and starting from a direct grasp of the inner condition, an internal psychological path. Both are frequently employed, and both are necessary for versatile acting. The point is to focus attention on the direction of flow. One direction is from physical expression toward inner form, the other is from inner form toward physical expression.

A NOTE ON OBSERVATION AND IMITATION

If an actor's art largely consists of recreating other beings, movement studies offer an immediate and direct access to these others. The classic technique for finding models for re-creation is observation and imitation. What one observes is an amalgam of general types (soldier on leave, brisk businesswoman, smart-mouthed street kid, and so forth) and peculiar instances (the wino who slumps along looking behind him, the suburban woman with the frank stare, and the little old lady who hums to herself and smiles in all directions). One can at first be blind to anything but the types or be bewildered by unrepeated individual cases seemingly impossible to type. Observing the rich exchange between "type" and "individual" requires practice and work.

So, first one must learn to focus and structure one's observing. Generalities and typological assertions are not to be trusted, really, yet one can discover a surprising amount of truth in trying them on. Let us look at the old favorite—the comparison between the infant and the old man, two semi-hairless, physically feeble creatures at opposite ends of a lifetime. One can observe in the infant his precarious legs, unsteady balance, free but slow arm gestures, and curved but supple torso. In the old man there is likely a similar leg instability, another kind of torpid arm movement, and a sagging, curved torso. So far so good. But beyond these striking similarities are some obvious differences. The elderly's hesitant and sharp gestures, the fact that his torso has now been bent permanently into that curve, and his basic fragility, all contrast with the soft resiliency of the child's movement. There is enough truth in the comparison, then, a sufficient analogy, to make a good, useful exercise from it (try on old age and then do an infant; note the similarities and differences).

In the differences that close observation yields lie the most interesting discoveries. Special points of focus can produce new systems for typing. Look for different kinds of mouth movement, eye work, fingering, pelvis positioning, buttock swings, and so on. One observation technique is to watch necks one day, elbows the next, and so on. The closer one focuses the observation, the finer and more fascinating the data observed. It all depends on what you need to look for. A model for a business executive in a play? Styles of running? You must be explicit in knowing what you are looking for, or else you will drown in both types and particulars. A system of mental (or written) cataloging helps organize and retain the data.

Immediate imitation is a sure way for strong retention. Copying the posture of the woman next to you on the bus may prove embarrassing, but getting it at once is necessary. A safer method is to follow your subject down the street—at a considerable distance, of course. Working in teams and comparing and checking versions also helps. Something like a mental catalog of physical movement can be created and stored away for further use. A long and close observation and imitation session, such as with a mail carrier or police officer who is exposed to daily scrutiny, can actually so involve you that you will develop a certain raw empathy, a kind of identification with that person, not unlike what one does in developing and getting to know a character one is getting into for a play. In a way, this phenomenon is rather like the basic activity of the "doubling" exercise in sensitivity training, wherein the members of the encounter group closely imitate one another in order to get a little better feel of what it is like to be in each other's shoes. Viola Spolin's mirror exercises can also establish this kind of raw empathy. But once an actor knows himself, the basic goal is to get outside himself, to discover other ways of being and moving.

Walks

The simplest and least analyzed stage movement is the simple walk, yet it is usually the first movement an actor makes in a performance, and it tells the audience how far she (or he) has gone into a role. If she is the least ill at ease in the role, or still groping for the role's center, the walk will give it away.

Let us encourage a healthy and freeing self-consciousness concerning walking. First, take the normal, customary walking style. The actor or the instructor should perform an analysis of it, noting all the peculiar mannerisms. It is helpful if actors training together analyze one another's walks as well. Of course, once the idiosyncrasies are pointed out, we must try to eliminate any glaring problems, and this will take a number of sessions over some length of time. But the advance toward a "pure walk" (of some approximation) can be speeded up by experimenting with exaggerated walks: walking with extreme tension, like a mechanical monster or a stick man; with utter relaxation, almost collapsed, like a monkey; with the weight way back on the heels, always teetering on an invisible edge; with the weight slugging forward; stylized mincing; horse-like loping. The list is long, but the point is that experimenting with exaggerated walks helps one feel how an ideal walk must be performed, reinforces alignment work, and should increase the range of styles at the actor's command.

An observation exercise will help these lessons to take hold. The actors might go out into the streets, shops, and parking lots to observe many kinds of interesting walks. A useful way to structure an observation is to look for different types by age grouping. One might start with a toddler, move up a few years for the next grouping, and find characteristic samples of major age classes for young men or women, middle-aged adults, and elderly people. The age classes are not definitive, for social classes and the sexes have their own walking "imprints." Environmental or psychological variables add to the age factor. So try to deal with examples that strike you as representative. An interesting moment to capture is when a little girl begins to imitate how a woman walks.

A sample observation assignment might call for these walks and walking situations:

- A baby learning to walk
- A child confronting a strange adult
- A youth walking up to a member of the opposite sex
- A middle-aged person at work, on a lunch break, or running for a bus
- An elderly person crossing the street, anxious to make it across before the light turns.

Always use a specifically observed person in a specific situation—for example, a male construction worker talking with a foreman, or eating his lunch watching females pass by on a sidewalk. Then bring the persons observed into class and render their walks as faithfully as possible, trying always to communicate to classmates all that is specific about him or her (arthritis? just paid? walking in a drizzle?) and about the specific situation. If the renderings are successful, the lesson that emerges concerns just how much we can read of people by their ways of walking.

This exploration deepens the actor's ability to observe and draw from everyday experiences. It should also encourage a reluctance to generalize about movement styles. There is no such thing as the baby's walk or the old man's totter. In the specific texture of each person lies all that is interesting and important as resources for future roles. If some provocative discussion fails to emerge from the sharing of this exploration, consider it a disaster.

WALKING SITUATIONS

Keep the characters you have discovered in your observations, for you are going to know and do them well enough to proceed to place them in new and different situations.

This exploration involves a quick demand for a specific new situation, activity, locale, and so on, and the actor's ready response. Usually a minute or two should be the maximum amount of time to think about it, for if the character's walk has been carefully learned, no more time is needed.

Here are some sample situations: going shopping on a rainy day without an umbrella; walking along a beach full of deeply browned sunbathers without a tan of your own; walking along and building up confidence for some challenge ahead; walking into a party full of strangers; walking away from a street fight you observed; walking through a grocery store at peak shopping hours; walking by a policeman just after you have jaywalked, unsure whether he noticed or cares. In making up your own situations, you should try for those that have their own kind of implied drama, tension, and conflict.

Music Improvisations

This improvisational exploration is an ideal change of pace, useful during the course of training when free, opening-up work is needed to refresh actors from working within restricted, other-oriented projects, such as the observation series. It also helps to create a sense of ensemble among actors training as a group.

Based on a selection of different kinds of music with various interesting textures, feelings, and tones, the exploration consists of listening to and absorbing a piece of music and then responding to the music physically. This is not to illustrate music; rather, the point is to allow the music to drive one toward a certain kind of physical expression and response, shaping and communicating its essence— what the music makes you feel or think.

Start off relaxed, on the floor, in a neutral state. Lights may be dimmed. Then, let the music take over. At the end of the music, follow through with your actions until you have resolved the emotion or image; then, relax back onto the floor and allow the images, impressions, and tensions to drain away from you. Find your natural breath rhythm. When you are back to a neutral state, sit or stand up. Often lively discussion will follow.

Sometimes an interesting single recording or composition works well. A tape of various pieces also works and provides for more stimuli. Many different types of music can be used for this purpose—for instance, non-vocalized rock compositions such as "Echoes" from the Pink Floyd album *Meddle;* sophisticated musical theater scores, such as a selection from *Leonard Bernstein Conducts His Music for the Theater* (Columbia Masterworks recording); jazz recordings such as a selection from Yusef Lateef's *A-flat, G-flat, and C* on the Impulse label; George Gershwin's *Rhapsody in Blue* or *An American in Paris,* although perhaps too well known, have enough different levels for an interesting experiment. Music from ballets such as Sergei Prokofiev's *Romeo and Juliet* can be used as long as the passages are not too didactically balletic to be sources for pure non-intellectualized movement. The key to selecting music for the musical improvisation is not to have a too-specific spoken message ("Hold me in your arms and tell me you care," and so on), nor an identity that is too specific to be taken out of context (such as well-known theme music from James Bond films, *Doctor Zhivago,* and the like). The music should be a surprise to most of the participants (to say all would be asking too much) and have clear, universal messages. The selections should also evolve; there should be changes in the music that are either inherent in the compositions themselves or built into the arrangement made for the particular recording.

Selection of musical compositions can promote understanding of all aspects of movement training. Thus this single approach can be adapted so that there are an unlimited number of uses for this exploration, which fits in well with space, time, and emotion explorations. (See Chapter 6, "Playing Teddy," for an illustration of musical improvisation.)

Analysis: The Elements of Movement

Whereas the vocabulary of anatomical parts allows us to say precisely what in our body we are moving (lower leg, middle back, rib cage and so on), we still need the further refinement of perception provided by basic terms of pure movement. To describe movement in terms of where, when, and how the body is moving, we must employ three elements of perception: *space, time,* and *energy.*

Again, I must sound a major theme: Because physical expression and physical movement are little observed, seen, and understood, we must focus on how we begin to see. Our first need is a language (terminology) and classifications of movement that will organize what we see and so allow us to perceive. Rudolf Laban was one of the first to systematize a language, with his meticulous graphing of exact and minute combinations of space, time, and energy. His disciples proceeded to organize this system in detail and have produced *Labanotation,* a detailed, symbolic language for seeing and recording explicitly all the movements in a dance. In stage movement training we do not need the whole elaborate system; we need only the basic concepts and an understanding of the elements underlying each. The intent of the following explorations is to wed the anatomical movement vocabulary to the pure movement terms, both intellectually and kinetically, with a transition into the emotional.

A thorough discussion of space, time, and energy does not immediately follow, for the process we are concerned with requires us to explore other elements between these three elements (contrary to the Laban method). That is, a time interval between each section of study based on the three helps actor and instructor alike to focus more finely on the pieces of the puzzle. Space is dealt with immediately after the following exploration; after that are in-depth discussions of energy and time. In introducing any one of the three principal elements, I reinforce the concept that they are all essential to movement. Eventually I will discuss and analyze them as they relate to each other, but in the early stages they must be dealt with individually; otherwise the actor will get confused or feel that the material is too esoteric for serious consideration.

Space Explorations

Let us first analyze space. The most basic feature of our environment is the physical space we occupy: it, in turn, occupies us. Space is around us and inside us; we move through space and space moves through us. Space is extremely flexible in that we can make it appear or disappear by the way we move through it. We have feelings about ourselves in space. We are sensitive to people and objects outside ourselves in space. We develop a response to other people's use of space and its effect on us. The way in which we relate to space is an important part of our expressive behavior.

We can best conceive of space through these frequently cited subcategories: *direction, range, level, design,* and *focus.* The first, *direction,* characterizes the path of movement, whether forward, back, diagonal, circular, curved, or zigzag. *Range* indicates the amount of space used. *Level* tells us the altitude of the moving, standing, sitting, or lying down body. *Design,* a more ambiguous concept, tries to communicate the whole pattern of movement, both in terms of one body and a group of bodies and the shapes that they make. *Focus* designates the point to which the attention of the viewer is drawn.

A General Space Improvisation. In the warm-up for this exploration it helps if attention is called to the five aspects of space and how space is used in the exercises. Specific space exercises may also be devised.

The actor begins in a supine position, with eyes closed and the body in a neutral state—that is, mind cleared and tension drained. The movement training instructor must talk the actors through this exploration.

1. First, become aware of the body in space: the space it occupies and the space surrounding it. Don't touch or move the body; just feel it in space and its relationship to others in the room, the space all around and the space inside you. Feel the head in space; feel the rest of the body and its space—again, without touching it. Feel what it would be like to move in space, but do not move. Imagine the sensations of your hand moving through space, but do not move it.

2. Now begin to move the body in space, first in isolated ways, such as moving just the hand. Then go through the rest of the body in the same way, adding parts and eventually working up to the entire body in motion.

3. As you increase the movement, sitting up and then standing, begin to become conscious of the levels of space, the directions, the range, the shape, and the design.

4. Once in a standing position, sense the differences in non-walking (stationary) and walking (locomotive) movement. Try to float through space and feel its lightness. Try shaping space with your body, soak it up, touch it, pat it, slice it, mold it into a ball, hug it, feel its texture and sense your body in it. Penetrate space with your body, push it, and so forth.

5. Now explore making shapes, designs, or patterns with space and the body. After a while, each actor should become more aware of the other shapes in the room and begin some reciprocal shape-influencing. Continue this improvised reacting.

6. Upon command and without warning, all should freeze in their individual shapes. Make a brief study of the frozen state: the shape of your own body, how it relates to the total design of the room, how it relates to specific other spatial shapes. Now "unfreeze" and follow through with the movement patterns, bringing them to a kind of completion.

7. Place yourselves at random in the room. Begin to walk toward someone in the room, then move away from someone. Now around; through, over; with; against. Now touch the environment with as much of your body as you can: slither, crawl, roll.

8. Now stand, eyes closed, and begin to move around the room, but try not to touch anyone. Use your other senses to feel people near you, to feel all the space you are moving through. If you collide with a person or object, you must identify that object or person with your eyes still closed, and then move on.

9. After a while, the command to freeze again begins another study period. Your eyes remain closed. Try to identify where you are, who is nearby, what the room now looks like.

This exploration offers a great opening-up experience to the element of space and may be returned to later.

Shapes in Space. This is an exploration of two principles of design and their opposites: symmetry and balance.

Begin with individual explorations of balanced movements, on all levels, stationary and locomotive, in various ranges. Here is a useful way to begin: Imagine the body cut in two in a vertical plane, thus creating two halves to be balanced or unbalanced. Stay balanced, even in transitions from sitting to standing. This is not weight balance, but *design* balance. You will note how difficult it is to hold a balanced design, for most moving requires a symmetrical-asymmetrical flow. You will also probably find holding a balanced design boring.

Now move to easier, more normal, unbalanced and asymmetrical designs. Note the increased amount of freedom in moving. After a while explore both balanced and unbalanced designs; work individually, then in groups.

Filling in Space. Pair off: one actor becomes A, the other B. The typical pattern has A make a shape with her (or his) body, then B relates to that shape by fitting into the enclosed space so created. As B fills that space, A then fits herself into the open space B has just created. Then B responds, and then A again, and so the process goes on, until both are too tired (or tangled) to proceed.

Next, pairs should pair off, so the pattern becomes A-B-C-D. Eventually the entire class should be joined into a chain of filling responses, a single, long, flowing sculpture from A to Z.

Direction, Level, and Range. In the warm-up for the day, pay attention to three aspects of space, direction, level, and range in the selected exercises. Note the range factor from a demi-plié and to a grand-plié or the levels in jumping.

For *direction,* actors should freely explore all the different directions the body can take, moving across the floor or standing still: Take four steps forward, four at a right diagonal, four to the left, four at a left diagonal, and so on.

For *levels*, working on falls is excellent. But remember it is wise to work with gymnastic mats or mattresses, especially in the early work. First do a knee fall—a continuous fall a bit to one side with one arm out to catch the weight, starting with knees on the floor. Then repeat the process, falling to the knees from a standing position. Then do a walking fall, a trip or a slip. Enact being clubbed from behind, shot from the front, and so on.

For *range*, a set of basic folk dances makes the exploration fun and culturally informative. In performing the *Korabuska, the Teton Mountain Stomp,* or the *Miserlou,* a rich assortment of range is evident (see Jane A. Harris, Anne Pittman, and Marlys S. Waller, *Dance a While: Handbook of Folk, Square, and Social Dance,* 3rd ed.) The steps of any dance yield useful range and direction experience. Ballroom dancing works equally well.

The sum of activities to develop direction, levels, and range awareness is enormous. Be creative.

Spatial Relationships. Pair off and invent a relationship (mother-daughter, brother-sister, boss-employee) and then set up a situation (confrontation, lovers' quarrel, celebration). Then, with the situation set, lie on the floor, clear the body, and in a neutral state think out the situation you have developed. When ready—when the internal aspect of the role and situation becomes felt— get up and begin to move around in this situation. Relate and react to one another, not miming, but reflecting the essence of what you feel.

Now clarify the relationship without the situation (that is, the roles of the lovers, friends, parent and child); avoid pat situations such as an argument or comforting one another at a funeral. Let the situation evolve out of the movement; be sensitive to how the other person seems to feel her or his role. For example, a mother may be anxious, bitter, or frustrated—there are all kinds of mothers.

For both explorations, while inside your role try to note how the spatial relationship changes, depending upon the course of the interaction.

Gatherings. Invent any specific kind of gathering or group affair—from a family picnic or class reunion to a town meeting or a group of witnesses at a fatal accident. What is important is that within this agreed-upon situation, each actor assumes a particular role, character, or personality type.

There are two variations:

1. In a gathering of strangers, each person keeps his identity to himself, except as he reveals it in his movement and his spatial signature.
2. In a gathering of acquaintances or intimates, all identities are known (perhaps assigned) and are important to the spatial drama. It is necessary that Aunt Clara know who her niece Bess is.
3. There is actually a third variation in which individuals take turns being ghosts or invisible nonpersons who float through the gathering able to

observe without performing in their own space. The point of this exploration is to observe spatial relationships without overly intellectualizing them, and to observe yourself and your use of space. It should be exciting to observe the dimensions and patterns in all the contacts your character has in the gathering.

Before beginning, work into the identity as you did in "Spatial Relationships." At the end, have a long and detailed discussion.

This exploration might be returned to later, after working on abstractions, trying the same activities with the abstract identities.

Essence Study: Abstractions

Essence study involves seizing on the essence of something, capturing the epitome of an emotion or thought or gesture, getting into the center, or passing through external barriers that either reflect or disguise the center. When I conduct an essence study I assign actors the task of finding, through movement, the essence of an emotion, an animal, a poem, or a line from a play, and so on. An essence study may be used by the actor to discover things about her own life (as I ask her to do in the first part of training), or about a character, a play, or a scene (as I help her do in the second part of our work). By seeking the essence of a physical or mental occurrence the actor is forced away from the literal context and the outer form of the episode into an abstraction; she finds its universal or essential qualities.

You must understand that essence movement is not at all literal or realistic. It would not be used in our everyday life. It is the embodiment—the physical expression—of the human being's experience of a thought, thing, emotion, or desire. It is difficult to describe because it is not meant to communicate an idea (like "Come here" or "Hello"), or to achieve a physical result (like picking up a book, or combing your hair). It is primal, universal movement whose purpose is to allow the performer of the movement to embrace the totality of a living moment: its emotion, desire, and intention.

It does communicate, very effectively and immediately. Its message is best understood, however, by the participant, the person actually doing the movement, because it is her total organic history that is involved. And it is this multilevel reality of human existence which speaks to the person involved in the essence work.

The act of abstracting here stands at the opposite end of the spectrum from the imitation of physical mannerisms in literal detail. We are trying to get through the outer trappings into an intimate grasp of the inner nature of experience. In physical movement, gesture, and expression, abstraction is not an enlargement any more than it is a duplication. The essence of a handshake, for example, is not larger, more sweeping swings of the hand. That is merely blowing it up. To get at the handshake's essence, the best thing to do is to transfer the movement from the hand to another body part—say, the foot—or into the whole body. Thus, the foot has a better chance of abstracting a handshake than the hand, since there is less danger of simply exaggerating.

This is not the beginning of surreal (or weird) exercises for a stylized, perhaps expressionistic, acting style, but, rather, the beginning of the most serious and potentially most rewarding portion of movement study. One reason this exploration is useful is that it helps actors to break down their preconceptions. It helps them understand in an immediate sense that familiarity with a thing is not the same as knowing it. By forcing them to abstract simple movements, I force actors to study their kinesthetic awareness of the movement as well as the meaning implicit in it. Any kind of acting requires the penetration of externals that essence studies provide.

In all the work preceding this portion of study, there have been several guiding principles that essence studies help to focus for the actor and instructor alike. First among these principles is the concept of *organic movement.* This simply means movement that flows naturally from the organic unity of the mind, spirit, and body. In all that has been presented thus far we have been involved with helping actors understand and trust this organic unity, with the ultimate design of providing the tools for understanding their truth, to aid them in acting their roles.

The essence study is both teaching aid and tool for the actor. By striving to master the subtle intellectual puzzle it presents, actors will awaken new pathways to their own psyches. Once conquered, the essence study becomes a valuable psycho-physical tool to unlock the secrets of a character's inner reality. This is important because what we are ultimately doing is aiding the actor to convince an audience that they are observing the organic reality of that character—not to "wow" them with a virtuoso performance.

This is the one tool I have found to be most effective at awakening in the actor a profound, reliable sense of the psychological reality Stanislavsky sought to awaken in his Moscow Art Theater troupe. It is effective because it involves more than just the mind; it involves the total being and total commitment.

The technique is, at its heart, pure and simple. When the tool is understood, it cuts through all lies and rhetoric to find the startling and simple truth beneath all the words.

First things first, however. Let's start by focusing on the thing the actor must know first, and best—himself or herself. To help the actor to do this we continue to do what we've been doing all along: We take away the actor's personal props. In the initial stages we were (and continue to be) involved in removing the actor's personal physical quirks (that is, the slouches, poses, tensions, bad breathing techniques, and other personal movement traits) that would inevitably prevent him from assuming any role but his own on-stage. With this later period of study we are attacking the actor's mental props (that is, those subconscious assumptions that support all our daily activities).

The reason we do this is that, although assumptions are useful tools to a reasoning and highly adaptive social animal like *homo sapiens,* they are very often taken for fact by the mind that formed them. This misleads the performing artist, because *assumption of fact* is not the same thing as *knowledge of fact.* If the artist does not know the difference between assumption and knowledge, how can he be expected to breathe life into a character he is doing? The usefulness of essence studies is that they aid in the discovery or revelation of the truth.

Regarding where this mode of study is leading, it should be pointed out that essence studies will be used in almost every succeeding phase of training. For analysis of energy, emotion, intention, time, and many other topics, essence studies will aid actors in focusing on each individual concept by freeing them from the need to relate each term to a specific, realistic situation. This allows them to explore with mind, spirit, and body in a more open manner while maintaining a feeling of being firmly grounded in an intelligible, organized system of study.

In fact, they are following an intelligently organized system of study, and it is no mere coincidence that essence studies are introduced at this time. If the actors have been assiduously applying themselves to the program thus far detailed, they are now ready to move into a more challenging, thought-provoking, and more creative phase. And the best place to start is in an area of focus they are already dealing with—their own bodies.

Gesture

The easiest and most revealing way to approach essence studies is to begin by using them to help analyze gestures.

INTRODUCTION: ESSENCE/GESTURE

We will begin by comparing the results of an external method and an internal method.

1. Try first the externally derived essence of wringing your hands. First, wring your hands, and watch them as they move. Try to find what is *essential* to the movement: What makes the movement what it is? When you have found it, abstract that essential quality by giving that movement to another body part or parts. Do not settle for the first movement that pops into your mind and body; experiment with different movements until you feel you have grasped the essence of the original hand movement in at least three abstractions of it.

2. Now empty your mind, spirit, and body. Come to a neutral position and breathe deeply in and out several times. Clear yourself of all unnecessary tension and relax. Now try to find or create within yourself a situation in which you did, or most probably would, wring your hands. Do not do the gesture until you feel you must, or until you feel it will help to understand the emotion. When you feel the wringing to be part of the situation, to be essential to the episode, try then to abstract it. Find the essence of this. Change both the emotion and the feeling that the movement is an integral part of the emotion.

   When you have done this, relax. Clear yourself. Breathe deeply.

3. If you committed yourself to the task both times, you probably found different essences for what amounted to the same gesture. This is normal. Why? Because of the different approaches. You may feel one approach worked better for you than the other, that both revealed something different but worked equally well, or that neither approach had an effect. Whatever you discover will almost certainly be unique to you.

   But remember, this is only the first crude step in a very elemental level. Immediate or profound results are not expected, and complete comprehension of the benefit, concept, or goal of these essence studies is impossible. All that is important for you to do at this stage is to commit yourself fully to each one you do. The questions you have will be answered by your own effort.

A reminder: *Which* gesture one uses and when one uses it are stage business concerns, best handled by the actor and the director in rehearsal. Here we are concerned with developing some experience in the origins of gesturing and, especially, how gestures are performed. Of course the primary *how* is answered by these principles: precision, sequence, and clarity. Whatever the gesture, and however derived, the audience must see it clearly. On-stage, one can exaggerate and enlarge a gesture, but except in certain comedy or campy melodrama, this broadening creates a false, stagy effect. Slowing it down slightly increases the visibility more than enlarging it. Breaking a gesture down into its component moves helps one get that slowness without a lethargic, slow-motion look to it. It also ensures precision. (For instance, you can think of lighting another's cigarette in four steps: hand to pocket, pull lighter out, bring it up to the cigarette, and flick for flame).

   The full meaning of how a gesture is performed leads us into observation studies, psychology, anthropology, and characterization. What are gestures? They are not the units in the special language of mime; nor are they the elaborate punctuation of stage speech. They are fairly specific actions of the body, often surrounded with oversignification or indirect revelation, and they occur in everyday intercourse.

GESTURAL CATEGORIES

Here are some of the major categories I work with in analyzing gestures:

1. Functional gestures: Gestures that achieve a simple, specific purpose—for example: combing your hair, scratching where you itch, looking at your wristwatch to check the time, brushing your teeth.

2. Conventional gestures: Substitute an unreflected movement for speech—for example: a nod means "yes," shaking your head means "no," shrugging the shoulders means "I don't know," or "Who cares?" and so on.

3. Social gestures: Ritualistic communications between members of the same society. Some seem almost universal (waving hello or goodbye, putting one hand straight up at face height, palm facing another person to mean "listen" or "quiet"), but there are many social gestures not shared or generally understood between one society and another, or even between one generation and another. For example: American youth of the 1940s used the "V for Victory" to signal their desire and commitment to end World War II by armed victory, whereas their children used the same signal to mean something far different. Initially, the parents were confused, and even with comprehension mutual understanding of the gesture was not universal.

4. Nonfunctional gestures: Repeated unconscious routines—for example: nonfunctional licking of the lips, twitching of the face muscles, drumming fingers on the table, and so on. (Note: Many of these gestures are of the type that annoy a second party when performed for a prolonged period in close confinement.)

5. Emotional gestures: Gestures that replace language when verbalization is impossible or not needed—for example: holding hands; raising a fist; kissing; opening the hands in shock or surprise, and so on.

6. Shadow gestures: These gestures may accompany language or be silent, but are nonverbal expressions of inner emotional activity not necessarily intended to be communicated—for example: a young boy's squirming in the chair while waiting in the principal's office; nail biting; wringing of the hands, and so on.

The purpose of this classification is only to enlarge the awareness of the kinds of gestures one has to work with. There are probably a number of ways to classify gestures; this is not intended to be the last word on categories. But to help actors understand some differences between gestures, it is helpful to establish some of the causes, motivations, and origins of the various body movements we call gesture. It helps actors to focus on a specific range of meaning for each study rather than to attack the subject on the broad front.

Each gesture that we do takes on meaning according to the timing and manner of our performance. A nod can mean anything from "I am happy to see you alive today" to "I fully intend to destroy you if I can," and it is in most cases a conventional gesture. A nod can be a function gesture (in the case of a person who simply nods all the time for no apparent reason); it may be a shadow gesture (in the case of a defendant awaiting trial nodding to keep his or her spirits from lagging); it may even be a functional gesture (as in the case of a person trying to stay awake during a lecture).

Any kind of gesture can be performed consciously or unconsciously, reflexively or nonreflexively. A shadow gesture, for example, probably arises both reflexively and unconsciously, but one can also manipulate gestures. In fact, most people manipulate their gestures automatically through the course of the day as situations change. A person can play with a twitch of consternation to make it into a conscious sign the receiver will properly read as "beware." One can generally predict an intimate's gestures, for they become so familiar and consistent. Yet they do vary as we might expect, from situation to situation. For example, at home John Doe may employ medium-range gestures in a straightforward manner, whereas in his office they may grow large and percussive. When he consults his auto mechanic, they may become little and tentative. There are no firm rules for analysis. The point of this exercise is to savor the fascinating variety and nuance of gesture.

In terms of a gesture's meaning, we must consider its psychological sources. Broadly, we can distinguish two sources: (1) the desire to *express,* and (2) the need to *conceal expression.* In peak moments of elation, rage, and horror, our gestures unfailingly give away our inner state by their direct, unpremeditated execution. When "our heart goes out to" someone, very likely our arms do too, revealing a natural flow of feeling outward. Here the gesture arises in our desire to express (push out, via gesture) what we are feeling or thinking.

Yet conditioned as we are by social instruction and experience not to feel things too intensely—at least not to show our feelings—we as frequently use gestures to hide our feelings. We are not just considering situations where one of our hands covers a yawn or expression of shock or hides our tears, but, rather, all the gestural activity that creates and maintains our social mask. Partly this is our public face, the one we don in elevators, with sales clerks, and to anyone who seems to be pointing at us or talking about us in our presence. But the major feature of the social mask is its presence in even very private or intimate contacts. Immobility, a walling out of intrusions and expressions, has long been almost a cultural ideal in many civilizations and cultures, including modern Western social behavior.

Yet it is misleading to simplify the two sources of gesture into true and false categories. Our inner, *true* insecurity, for example, frequently produces false, protective, and immobile masks. So the outer face, although frozen, is not a false, merely external gesture, because freezing expression is an accepted protection. Generally it is true that our social and external masks keep us apart (even our sexy neighbor with the permanent smile of hello is really keeping his or her distance) while gestures that express from within do reach out and establish contact with others, whether in anger or compassion.

This discussion is not to set up specific acting projects or movement explorations. In part it is meant to confuse—that is, to illustrate the inherent complications in studying gestural phenomena, all the rich, fascinating particulars and the problems in theorizing about them. For example, the common distinction between gesture and words: Actions have always been thought the truer expression, but we all recall times when our words spoke more accurately than our gestures. There are other occasions when gestures may be in conflict with one another— one betraying an inner desire (hands groping or patting), the other a social pose (body erect and face expressionless). Then there are less dramatic contrasts, such as an apparently relaxed slouch, legs casually crossed, foot slowly swinging, while the fingers tap out a staccato impatience on the table.

There are obvious exercises, explorations, and acting projects galore in this material, but perhaps the most useful way of dealing with the world as a swirl of gestures is to try to feel the truth and appropriateness in all the experiments you do with them.

GESTURE EXPLORATIONS
Begin a series of explorations with *functional* gestures, as follows:

1. Do a functional gesture. Scratch an itch, comb your hair, pull up your socks, adjust your shirt, fold up the cuff on your shirt sleeve, or some other functional gesture. *Do not mime it.* Do not, for instance, "pretend" you are brushing your teeth (if you have no toothbrush) or opening a door (when there is no door to open).
2. Observe the movement from the outside, and then try to feel what you are doing from the inside. Do it several times, each time observing from a different perspective until you understand it.
3. Once you feel you thoroughly understand it mentally and kinetically (how it feels to actually do the movement), experiment with different movements that embody the essence of that understanding. Explore it in all your body parts, and then in your whole body so that your whole body understands the essence of that gesture.
4. One by one present your studies to the group. Each person will do the gesture he or she has selected, and then present its essence. Each person will do the essence several times using different combinations of movements which carry the essence of the original gesture. (One set of movements may feel or appear to most embody the essence, but to keep everyone from settling for easy answers, I demand more than one essence.)

The discussion for this exploration should focus on whether the movements discovered by each participant carried the same sense of purpose, or bore any relationship to the original gesture. Oddly enough, even in these initial stages actors will find it fairly obvious which people have understood and succeeded in presenting the essence of their gesture. The same sort of mental and physical tensions are involved, after all (though displaced to other body parts or reorganized temporally), and by the very commitment to comprehend, any serious actor will be able at least to transpose the superficial realities of the simple movements involved.

Other topics of discussion should touch on the desirability of movement that has follow-through (actors should never be allowed to drop off movement in the middle of a phrase), and that seems to come from the center. This should not be an important part of the discussion, but gentle reinforcement in a wide variety of activities will help to ensure comprehension and appreciation.

Now do the following to explore *conventional* gestures:

1. Do at least five different conventional gestures. Shake your head "no" or "yes"; gesture "I don't know"; "Go away"; "Get away from me"; "Come here"; "What did you say?"—each without any verbal utterance.
2. Choose one of these five and, as with the functional gesture, execute the movement several times, looking at it in different ways (what does it feel like; how much tension is involved, and where; what does it look like?) until you understand it. Find the core of the gesture.
3. Find the essence of this gesture. Try to find different qualities that may, at first, have been hidden from you by refusing to settle for the easy answer. Ask yourself "What is there in this gesture that I haven't noticed already?"
4. Again, everyone will present their studies to the group. Start with the movements you feel most embody the essence of the original gesture. Do the essence twice, then do the gesture. Finally, repeat the essence.

After each presentation (which includes the essence done twice, the gesture, and the essence again), discussion of the ability or the inability to find the essence will be followed by that actor (whether or not the others felt they captured the essence) presenting at least two movement sequences that she (or he) rejected in favor of the sequence presented. In this way the entire group will have the benefit of having their choices and efforts discussed openly in the same terms. The instructor must keep the discussion focused firmly on the goal, to help actors understand the value, purpose, and meaning of the essence studies, especially as a tool to reveal the true nature of the (in this case) gesture.

Any number of gesture explorations can be devised, and each should be useful. Gesture assignments encourage follow-through improvement, help to get movement started from the center and the core, underscore the effectiveness of a few movements well done (the *economy principle* that helps one cut down on gestural flailing), and are valuable practice and research for characterization.

Fragments/Follow-Through. The purpose of this exploration is to teach follow-through in physical movement. But we will approach follow-through by comparing it to its opposite—fragmented movement—which is interrupted, incomplete, contextless movement.

1. Begin by creating and moving around in jerky, "percussive" fragments. Do this alone but do the fragments as though relating to other people. There should be no completion of a fragment nor any transition between fragments.
2. Now do movements in which you are thinking of the natural follow-through and completion. Try for a smooth flow in which all your movement phrases join a larger line that continues from the beginning to the end of the experiment.
3. After working alone on both fragments and follow-through, work with a partner, making a movement conversation in which you talk in both fragmented and complete movement phrases. You are working here on the essence of a conversation (not indicating or signaling), which is an abstraction exercise.

   Note: When some clear communication has you readied, slowly ease into a transition toward a realistic conversation with everyday gestures, and actually begin to verbalize, to converse, with each other. This is a subtle transition. Complete your silent, abstract conversation; don't break your conversation, but work together toward the easy and natural drift toward conventional gesture and speech. You should feel the sense of follow-through in this very process.
4. A "take-home assignment": Take a sentence or two from the dialogue of a scene you are already working on, perhaps a troublesome passage. Prepare an abstraction of those lines, the essence of the movement that underlies the words, and be ready to do that movement with the words. Also prepare a conventional and realistic version. In training session with the group, you will perform both. By working with just a brief passage, we enjoy the greatest opportunity to get the words and the movement to flow together, one following from the other. Having dipped into the essence of the situation, the actor should have a firm inward grasp of the words and realistic movements that flow out from the center.

Haiku Exploration

This exploration prompts the actor's creativity and reinforces work in abstraction. The haiku is a special form of Japanese poetry: very terse (three lines, seventeen syllables) yet highly patterned (five syllables in the first and third lines, seven in the second); it is also a dramatic form of poetry, with each line often taking a sharp turn in idea, with a minimum of explanatory transition. Thus the haiku offers, as it were, a series of empty spaces within its intricate and usually concrete structure of images, spaces to be filled in by the reader's imagination. A highly evocative and stimulating kind of poetry, haiku is well suited to our study of abstracting essences with the body.

Let us examine some sample poems to see the kinds of patterns we can work from.

Tremble, burial mound—
my lamenting voice—
the autumn wind.

Bashō

Note how each line evokes its own image and action. As we shift from the image of a trembling mound to the voice in opposition, we are combining unlike entities (a trembling voice with ground that trembles); yet, in the desire to see the earth shake in sympathetic grief, we also see a poetic identity between voice and ground (mourner and the earth that holds the beloved dead). Then, we pivot on voice to wind, and we see a new association: the voice of grief is the voice of autumn, its cold and sad wind. Another interpretation (perhaps more accurate from the point of view of the poet) is to imagine the "trembling mound" not as earth, but as a funeral pyre. In that case the trembling would be the actual physical trembling of the wood supporting the body just before its collapse. In this interpretation the combined images imply the similarity of the crackling weakened wood to the mourning voice to the cold and bitter wind. Neither interpretation is necessarily correct, nor is "correct interpretation" important. But in either interpretation, the density of the language is important. Thus, with the shifting perceptions we have a dramatic buildup to the final incorporation of all three images as a poetic whole.

The lightning flashes,
zigzag-piercing the darkness
a night-heron's scream.

Bashō

Again we have a second-line pivot: lightning pierces, and so does the scream. Each image is succinct but vivid. We see lightning; we see and perhaps feel the piercing; and we hear the scream. Yet while the imagistic picture is specific and hard, it opens up into metaphorical suggestion well beyond the perception of a scene.

For I, who am leaving
for you, who are staying
two autumns for us.

Buson

This poem implies a dramatic vignette. We contemplate the paradox that one season is divided by the parting of intimates.

> I feel a piercing chill:
> in the bedroom, my dead wife's comb
> under my bare foot.

Buson

Indeed, a whole scene of poignant drama is imagistically sketched in this poem with that final, mundanely haunting detail—he is stepping on the comb. The "hurt" is considerable. Consider the differences created by these two equally sound translations of the same haiku by Buson.

> A:
> This morning's breezes—
> I can see them rippling
> a caterpillar's hair.

> B:
> See the morning winds
> how they are blowing the hair—
> a caterpillar?

Can you see the scenic quality of A? We see motion first, then rippling effects become visible, and, in a close-up, the "fur" of a caterpillar. All along we suspected it would be grass and are pleasantly surprised. But B depends more on rhetoric—that is, we hear the poet's voice as he moves us to his surprising query, whose answer must be "yes."

For further haiku, consult a good collection with translations in modern English. *An Introduction to Haiku,* by Harold G. Henderson (New York: Anchor, 1958) is a useful collection. You can even compose your own.

Now that we have the medium, let us proceed to a haiku exploration.

1. Get into groups of three to five. Select a haiku and analyze it for five or six minutes, deciding as a group how it works and what is essential in it.
2. When decided, begin as a group to prepare a version of its physicalized essence, exploring physically as a group. Be sensitive to the technique of the poem, but do not try to illustrate it literally. Seek the essence of the images and its pattern of unfolding. Remember the quality of surprise, for example, and the way the three lines build into a single effect.
3. Keep what works, throw away the rest, until your physicalization carries the same message as the poem. You should need about fifteen more minutes.
4. For presentation to the group, the haiku can be read before, after, or during the presentation.

5. A discussion should follow the presentation, so that the problems encountered in the poem may be compared to the results. A take-home assignment should carry the work over to the next meeting. Have each actor select a haiku and prepare its essence for the next meeting. Presentation should be of the same order as for the groups.

Energy

To restate an earlier theme, there are three elements in all movement—space, time, and energy. Only space can be specifically measured by our senses. Both time and energy are hypothetical and only dimly understood concepts that most branches of education do not even consider as relevant. This is no less true in the study of theater arts in general. But any serious study of stage movement must deal with these concepts. Time and space exist without us, but without energy we could not move, and so we would not exist at all.

Before I begin this portion of study, I always ask actors: "When you think about energy, what terms or images come to mind?" Typical answers are "solar power," "atomic power," "the sun," "horsepower," and so on. Occasionally an actor with a scientific orientation will say "Energy is the capacity to do work and overcome resistance." I have had no one, in all my classes, come forward with a practical definition that would be useful to a dance or theater artist. Why should they? There is no generally accepted method of dealing with this phenomenon outside the work of serious modern dance theorists and practitioners. Indeed, my understanding of the elements of energy come from my studies of Laban and modern dance as affected by my theater studies, and the practical definition I derived is the one I apply with actors.

Briefly, we never see energy. All we ever see is the result of energy: We see the light bulb glow when we throw the switch; the water wheel turn as the current spills over the paddles; the trees bend in the wind; the car speed away—but we never see the energy that causes these things to happen. Our eyes are not equipped for that. Let us then concentrate on that which we can see.

ENERGY QUALITIES

In all movement we can see evidence of six types of application of energy. By the outward appearance of the movement, we can understand how the energy is being applied. With this visual evidence we can qualitatively define the six different types and illustrate and validate each through human movement.

1. Sustained or lyrical: This is a constant, even flow of energy, which produces movement identified by its smooth, unchanging dynamic. Whether the person is moving fast or slow, no noticeable change occurs in the speed, rhythm, or effort needed to execute any movement in the phrase.

2. Percussive: In contrast to "sustained," this is energy that strongly pulses, at regular or irregular intervals, to produce sudden and dynamic changes in the speed and rhythm in which the movement is executed and in the amount of effort needed. There are sharp, sudden changes in the dynamics of the movement.

3. Vibratory: This is a kind of cross between "sustained" and "percussive," in that the energy is applied continually, but dynamically changes direction and intensity at regular or irregular intervals at a speed and rhythm too fast to be either "sustained" or "percussive."

4. Suspended: This is a sort of hybrid of "sustained" energy that produces a unique visual impression quite distinct from normal sustained movement. Here the energy is constantly and evenly applied so as to combat just barely the forces of gravity acting upon the body. It produces the visual image of a body rising slowly, or suspended at a height and altitude that it can barely sustain.

5. Collapsed: The exact opposite of "suspended," this and the preceding type are almost inseparable in human movement. One cannot suspend indefinitely; eventually one must release or discontinue expending energy, and when that happens the body "collapses." This may be done slowly ("sustained") or quickly ("percussive"), but the end result is the same: The body falls back in on itself and down toward the ground as gravity takes over.

6. Swinging: This is a particular kind of dynamic interaction of "suspend"/ "collapse," and "percussive"/"sustained." Energy is percussively applied at the beginning of the movement phrase, and the body collapses progressively in a sustained manner until it rebounds up into a suspended quality as gravity in a gradual, sustained manner takes over once again. Then the next movement phrase begins again with another percussive surge of energy.

In our everyday experiences we can find each energy quality employed in the movement of the people we encounter. Certain mental and physical states tend to produce the same energy quality in people's movement regardless of race, sex, or other characteristics. Anger tends to produce percussive movement. Cold, fear, or intense anxiety tend to produce vibratory movement. A person trying to make a decision, or trying to hear urgent cries for help almost invariably suspends the body and holds very still so that the senses and mind can most efficiently function. Gaiety, especially in small children, leads people into a swinging, carefree bodily carriage. Formal occasions requiring solemnity seem to dictate sustained movement in most individuals, whereas despair, gloom, and defeat seem to leave people collapsed in on themselves and slumped carelessly on furniture. Even certain combinations of qualities can be predicted if the physical state is known. Observe a person in an extreme state of intoxication and you should be able to note a very clear combination of suspend and collapse qualities operating as he or she struggles to remain erect and even to appear sober.

Of course, there are exceptions to these generalities, and there are many other kinds of mental and physical states that can produce each of the examples offered, but we are not in the business of cataloguing here. The business of theater artists consists partially of making accurate and meaningful observations in the world inside and around us. These concepts of energy qualities are one of the most useful tools I have found to aid in this process of "seeing."

All that remains for the stage movement instructor, actor, and director is to find a way to make this new tool work for them. That is what this period of study is designed to permit. The way to proceed is to place the preliminary observations on the individual.

Every person tends to have a distinctive energy pattern, with perhaps a single dominating quality and one or two complementary qualities. So an untrained actor with a percussive dominating quality may have difficulty basing actions on a swinging or sustained quality. Exploring all the ways energy is released should give an actor a greater range of energy choices, provide her (or him) with a more supple body, and thus increase her range of character choices. (A public figure or entertainer can develop or cultivate a movement personality, stressing one of these energy qualities. Don Knotts did so with the vibratory quality; Jay Leno, like many stand-up comedians, has developed a swinging one. A parlor game is inherent in this material: Was Richard Nixon's gestural style "percussive"; is Bill Clinton's "sustained"?)

Whereas an actor may become president, one-dimensional movie star, or nightclub entertainer, it is desirable that all serious actors will attempt to do more than drag the self-same mannerisms, complete with immediately recognizable energy quality, into every role they attempt on the stage or screen.

ENERGY TRANSFORMATIONS

The movement instructor can tailor warm-ups for this unit to reinforce the concept of the six energy qualities. Take note how the plié or knee-bend is done with sustained, even quality, and the four-count stretch with a percussive one. But to enhance the reinforcement, one can tinker with the exercises in unaccustomed qualities, so the four-count stretch might be done in a sustained or swinging manner. As has been said before, one should try to invent and adapt exercises to suit exploration topics, and exploration topics to suit actors' talent, attention, and capabilities—so that the instructor uses previous lessons to help guide and focus the next or future topics.

General Improvisation (Short Form). This is the introduction to energy that each group of actors in training receives. Before any warm-up, with no prior discussion I inform the group that the next period of study is to be energy. I then ask the question: "When you think of energy, what terms or images come to mind?" All responses are valuable, even when actors are at a loss to say anything. This is neither unusual nor unexpected, because, as noted above, most people have not thought in depth about energy.

Once the actors have said all that they can on the subject, I explain that all movement occurs as a result of certain applications of energy on matter, and that we will analyze energy in terms of the movement qualities caused by the various applications of energy we employ to effect movement.

This general improvisation will be repeated at the end of the warm-up to reinforce understanding of the six energy qualities. The difference is that more time will be spent on each quality because we do not want the actors to do any really strenuous movement before they are warmed up. So this initial exploration for each quality should be no more than thirty seconds, just enough to acquaint the actors loosely with each one, while limiting the risk factor. After the warm-up several minutes of exploring each quality in the same general manner will provide the actor with a less superficial grasp of the subject.

Sustained or Lyrical. This is a smooth even flow of energy that results in a similarly smooth, even flow of the body.

1. Try moving your arm in a sustained or lyrical manner. Notice there are no sudden changes in direction or dynamic.
2. Move other parts of your body in this quality. Explore the range of movements you can use with your head, torso, legs, and hands and still maintain the lyrical quality.
3. Now explore with the whole body. Do not feel tied to one spot on the floor. Don't stay small and tentative in your movements.
4. Speed up your movements as fast as you can and still keep the movement sustained—free of jerks and stops. Don't make them all slow, as in a dream.
5. Let yourself go. Trust your body.

Now let's move to a quality opposite this one in feeling.

Percussive. This is just what the name implies: dynamic, powerful changes in the application of energy that causes sudden, abrupt, or jerky movements. Explore the use of percussive movements with your body. Really let go with this movement, then bring it to a halt.

Vibratory. If you move in a long series of very short, jerky percussive movements, a vibratory quality is produced.

1. Try vibrating just your hand; your head; your leg. Now vibrate your whole body.
2. Feel how much energy is needed to maintain this for any great length of time.

Suspended and Collapsed. The next two qualities operate together. They are suspend (I suspend my arm) and collapse (I let my arm fall to my side.)

1. Suspend just your arm. Hold it there. Eventually it must collapse down. Let the energy go.

2. Explore suspend and collapse in various parts of your body. Suspend just a finger, then let it collapse. Now your hand, your head, your upper body. Explore easily.

This is the normal interaction of suspend and collapse. Let's move into the last application of energy on the body, which is another type of suspend/collapse.

Swinging. Swinging starts with suspending, and with just a slightly percussive motion proceeds to collapsing and rebounds to suspending. Then the cycle starts again.

1. Swing your arm.
2. Explore swinging in various parts of your body. Isolate the quality in your head, leg, and upper torso.

Now go into the warm-up, paying attention to these various energy qualities as we use them in the exercises. Discussion of the six qualities does not occur until the end of this first session. The introductory material I have included above (that is, for the reader) is unnecessary and undesirable for an actual movement training session. Once this initial exploration has been coupled with the ensuing warm-up and the following in-depth exploration, actors will have a more immediate understanding of energy than any amount of discussion would provide.

At the end of the warm-up during this introduction, the three frustration jumps should be performed in any three energy qualities the individual actor chooses to employ. From the position of total collapse at the end of the three jumps, I then move once again into the general improvisation, but this time actors will explore each in depth.

General Improvisation (In-depth). First, bring yourself to a neutral state. Allow your breathing to return to normal, release all tension, relax into yourself, and clear your mind. (Use the breathing exercise on page 35).

1. Once your breathing has returned to normal, rise, in a sustained application of energy, into your natural alignment, and check your alignment by pressing up through your feet.
2. Now begin exploring a sustained application of energy.
   a. Isolate movements in your hands, then incorporate your arms.
   b. Isolate the movement in your legs, your head; then just your torso.
   c. Now involve the whole body. Don't allow yourself to stay rooted to the same spot. Let the movement use various ranges, levels, and directions in space. Use the entire space in your exploration.
   d. Don't make all the movement slow and dreamlike. You can move fairly fast and still give the movement a sustained energy quality. See how fast you can move and still be sustained in your movement. What kind of movement do you have to use to do this?

e. Now explore sustained movement in any way you wish. Pay attention to how this affects you internally.

3. Let's move to percussive movement.
   a. Try freely exploring a percussive energy quality.
   b. Take the time to explore it in a variety of ways. Don't be satisfied with one way of moving percussively.
   c. Does this affect you differently from moving in a sustained manner? Let the way this movement affects you guide you. Keep the movements abstract. Just let the essences of your emotion dictate your movements.
   d. Now release that emotion and shake out your tension.

4. Move on to the next energy quality, vibratory movement.
   a. Try vibrating various body parts—hand, arm, foot, head, and so on.
   b. Take the vibration into your whole body. What feelings does this elicit?
   c. Explore vibration any way you wish, and allow your feeling again to guide your exploration.
   d. Relax. Vibratory movement uses much more energy than the others, so it is difficult to sustain for long periods.

5. Now let's turn to suspended and collapsed movement.
   a. Start exploring with just a finger. Lift it up, and let it collapse back into place.
   b. Add other fingers until you have the whole hand suspending and collapsing.
   c. Slowly add on body parts suspending higher and collapsing lower until you collapse onto the ground.
   d. Explore this now freely and see if it will elicit some sort of feeling tone in you. Then let that feeling change and guide your exploration.
   e. Release that feeling, shake out your body.

6. Let's go to the last energy quality, swinging.
   a. Try swinging your arm. Add the other arm, and let the torso swing with them. Finally, the head joins in.
   b. See if you can keep the sense of the swing as you move around the room. How can you move across the floor to the other side of the room and keep the feel of the swing? Try different ways of moving in various directions and still maintain a swinging quality.
   c. Explore it any way you want to. Let the body take over.
   d. See what kind of feeling tone this brings out of your body.
   e. Let the feeling help your exploration.
   f. Now relax, shake out your body.

7. Summation: By now you should be able to see that the different energy qualities do affect you emotionally, especially when they are used as broadly as we have here. But the effect is still there on both subject and observer even when the movement is much more subtle. To prove this, the next exploration will be geared to revealing the truth of that statement.

Energy and Gesture. Choose some functional gesture: scratch your nose, brush your hair out of your eyes, pull up your socks—anything that you do normally every day.

1. Do this gesture several times, trying to notice how you do it. What kind of energy is involved?
2. Are you performing it in a percussive, sustained, or vibratory manner? Why? What other ways could this same gesture be done?
3. Try doing this same gesture in a vibratory manner. How does this change the way you feel while doing the gesture?
4. Now use percussive movement; lyrical; suspended and collapsed; swinging. Do each several times while trying to sense the difference in your perception of the gesture.
5. Now do the gesture again the way you normally do it. Ask yourself, "What is there in the performance of the gesture that is me? Why do I perform that gesture with that energy quality and not another?"
6. Take another gesture, this time a social gesture. And repeat the process (steps 1 to 5).
7. Notice the similarities and differences in the energy applications of your functional and social gestures. Can you identify the reasons for both the similarities and the differences? How? Why? Depending on the time available and the capacity of the participants, this as well as the next two explorations ("Walking/Energy," and "Internal/External Dependence") could be combined with the general improvisations to provide an excellent introductory session on energy. In many cases, however, these explorations will have to be spread out over two sessions because of time constraints and actor endurance levels.

Walking/Energy. For this exploration, you will try several different energy qualities to bring about various styles of walking.

1. Walk around the room as you usually do. Note your use of energy.
2. Now make your walk take on a percussive quality.
3. Change to a swinging quality. Try several different ways of walking in a swinging quality. What different images come to mind?
4. Move into suspending and collapsing. Note the changes and the similarities, if there are any.
5. Vibrate in your walk. You may have difficulty walking in a vibratory manner but try it different ways. It is possible.
6. Now walk with sustained energy and a complete change in the feeling tone. Don't just move slowly. Try walking at different speeds and still maintain the sustained quality.
7. Now come back to your normal walk. Do you notice anything new about your use of energy?

Internal/External Dependence. Before launching directly into the next exploration (as I would in an actual class), it is beneficial to note several observations about the relationship of internal and external realities. As has been discussed earlier in this book, all actors do not work the same way. Even using the same tools, no two actors will approach the project of revealing the secrets of a character in the same way. To restate a previous theme, there are only three basic approaches to characterization:

1. External to internal: An actor can put on the mask, say the words, and try to discover what the external manifestations indicate concerning what he (or she) is feeling. Why does he look the way he looks and say the things he's saying? Thus, the external informs the intellect, which sculpts the internal reality.
2. Internal to external: He can build up such a wealth of emotion, compassion for, and understanding of the character (through the use of native empathy, sense-memory, and other tools) that his inner reality radiates outward. So the internal reality defines the external appearance.
3. External and internal: An actor can use one, then the other, or both at the same time, allowing both to affect each other.

In most cases (even though most novice actors do not realize it) actors tend to be extremely pragmatic and use anything that works for them. That means that actors tend to approach roles both from the inside and from the outside. Oddly, many actors choose to believe totally in one method of working (external to internal or internal to external), so much so that they are blind to and feel incapable of working in the other manner. This is a great problem because it inevitably makes an actor either unsure (because he realizes his crippling inability), or grossly overconfident (because he is blind to his lack of perspective). The interlocking approaches serve to provide for perspective, balance, and a fail-safe system that mutually benefits and reinforces decisions and their execution. Without this system any actor is at a great disadvantage.

There may be many reasons for actors' falling into this, but principal among possible explanations is the pragmatism I've noted: Because actors use what works, many actors who have found early success (not always the best gauge) using the mask approach scorn any other, and those who have learned to "spill their guts" disdain their "empty technician" friend's approach. What is so strange about this phenomenon is that most of the people who have this attitude have either never tried "the other" approach, or have done so with such a jaundiced eye that they poisoned their sensitivity and so doomed the attempt, thus "proving" to themselves that the attempt was useless in the first place!

Although there may be no cure for these extreme cases of jaundice, the majority of actors should find the following exploration very illuminating and helpful. This is a rare opportunity because actors have very few situations in which the two approaches are so clearly delineated: they are attempted in the same narrow band of time under a single exploration that is specifically designed to reveal the positive values of both. Intellectually we may understand the relationship of form and content, but here actors have the chance to discover, in very immediate (emotional and physical) terms, some of that reality within themselves.

External to Internal Approach. The exploration begins in a relaxed state on your back.

1. Breathe deeply. Clear your mind and body of all tension. Bring yourself to a neutral state.
2. Choose at random one of the energy qualities (if you choose suspended, you must do collapsed also) and try to feel what it is like to move with this energy quality without actually moving.
3. Now begin to explore moving in this quality. Take your time and explore it fully.
4. Let it affect you emotionally. What kind of emotion or memory does this call to mind? Allow your movement to change as you discover an emotion that fits that quality.
5. Do not change the basic quality. If you are moving percussively, continue moving percussively, but let the percussive quality be textured by the emotional tone.
6. See if this problem or emotion will work itself out. Follow through with your exploration while you try to discover the natural conclusion to the emotion or situation. Let the quality change.
7. If you feel like relating to those around you in essence form, do so nonverbally, but if you do not wish to relate to others around you, you don't have to.
8. Allow the tension to drain from you. Relax onto the floor. Don't just let it fall off. Follow through with your situation and its resolution. Take your time, but don't hold onto it. When it's over, it is over. Just relax. Breathe deeply. Clear yourself. Bring yourself back to a neutral state.

Internal to External Approach. In your relaxed state, search your mind for a situation or experience that caused you to have a strong or very definite emotional reaction. This could be a happy or sad, angry or joyous experience. It could be one that made you feel empty, confused, anxious, or hopeless; or it could be one that made you feel just the opposite. If you are depressed today, don't pick one that will aid your depression. That is the only restriction on the memory you can choose.

1. Fill yourself with the memory of this experience. Try to see the place and people; hear the sounds. Can you recall any smells or other textures of the experience? What caused the emotion? Try to feel the emotion that was caused by the episode you experienced.

2. Once you have a firm grasp of the situation and the emotion—once you have filled yourself with it, and are ready—allow your body to respond to the stimulus you are feeling. Let the situation or emotion suggest an energy quality to help your exploration of it.

3. Do not rush yourself. Take your time, and keep the movements free and abstract. See if your movement can help in your recollection of the event.

4. You can respond to people working near you if they aid in the exploration. See if there is someone who seems to fit into the recollection—an opponent, a friend, a lover, Mother, Father.

5. See if you can find a resolution to the situation. Follow through, and don't impose an artificial resolution. Let it work itself out.

6. When you have gone through either to resolution or realization of stalemate, let yourself slowly release the situation, allow the tension to drain from you, and collapse gradually back onto the floor.

7. Breathe deeply, clear yourself. Come back to a neutral state. Relax.

If this exploration ends the session, the discussion will probably center on the question of which method worked better for each individual and why. It is important to point out that neither one is *the* way of working; both are acceptable. If one works inside to outside, the exterior manifestation of the internal reality is as important as the ability to conjure the internal reality. And if one works outside to inside, the outside is only a shell. Without the inner reality to fill it, the performance, the character, the actor is hollow. Either fault is really only the age-old problem of "sound and fury, signifying nothing."

ENERGY COMBINATIONS

Occasionally an actor will be cast as a character whose major obstacle is himself (or herself). The character must conquer fear or must try to appear calm although he is quite agitated, or perhaps has conflicting desires about the presence and actions of an aggressive member of the opposite sex. The problem of how to physicalize and make this visible to the audience in a realistic or believable manner is sometimes impossible to solve for untrained actors. This exploration is designed to provide one possible tool for dealing with this problem. Aside from that, it is a challenging and creative tool for fixing the comparisons and contrasts of energy qualities and demonstrates the need for disciplined concentration in the acting craft.

External to Internal. In the following, you are going to try to draw upon two energy qualities simultaneously. First relax onto the floor and clear yourself. Breathe deeply and release all tension.

1. Select two contrasting energy qualities at random. Stay relaxed.
2. To perform with both energy qualities simultaneously, you may have to put one energy quality in one part of your body (say the right side, or from just your hips down) and the other quality in another part.
3. When you think you have found the proper body parts for the energy qualities, begin to move around in these contrasting qualities.
4. See if one will take over dominance. See if there is a resolution to the problem of the two qualities working simultaneously.
5. Is there an emotional state created by this problem? See if this can be resolved in any way.
6. Follow through until there is resolution or stalemate. Then gradually release the tension and the problem and come back to a neutral state.

Internal to External. This time, recall a situation in which you experienced conflicting desires or emotions.

1. Fill yourself with your chosen situation, and when you are in touch with the emotions it has created, begin to explore the situation physically.
2. See if one emotion can cause one type of energy quality and the other a contrasting energy quality. (Suspended energy and collapsed energy are two separate qualities for this exploration.)
3. See if you can find a resolution of your problem.
4. Does one emotion and energy quality win out or suppress the other?
5. Follow through until there is a resolution or stalemate. Then gradually release the tension, situation, and emotion and relax back onto the floor.
6. Clear yourself. Breathe deeply and relax. Bring yourself back to a neutral state.

This is a perfect time to do a movement (music) tape, to allow actors to explore their energies and emotions freely. This exploration is an excellent prelude to "take-home" energy essence study.

SELF-DISCOVERY: AN ENERGY ESSENCE STUDY

This take-home assignment is a study of one's own characteristic energy quality. We all have a dominating energy quality, a product of our personal psychology and socialization. Usually, individuals primarily employ some dynamic blend of two primary energy qualities. Rather than a single energy quality, most people tend to use a combination of "the *me* I want to be perceived as being" quality (that is, perhaps, a sustained and emotionally controlled person) that is just as much a part of their natural energy quality as "the *me* that I want to keep people from seeing" quality (that may be a percussive person, driven by ambition and perfectionism). The two qualities, whatever they are, work together—not usually in the manner of Jekyll and Hyde, where one dominates for four hours and then the other takes control—but in a more subtle and efficient way, depending on the nature of our changing reality.

From the information learned in the previous explorations and from the knowledge you have gleaned from years of living with yourself, prepare an abstraction of your own basic movement quality, a brief, perhaps half-minute study that reveals your employment of your one or two primary applications of energy in a typical day. Prepare both the essence and the realistic manner for how you walk, sit down, put on your coat, and so on. Be sure not to over-intellectualize this assignment. Remember, you are you, and the knowing will reveal itself externally.

At the next session, after the actors present their energy essence, they should move into a realistic walk in order to show how the energy qualities carry over into normal movement. The session should end with a discussion period and actors should critique and compare notes on how accurate or revealing the studies were.

We will return to energy in the applications phase (Chapter 5).

THE ACTION-VERB APPROACH

This is a movement study inspired by Archie Smith's graduate acting class at Penn State University in 1976. This class, working improvisationally, seized the basic activity of a scene and expressed a capsulized version of that activity in action-verb units: *kill, seduce, surround, flee,* and so forth.

Specifically, the action verb can be effectively used to focus a line, a word, or even a pause: conceiving that small unit in terms of specific and graphic physical gestures or actions you would like to use with a given character, you use the word and/or body language to perform the action in a manner consistent with the script. (For example, you would not express a socially acceptable action by enacting a criminal one.) The actor may subverbally conceive an action verb in this manner: "With this (word, line, glance, stare, wink, shrug, pause, etc.) I (the character) am going to (kiss his cheek, kick her in the belly, stroke her face tenderly, shove a knife into him, spit in his face, and so on)." In this case, the more specific the naming of physical action via the action verb, and the more organic the connection between visualization and emotional justification, the better the tool. As long as the actor is working in essence and is trained to avoid harming another actor, this is a powerful, useful tool. The purpose of this exploration, then, is to help the actor gain easier access to the action-verb activity by working on its physical essence.

With a partner, set up a situation or work from a scene and prepare action-verb capsulizations. Begin on the floor, lying close enough to one another to sense the other's presence. Attain a neutral state. Then let the situation and action verb soak in, until you have a strong inward sense of it. When ready, begin to move around, developing the feel of the action verb. When plugged into yourself, begin relating to the other and follow through with your action as long as you can. Generally, most situations and scenes demand a winner, one whose action verb defeats the other.

Variation 1. When ready, move gradually from the physical abstraction into a realistic version of the imagined situation or the scene itself. Verbalizing is helpful, but if a scene is used, verbatim dialogue need not be essential.

Variation 2. In the middle of a successful abstraction, the pair will be commanded to freeze. Then roles are reversed. If the interplay has been intense, each will be familiar enough with the other's action verb and physicalized identity to effect a smooth exchange. After this proceeds well, do another freeze, and then return to the original role. After a while, do a slow transition into a realistic vein with dialogue.

LINE ESSENCE STUDY

The purpose of this exploration is twofold. It is designed to help the actor get to the core of a line of dialogue and to achieve the organic movement inherent in the line.

As a take-home assignment, have the actor bring to the session a line from a contemporary play that the group has not worked on previously. There are three steps. It is very important that once the actors begin they go from one step to the next, so there is no time for the mind to monitor itself.

1. Essence movement: Begin by lying on the floor in a relaxed, neutral state. Think about the line of dialogue; pack your mind with all the particulars of the line. Allow your spirit to be affected by the line and let it connect your mind with your body. Let your body react by physicalizing the essence of the line and its core. Do not indicate, mime, or "act out" the line. Trust the mind-body-spirit connection, and let it happen.
2. Essence movement of dialogue: Immediately repeat the physical essence study and then, without pausing, vocalize the dialogue. Let the line flow organically out of the movement.
3. Realistic: As step 2 is completing itself, go immediately into a realistic delivery of the line. Do not impose any movement; just trust and allow it to happen. The purpose is to go from one step to the next without hesitation, so that the organic connection is not broken. This prevents the mind from monitoring itself. If you sense the actors not carrying over, especially from steps 2-3, have them go back and repeat the last two steps. Guide them to trust their essences, to avoid indicating, and to immediately flow one into the other. Remind them not to struggle or force this process, but to let it evolve.

As a take-home assignment, have the actors prepare another contemporary line essence study at home to share with the group. Once this process is understood, you can expand the assignment to include classical drama and various genres of drama.

This exploration can be used periodically. It is valuable when an actor is having difficulty finding movement for a particular line.

Time

Of the three primary elements of movement (space, time, and energy) time is perhaps the most difficult to deal with in stage movement. Time is conceptually more difficult than the other two elements because, while you can see and even feel space and see the effects of the application of energy, time is neither tactile nor, in most cases, easily controllable. In fact, time is the most intractable concept mankind possesses simply because it is so subjective. One person's estimate and perception of the passage of time is so radically different from another's that without clocks there could be no agreement about the amount of time that it takes to read from the start of this paragraph to the end. Do you know how long it took you?

Knowing that our sense of time is almost entirely subjective, however, is the key to unlocking the secrets we as theater artists need to reveal. What we are looking for, then, is not the precise measurement or quantitative analysis of time that scientists desire; what we need are tools to understand how our perceptions of time are affected.

Fortunately, there are many things that we already know about our perceptions of time. For instance, we know that when we are bored and have nothing to do, a minute can seem like an hour. We know that when we are late for an appointment and are stopped at a red light, that same minute can seem like an eternity. When trying to write a paper that was due last week, the minute spent agonizing over the choice of words, or looking up a spelling, can flash by without our notice. Rushing to catch a plane leaves us wondering why our watch suddenly speeded up.

We all know, in short, that our sense of time changes with our emotional states and the situations that cause them. Oddly, most of us tend to forget that time is more complicated than our watches, bus schedules, and calendars lead us to believe. One minute is not the same as the next; one day is totally different from the one before; and one year in the life of a three-year-old is altogether different from the same year for an octogenarian.

Even within the same event there are contrasting perceptions of time. In the first year of Ronald Reagan's presidency, as he was walking jauntily out of a Washington hotel with his entourage, a would-be assassin stepped from the crowd and fired his revolver at the President. It is obvious that the assassin's time sense was dramatically different from that of Reagan, the reporters, his entourage, and the casual onlookers clustered a few feet away. Once the first shot was fired, however, the "Sunday morning stroll" atmosphere rapidly vanished and time condensed. Before the shots there was "all the time in the world" to do what everyone needed to do, then in less time than it takes to think the word "assassin," there was not enough time to do anything—to duck, to dodge, to evacuate the president, to stop the attacker. The film and videotape revealed all this in detail, revealing even the cameraman's wince. Each person perceived and reacted to the threat in his own way at different times.

So how do we deal with time in stage movement training? What terms do we use, and how can we manipulate our sense of time to further our understandings of its many facets? Thankfully, there is at least one group of artists who out of necessity have spent centuries dealing with the problem of time, and it is in their direction that we, as theater artists, must turn.

Musicians have, probably since before the invention of musical notation, been involved in the process of defining and manipulating our perception of time. The theoretical basis is so firm by now that both dance and theater artists can and to varying degrees effectively do use at least the basic principles of music theory.

FIVE BASIC PRINCIPLES OF TIME

There are five basic principles I use in explorations of time. Although the theory comes primarily from music, the application of that theory can be expressed in terms of movement. And although the description of phenomena may seem at first purely external, keep in mind that, as with all elements of movement, in reality it is merely another way of describing the external manifestation of some internal state.

1. Duration: How long it takes to complete a movement, or set of movements.
2. Tempo: How fast a movement or movement phrase is completed; speed.
3. Rhythmic pattern: The regulation of tempo and duration of movements into ordered sets.
4. Accent: The emphasis within the rhythmic pattern of movements. The strongest and most significant movements in a movement phrase.
5. Counterpoint: Two or more contrasting sets of time elements existing simultaneously, either within one person's movement, or between two or more people (for instance, one person rocking languidly in a chair with his foot rapidly tapping the floor; one person moving slowly, another quickly, and so on).

While these definitions seem fairly simple, confusion sometimes occurs when actors ponder the difference between duration and tempo. Partly this is so because they are in some sense similar and can be used to describe the same event. They are dramatically different, however: tempo is concerned with speed (how fast the car was going); duration is concerned with length of time (how long it took the car to get there).

Accent can be a tricky concept to explain, but it becomes much simpler by demonstrating. Have actors clap their hands four times, keeping the sound at a constant level. Note the lack of accent. Next have them clap their hands four times trying to make the sound loudest on the last clap. Now note the accent or stress placed on the last clap. The last clap, then, is one example of a movement that is similar to other movements, but different because it used more energy and larger swings of the hands, and produced a noticeably louder sound. You could note that even without the sound, the movement would still be noticeably different from the others and so is still accented.

Once actors have learned this, you can have them move forward around the room in a walk, placing emphasis on, say, the first step out of each four. (*one,* two, three, four). Then you could have them try the same pattern, or another accented pattern, in other parts of the body (say, one, *two,* three, *four*). These three definitions are fairly easy to communicate even to the uninitiated actor.

Before moving on to the major problem of defining rhythmic patterns, let's acknowledge and further develop another musical concept that has just been introduced. By placing four regular pulses of movement of the same duration in a sequence, we have created a time pattern called a *measure*. Specifically, the pattern established above is 4/4 time (simply four beats to a measure). This is so frequently used in music that it is called *common time*. Emphasis or accent can occur on any of the four beats, and it is still 4/4 or common time. There are many other measures or time signatures that are used: 2/4 (two beats to a measure), 3/4 (three beats to a measure), 6/8 (six beats to a measure), 5/4 (five beats to a measure), and others. But the basic principles apply to each. By placing a limit on the number of beats you will consider as a unit and then repeating the unit, you provide yourself with a frame of reference, a measure by which you compare and compose the elements.

Now, to eliminate another possible problem that may develop, let's state here that there is a fairly broad spectrum of tempo (speed) at which these accented or unaccented patterns may be played and still remain essentially the same structurally. Watch what happens to the feeling tone, however, when the tempo is increased. Each beat remains the same duration relative to the next within a given measure, but the faster the tempo, the shorter the duration of each beat and measure. Take the Plains Indian drumbeat, a cliché in Hollywood films (*one,* two, three, four) from a very slow tempo gradually to a very fast tempo, and it turns into a speeding steam locomotive. It is still 4/4 time— the accent remains the same, as does the rhythmic pattern—but the internal feeling evoked is totally altered, along with the movement quality of improvising actors.

To change the rhythmic pattern within the 4/4 time frame, we must add one further consideration: Let's change the *duration* of one or more of the counts or numbers within the measure. Take the unaccented pattern "one, two, three, four" and elongate the first count so that it is exactly as long in duration as the first two counts (one and two) combined. The pattern thus produced would be "one, three, four" and so on. Count two is counted (there are still four beats to the measure); it is merely hidden, by being included in a longer count. Another way to alter the duration of the numbers is to shorten the duration of one or more numbers by one-half so that count one, for instance, has two equal pulses in the same duration as it would normally take to count one. The new rhythmic pattern thus produced would be *one-and, two, three, four.*

Frequently used rhythmic patterns using this system are:

One-and, two-and, three-and, four-and
One, two-and, three-and, four
One-and, two, three, four-and
One, two-and, three, four-and

Notice that none of these is accented. Accent, as we've noted, can completely alter the feeling tone of the music or movement thus affected. Also, accent can be placed on any number or any corresponding "-and" (that is, on or between any counted beat). For instance: "one, two-and, three, four" can become "one, *two*-and, three, four" or "one, two-*and*, three, four." Notice, however, that while accent does affect feeling tone, the rhythmic pattern remains the same.

The last way to alter rhythmic pattern is by simply not playing a beat—by resting during that interval—so that there is a gap between numbers:

One, (hold), three, four
One, (hold), three-and, four
One-and, (hold), three-and, four

It must be noted that the rhythmic pattern in music is *not* the measure of the notes of what would normally be called the melody or harmony lines—it is rather the underlying *structure* of the music, the major pulse rate of the sound. Melody and harmony lines often incorporate either fewer or many more notes than exist in the rhythmic pattern, but both are inexorably focused, directed, and propelled by the basic rhythmic pattern.

So it is with movement. While every single heartbeat, breath, and eye blink may not occur simultaneously with the pulses of the rhythmic pattern, the basic kinetic orientation is aligned with it naturally and spontaneously as the mind-spirit-body connection functions in an interactive state too fast for the conscious mind to calculate or control.

Rhythmic pattern changes for two reasons only: when the time signature changes, and when the established pattern of beats within a single time signature changes.

Each of the five elements defined above alters our perception of time. This is rudimentary music theory that may, nonetheless, prove to be difficult conceptually, but it is universal and simple to respond to. Understanding them both intellectually and kinetically gives you more understanding and control of your perception of time. If the effort to understand intellectually begins to interfere with the ability to understand kinetically, you should stop thinking, and just feel. The concepts I use in stage movement training are really quite simple, but an actor with no prior exposure to them tends to suffer from the effects of too much intellectual effort and too little spontaneity. Obviously, actors who have studied at least rudimentary music theory will be, initially at least, better prepared to explore time in depth than actors who have not and who struggle to comprehend the concepts involved.

For the instructor, the key to teaching this section is to bring in an element of lightness so that the group relaxes into their own natural sense of rhythm, which in most cases is considerable. For the few who have no sense of rhythm no amount of browbeating will help them grow in this capacity.

The following sequence of explorations for approaching the subject of time is meant partly to inspire other adaptations of the theory more lucidly explained in other texts. Keep in mind that in movement training for actors the number of time signatures involved is small (usually 2/2, 2/4, 3/4, 4/4, 5/4, 6/8 will be adequate).

The reason for this is that, as bipedal creatures, we do not have occasion to use other, more complicated theoretical structures to describe movement that occurs naturally in our day-to-day activities. Everyone moves according to a personal time pattern, whether regular or erratic, fast or lethargic. For example, we can often identify others by their approach and distinctive sound pattern in walking. But it is important for actors to try out what it feels like to move in many time patterns that are not their own. The warm-up for "time explorations" should again be geared to focusing on the time elements in the exercises, so that the actor can anticipate the more difficult work later in the day.

Duration. This is an ambiguous set of directions, but you will know when you are sensing different lengths of time in completing movements.

1. Take a simple movement or gesture (say, opening and closing a door) and explore it with different durations. Then try other gestures.
2. Try walking, jumping, running, at different durations. The time it takes to move those three steps doesn't increase the number of steps.
3. Walk, stop, and freeze. Sense the duration of each. Move and freeze. Vary the duration of each. Feel the differences.

Tempo. Experiment with various tempos and how fast and how slow a movement you can execute.

1. Use a walk to improvise freely various tempos.
2. Perform a simple movement so fast your eyes can hardly follow it. Now repeat it as slowly as you can manage it. Then try it with an in-between tempo. Try other movements and repeat them using three speeds.
3. By yourself, improvise changing tempos abruptly. Effect a sudden transition from a dreamlike gliding into a Charlie Chaplin walk, for example. Then work with three tempo transitions, again abrupt and sudden, but with an intermediate tempo in between.

Rhythmic Pattern. Now try regulating tempo and duration into ordered sets, as follows:

1. Improvise rhythmic patterns with several parts of the body. For example: Take a 4/4 meter (the rhythmic pattern being 1, 2, and 3, and 4) and explore the head or the torso. Or try 6/8 or 3/4 and build combinations (head to torso to leg to arm, etc.) changing part on each count.
2. Now explore these rhythms, walking in different beats, or try a combination of walking, skipping, and running.
3. Take an everyday action, such as washing your hands, and explore it until you find its rhythmic pattern. Then alter that pattern.

Conversing by Rhythmic Pattern. For this exercise, find a partner. You are going to communicate with him or her by use of rhythmic patterns.

Use your whole body. Don't merely indicate. Think of and borrow from speech rhythms that fit certain emotions. Try anger, for instance, in a 1 and 2 and 3 and 4, at a fast tempo, with percussive movements.

This is an abstract conversation. When you think you are in tune with your partner, grade into a realistic conversation. Follow through to the end.

Accent. Like the strongest stress in the intonation pattern of an utterance, accent in a movement phrase organizes and focuses the whole communication. Since most accents are placed on the first beat in plain movement, it is important that you vary the accent pattern in the warm-up for this day's work.

1. Try one exercise with different accents: the pelvis rotation, say, with the accents moving from 2, 4, and 6, each rotation having a different accent.
2. Next, make up a simple movement pattern across the floor. Do it several times with different accents each time.
3. By yourself, explore in a free improvisation all kinds of movements and accents. For example, take an everyday movement, such as putting on your coat, and play with the accent in the movement phrase.
4. Take a piece of dialogue and play with moving the accent in both the speech and the accompanying movement. Work on dialogue and gesture as one. Usually physical accents occur with verbal stress.

Counterpoint or Conflict. Explore the conflict possible in a simple external manipulation of the body.

1. In this Grotowski-influenced exploration, you begin in a neutral state, standing. Oppose the right hand's slow, sustained quality with the left leg moving sharply. Add more combinations with conflict. Now work the upper torso against the lower body. Then return to a neutral state.

   Think of cutting the body in half vertically, left and right; make one side graceful, lovely, and elegant, with lyrical movement, the other side assertive, hard, vicious, perhaps percussive. Set up some opposition in the personalized states—a clash of movement qualities and feelings, between left and right. The two aspects must fight or clash, as you move around. Maintain a close concentration or you will lose the clean opposition. Continue until one side triumphs. Then hold this quality. Relax and release all tension. Breathe deeply, clear yourself.

2. Now lie on your back, relaxed and free of tension. Try to remember a situation in which you had an internal conflict. Perhaps it was something you wanted to do as a child, but were afraid of doing. Maybe it was having to make a decision between two equally pleasant options or two equally unpleasant options. Pick one situation you have experienced, and fill yourself with it. Without moving, try to feel the conflict within you as your desires, fears, and apprehensions do battle within you. Once you can feel the tension so strongly that you can no longer remain still, allow your body to move with the tension. Try to let the inner tension express itself in its essence through your movement. You can react to others or not, as you feel, but maintain the tension. Finally, find a resolution to the situation, or dissolve the tension.

3. Pair up with someone to explore counterpoint in pure movement—that is, movement that intends no specific verbal dialogue inherent in it. With each movement, respond to one another's movements, answering each other with opposing or counterpointed moves and patterns.

4. Still paired up, set up a situation of conflict within a specified personal relationship. This time the movement should imply inner states such as anger, impatience, love, and so forth. Begin by getting into a neutral state at a distance that is a little removed, but still near, your partner. Think about the situation until you begin to comprehend it inwardly. Then get up and move about with one another, abstractly at first, using the essence of the conflict. Then, when ready, gradually move from abstraction into realistic improvisation.

Your improvisation occurs first using *time* as the focal point, and then, second, moves to an internalized process. The analysis or revelation from the first part should show how external manipulations affect internal reactions;

the second part should reveal how the perceptions and use of time are influenced by internal states. This exploration is especially helpful when you are going for the inner nature of a scene in training or in rehearsal.

A MUSIC EXPLORATION

This is a summarizing exploration using music, incorporating all the elements of time you have been exploring. It works best using a tape-recorded collection of a wide range of music snippets—electronic, pop, rock, classical, primitive, jazz, and country (see the example in Chapter 6, page 198).

1. Move in time with the rhythm, whatever it is, breaking or transforming it. You may place accents against the natural accents in the music you are moving to.
2. Then work against the music, against the rhythm. If it is a percussive 4/4 rhythm, move into a swinging gentle 3/4, for example.
3. You may likewise concentrate on the tempo, fast music and slow movement, and so on, as you move.
4. Work with rhythmic patterns, seeing what types of things you feel when you follow exactly the rhythm being played.
5. Allow yourself to work alone or with others, either in counterpoint or in harmony. Do not feel inhibited by the orientation of the exploration; just respond freely to the stimulus around you.

ESSENCE OF SELF EXERCISES

Rhythmic Essence. We all have our personal rhythmic patterns. At home, alone, prepare a movement study on the essence of your own rhythmic pattern. Then add a realistic version of this pattern. Go back to basic movements to find it— walking, drinking, lying down. Recall your energy study for some help.

Presentation should start with the abstraction. Then, when the abstraction is completed, perform your set of realistic movements. Then repeat the abstraction.

Animal Essence. Also to be done at home, this exercise enables the actor to obtain his (or her) own external mannerisms as well as to hone in on his inner core. One animal may be chosen as containing both the external and internal elements of the individual, but in most cases two or sometimes even three or four different animals must be selected. For example, we have heard people say that a person looks like a panther, so sleek and agile. You want to find those characteristics of an animal that you think suit your external mannerisms. The goal is to explore these characteristics, not literally, but in essence. The same is true for the animal you select to bring out your internal aspects.

You can put this study together in the order that suits you best. You may want to begin with the external animal and go into the internal, or reverse the order. For some, the external and internal blend together, because we are both.

1. Begin by lying down in a relaxed, neutral position. Fill your psyche with the traits of the animal that have a specific meaning to you. Allow your spirit to connect your mind to your body. Let your body physicalize these common traits through abstract movement. Do not indicate or mime. Remember you are exploring the essence of the animal, be it the external mannerisms or the internal makeup.

2. Fully explore both the external and internal essences. Once finished, immediately walk around as yourself. Do not monitor your movement, but allow yourself to be free and natural.

3. As you walk, the instructor and the group will attempt to determine which study was your external and which your internal. Explain to the class why you selected the animals you did and what characteristics you share. Example: "My external animal is a panther, selected for its sleek and agile movement. My internal animal is a puppy because I am often playful, docile, and eager to please. However, the slinky movement of the panther also connects with me internally. I am often cautious and guarded."

By doing this exercise the actor discovers external mannerisms and internal makeup, as well as the connection between the two. Additionally, this exercise frees him to explore his deeper, primal self.

Emotion

Emotion is perhaps the most direct avenue of approach to characterization. It is certainly an inevitable step in the preparation of any characterization. But it is also the most obvious of the problems an actor can consider, and because it is such an important one, many actors never get beyond it. And because they never get beyond the question, "What is my character feeling?" the answers they find are quite likely to be largely arbitrary.

This is one reason why emotion is one of the last major areas I explore in my stage movement classes. To be sure, there are other considerations, the chief being the concept of the progressive acquisition of skills. Since this is a movement training system it has been important first to develop the ability to actualize *through movement* the various concepts the actor unconsciously employs in developing characterization. Now, having illuminated the darkened areas of the actors' perception of essential elements, they stand out in stark relief, and the actor responds spontaneously to them. We can now explore emotion and not worry how or even if these things affect the actor emotionally. Emotions become part of the actor's perception, as is natural.

Since every element previously explored has had an emotional reaction tied to it, actors should be more aware of the range and subtlety of the emotional response than if in the first session the instructor had said, "Let's explore emotion." Now when we explore this most obvious area of characterization, actors should have more information to draw from and be better prepared to use it effectively.

Lastly, in placing emotion near the end of this period of study, I have put early and continuous emphasis upon the fact that acting is *doing*. So many actors believe that all they must do is feel. But it is important for them to understand that emotion is only a part of awareness—part of an *organic* response (thought, emotion, action, or mind, spirit, body) to stimuli that helps to motivate actions. It is only through our perceived actions that others (especially audiences) can understand either our emotions or motivations. Just feeling is not enough.

Once an actor understands and is in command of the other primary elements of stage movement, this last very important area of awareness will be invaluable in completing the organic connection of mind, spirit, and body. The final pieces of the puzzle should come tumbling quickly into place with very little intellectual effort.

FEELING-FORM-FLOW EXPLORATION

In this exercise, you should develop the feeling of an emotion from some memories that make it your own.

1. First, lying on the floor, get into a neutral state, mind cleared, tension drained.
2. An emotion is suggested (joy, sorrow, love, hate). Let that emotion absorb your mind.
3. Get up and move about in the manner it seems to dictate. Let your whole body respond to the emotion. Heighten the feeling by expressing it throughout your body. Laugh or weep or cringe with the whole body.
4. Then localize your expression, just with the foot or the hands, laughing, raging, or caressing.

Once the emotion exploration has run its course, a group discussion will help sort out the individual and collective experience. An important topic to cover is the comparison of this emotional manifestation with a purely external one.

FORM-FEELING-ELICITATIONS

This exercise calls for on-the-spot sensitivity to named emotions. Respond as if each emotion were slapping you in the face, shocking you into a commanded state. As before, perhaps personal images, remarks, and memories will stir to life.

1. Assume a standing position, and work into a deeply relaxed neutral state, mind completely cleared.
2. The instructor will call out a series of emotional states (desolation, loneliness, inner warmth and security, and so on) and you will respond instantaneously, striking a shape, position, or movement that that feeling provokes in you.

3. Hold your response, but don't freeze. Move gently and slowly, keeping the emotional contours intact.
4. Meanwhile, reach inward to deepen the sense of the emotion. Let the form you are in seep into your core and elicit your most sensitive responses.

Proceed in similar fashion with each of the emotions called out. Then end the exploration with a discussion period.

EMOTIONAL ESSENCE OF SELF EXERCISES

Actors need to develop their own selves' emotional "through-line." This exercise enables them to tune into their emotional core (or spirit or gut, the paradox of who they are, both yin and yang). Emotions are primal and powerful. They are our feelings, our reactions to our thoughts, wants, and needs, and they cause us to act and react to situations in our lives.

Remember, the inner life extends to the external self: Thought (mind)—emotion (spirit)—action (body).

1. For each of us the process is different when we are dealing with feelings. Start by spending time alone and go to the quiet place inside you that knows, maybe through meditation. You can be lying down in a quiet space, walking in nature, or just looking at the sky or ocean—any place where you can turn inward to your emotions, feelings, spirit, to find your emotional through-line.
2. Now to your mind, your computer. Fill your mind with the specifics, and allow the spirit to connect the mind to the body. Let the body physicalize it, externalize your emotions through your body.
3. Your movement is organic, primal. You are congruent, both externally and internally. You are not combining memory with your movement; rather, the movement is coming from the core of your emotions.
4. Once the body has taken over, trust the connection, and explore each emotion. Do not monitor yourself. Let go, and go with the flow of your feeling.

Note to the Instructor. For the exercise to be clear to the group, the instructor must present it as specifically as possible in terms of the emotions, so that the body can be specific and clear in its movement. Usually, there are three to five major emotions, but remember you cannot generalize when dealing with people. Do what feels right for you (you know yourself). You should explore the emotional through-line in various explorations to enable the actor to deal with the power of the emotions and the emotional through-line.

Here are two exercises to help explore the emotional through-line.

Core Emotion. You might use sounds, if you wish, to correspond to your movements as you do the following:

1. Lie down in a relaxed state in a neutral position. Begin to fill the self with the particulars of the core emotions. Pack the self with as many things as possible to get to the core of the emotion.
2. Once the mind and spirit have connected with the body, let the body explore completely through the core emotion. Externalize your feelings with organic, primal movement.

Color—Energy—Emotion. Once again, color becomes a factor in relating the internal and the external.

1. Using an internal approach, select a color. In selecting, choose one for its strong emotional appeal and your feelings toward it.
2. Fill yourself up. Pack yourself with the particulars that that color evokes for you (such as texture, smell, sounds, feelings, events). Be as specific as possible with the who, what, where, and why.
3. When the mind and spirit have connected with the body, let the body externalize it through movement, letting the whole being explore the feelings and energy of the color and all that it means to you.

Tying It Together

TOTAL ESSENCE OF SELF

This exercise should be introduced in the training session and then be fully explored at home. The actors should bring their completed explorations to be shared with the rest of the group.

The purpose is to integrate the external and internal aspects of the individual into one essence study. The study is the composite of all previously explored elements. Up to this point, actors have explored their energy, rhythm, internal and external animal, and emotional through-line essence. Their intellectual and physical beings have gained understanding, and now is the time to trust in the spirit. Essentially, the actors have done the background research and now must tie it in together by trusting in what they have already discovered.

1. Lie down in a relaxed, neutral state. Clear your mind and body of any clutter. Journey back in your mind to the essences already explored. Think of what you discovered about your energy, rhythm, external and internal animals, and your emotional through-line. Trust in the discoveries you've made. Think toward the future, your hopes and aspirations, what you want out of life.
2. Allow your spirit to connect your thoughts and ideas to your physical self. Let the body react physically and explore the essence and core of these feelings. Leave yourself open to new discoveries. Remember that all these things are inherent in you. All you need to do is trust in yourself and open the door to discovery.

3. Now, using this foundation for your total self essence, the next step is to take yourself through this exercise again in a private environment. Push your boundaries and think of yourself as a limitless person, in order to fully discover the totality of your being through essence.

USING MUSICAL CUES

The activity of this exploration is your reacting to musical cues. Lie on the floor in a neutral state, cleared and drained, with the lights dimmed. Respond to the implied feeling or emotions of a musical selection, absorbing it and then letting your feelings flow into physical gesture and movement.

Your taped music may be one rich and provocative composition, or a medley of interesting pieces. Individuals respond variously to the same music, of course. Try only for the essence of the emotion. This is a free improvisation. You can work best by yourself. If some group interplay arises, you need not fight it.

From the frequent use of the musical-cues approach you can see my reliance on this exploration technique. This is because I have found music to be of great assistance in freeing actor's imaginations, spirits, and bodies; so that with the proper focus, the music allows the actors to teach themselves through an enjoyable, creative, and yet disciplined activity where they are free to come to their own understandings in their own way. This is the ultimate exploration technique, which can only be used after the early conditioning in body, spirit, and mind. It works well to record a tape of musical cues after a major unit of study such as Space, Energy, or Time.

It is not unusual for actors to request more frequent musical activities. It is important, however, that instructors not indulge this request too often, because it tends to allow the actors to rely too heavily on this tool. There are more important uses for the lessons they have learned than to allow them to revel in a good music tape. After all, these lessons were intended to be of help in specific acting projects, and it is necessary for the total, permanent acquisition of these lessons that actors begin applying their new-found knowledge, when it is ready, to acting.

ESSENCE STUDY FOR INDIVIDUAL PROJECTS

This exercise would be the final project for the first term of a movement training course. With it, the actors are given the opportunity to combine their own creative energy with essence study (see Chapter 5). They begin by selecting material that has special meaning to them. It can be a piece of music, a work of art, a poem, an excerpt from a novel or play—anything to which they feel a personal and emotional connection. It can even be something they have written or created on their own. It is important, however, that they keep their selection short in order to fully explore it.

The focus of this assignment is the actor's individual creativity in coordination with essence study. Essence becomes the explorative technique. The instructor should have the actors abstract and explore their selections. Then they can begin to think of how best to arrange these for presentation. This is where their creative interpretation comes into play. For example, while working on a poem, the actor might choose to first present the essence and then recite the poem. Another approach would be to perform the line and movement simultaneously, thus connecting organically. A third option is to have someone else recite the poem as the actor performs the movement. The options are limitless, and the actors should be encouraged to find their own way.

MOVING INTO APPLICATIONS

The best time to begin applications is after actors have attained a relatively firm understanding of the basic elements of space, time, and energy and have a firm grasp of the value and possibilities inherent in the essence work. Use of these basic tools is essential to their continued development, not to mention continued interest. Somewhere along the line actors are bound to ask themselves, "Fascinating, but what good is it? How can this help me in my acting?"

The answer is that these are tools that will eventually aid them in unlocking the secrets held within the words the playwrights provide. From these words actors must find the information necessary to bring the people speaking them to life. Whether the words provided are few or many, unlocking the secrets from them is not often easy. There are many systems the actor can use, but few proceed from a physical base, or even an organic base. Now actors have one, and in the next chapter I'll demonstrate how it works.

⁵ *Applications*

I may as well begin this second phase of training, concerning characterization, on a note of despair and then get on with the work. Certainly, there is no clear, straight, thoughtfully marked trail up the mountain to successful characterization. About brilliant, inspired acting there is always that ineffable air. Audience, director, and fellow actors will recognize it, but the actor in question may not be able to explain how he (or she) reached the peak of his capabilities. Our proper purpose, then, cannot be to lift the actor up to the summit, but to gesture in the general upward direction, and meanwhile to set about seeing that, like a mountain climber in training, he is given as many skills and experiences as are likely to prove helpful in the essentially solitary trek upwards.

The structure of this training underscores this process of ascent. I have referred to this method as the Triad, for there are three primary areas of focus. First we did the basic exercises; then the explorations; finally we do a number of applications, where we offer practice climbs so that actors can test their equipment and sense of direction. For this practice the atmosphere should be experimental (rather than success- or goal-oriented). This is still a period of discovery, and most of what the actors learn they will know only within themselves.

Let us use a definition of acting to focus our remarks. The philosopher Suzanne K. Langer in her book *Feeling and Form* (New York: Charles Scribner's Sons, 1953) usefully comments on the internal-external flow that lies at the heart of characterization:

> Since every utterance is the end of a process which began inside the speaker's body, an enacted utterance is a part of a virtual act, apparently springing at the moment from thought and feeling; so the actor has to create the illusion of an inward activity issuing in spontaneous speech, if his words are to make a dramatic and not a rhetorical effect.

In the chain of events that culminates in speech, we see an inextricable link between plain visceral activity and verbal expression. If speech does first arise in a mental act, it is only made possible through a physiological process. There are two kinds of internal origins, then, for articulation: the classic internal (emotion memory, intention, desire) and the physical internal (the body apparatus that shapes space and makes noise). Both thought and feeling are nestled within what you could call "gut," or visceral, life. This is what I call the organic reality. It is this verbal and physiological reality that stage movement training must work toward, because the whole body is involved in the physiological process of communication.

I would like to take Langer's statement one step further: Whereas the actor must at least create the illusion of inward activity, I believe that the ideal to work toward is not "the illusion of an inward activity," but rather the creation of an actual inner (or inward) reality that can be reflected outward. The illusion thus derives not from pretending that something is happening where there is nothing, but from the actor's creating an activity within him- or herself that is real and therefore similar to the character's inner state; the audience then believes it is perceiving the reality of the character. This is the "illusion," and it has no connotation of "trickery," no hint of "let's pretend." Something *does* happen within the actor, or the applause and the accolades are (perhaps subconsciously) solely for the actor's skill and not because the audience has been touched emotionally.

If actors strive for illusion—for tricking the audience—they only serve to distance themselves from the reality of the characters and the play; they become performers like song and dance teams. But if an actor creates an inner reality that an audience can perceive and that is appropriate—even necessary—for the character and his reality, then the actor can reach far deeper levels of the audience member's psyche and achieve a more lasting and truthful effect. Illusion has indeed played a role, but not in a self-serving or obvious manner. It is *this* illusion that a thinking audience accepts as necessary for theater. Respect for the audience and for the acting profession demands that the actor aspire to this level. Failing to achieve an inner activity, the actor can *then* fall back on "faking it," but that should never be the goal. This is not Langer's intention, but the clarification needs to be made.

Stage movement training justifiably concerns itself with aiding the actor to achieve the outward reflection of inner reality. But it should also aid in the creation of the inner reality, for that is not a creation of just the mind, but depends to a great extent on the mind-spirit-body relationship.

It is to this goal that the applications aspire. In this portion of study I try to help actors use the tools they have mastered to find a kinetic sense of a given character's reality, based on the mind-body flow connected by the spirit.

The Format for Applications

All the work we will be doing in applying the explorations to the problems of characterization will be performed on the actor's own time; the problems require too much thought and preparation to begin and end in training sessions with other actors. Moreover, the time with the group can be most effectively used if all the actors are working on carefully constructed studies. And even though each works alone, every actor is working on the same element of characterization. This arrangement allows a discussion and analysis period to take on more significance at this stage, when it is most needed. The instructor, freed from the role of constant supervisor and guide, can then operate more efficiently— here, as a critic and experimenter.

STEP I: CHOOSE THE MATERIAL

When the study of applications begins, actors are instructed to find a scene from a contemporary play that has two characters close to themselves in age. Then they should pair off and decide which scene to do and which character each will assume. It usually takes little time to decide because the options narrow considerably when the classics are removed from consideration (period and style questions are not really suitable for *basic* movement study, but rather confuse the issue), and age and sex are taken into account. The scene should be relatively short and balanced in respect to character interaction (let's have no dialogue-with-a-corpse scenes).

STEP II: WORK ALONE

Once the scene and characters are chosen, the work will at first be totally separate. There are many reasons for this: I want to focus the actors' concentration on different areas from those an instructor would ordinarily allow in normal scene study; I want to prevent one strong-willed actor from dictating ideas about characterization, the play, the scene, and even line readings to another actor; I want to interrupt the normal or habitual routine that actors, of necessity, fall into, so that they become more open to the work of their fellow actors; and I want to follow the path of development I have already explored. Yet the main reason that I ask actors to work this way is that I wish each of them to make their own choices free from consideration of how those choices affect the other actor or character. This gives a freedom not typical in normal scene study. It frees each actor to make initial discoveries unencumbered by consideration of anyone else.

STEP III: EXPLORE TOGETHER

After each actor has had an opportunity to discover individually the realities of the character (the inner activity of the character), then nonverbal exploration of the situation can proceed with the other actor, whose character she (or he) has observed but not helped to develop. Each actor's understanding of her own character and the scene can be significantly altered or enriched by this interchange. Also, while it may help sharpen the actor's improvisational skills, it will certainly reinforce the need for a continuing development of inner life.

STEP IV: ADDING THE DIALOGUE

A predetermined line-reading or vocal pattern can often inhibit or retard an actor's development of a character. If the line-reading imprints itself too heavily on the actor's psyche, she often finds herself incapable of making the subtle adjustments necessary to respond realistically—dynamically—to the changing nature of each performance. It may seem that to avoid such a situation I have taken elaborate precautions. That is only partially true.

It is more accurate to say that this is an elaborate process for revealing a truth that is elusive for many actors: *The words spring from the character's perception of the situation and the attempt to bring about a change in it.*

What and how a person says something depends on many variables. An actor can only know why a character says the words she says by knowing everything she can about who this character is. What she says and how she says it are determined by the situation. Since we already know what is said, and where it is said, the actor must supply the rest.

This entire process is an attempt to give the actor the ability to provide answers to *who* and *why,* so that *how* happens inevitably as a result. If that does indeed occur, that actor must surely have come to some better understanding and command of the mind-spirit-body connection.

Using this process, working together must take place under supervision, so that problems in the scene are not solved by discussion but by creative interaction—that is, with an exploration applied to the specific problem. For beginning actors it is most useful if a single character from the same play and scene remains the focus for the work in all of the applications. For an advanced actor there is some virtue in variety, shifting characters, scenes, or plays.

Working Alone

Once the material is chosen and partners selected, actors are instructed to keep communication between themselves about the nature of the material to a minimum. Discussion needs to occur only in the review of specific material in a day's presentation. Even then actors should be discouraged from trying to consciously incorporate or reconcile their partner's work. I tell them, "Don't worry about putting it together; we'll do that later. You work on your character, and you work on yours, and we'll all get to the scene together."

Because both actors are reasonably intelligent, working from the same script, and using the same tools under the same guidance, they can't be too far apart in their understanding of the nature of the problem after many weeks of study. Besides, each actor has the opportunity to observe his (or her) partner's work, and he (because I discourage conscious effort to incorporate this work) subliminally or instinctively develops an organic awareness of the character that evolves opposite his own. Almost all the work will be based in essence theory and will therefore affect each actor more deeply in a subliminal rather than a conscious manner.

Actors must be familiar with the entire play. Too many actors erroneously believe they can develop a characterization based on the evidence supplied within a single scene. The scene is the specific focus for the actor's efforts, but the character is most completely revealed by his actions during the entire play. And the scene occurs because of something that has happened previously and has consequences that the actor must be aware of; he needs to understand the importance of this occurrence to the character.

That said, where do we begin?

As we did in the explorations, here in the applications the path of attack is from external to internal, and primarily for the same reasons as before: It is less demanding, builds sequentially into more and more difficult tasks, and allows the actors early success so that they feel relaxed, confident, and prepared for the more demanding problems of working from the internal to the external. The first step, then, is for the actors to attempt to find the external elements of their characters.

APPROACHING CHARACTERIZATION THROUGH MOVEMENT

What is characterization? Characterization is the act or process an actor uses to build a believable, three-dimensional person who exists within a dramatic presentation. The most common problem beginning actors face in approaching characterization is that they attempt to create the whole at once—to grasp all the complexities at the very outset. As Charles McGaw and Gary Blake say in *Acting Is Believing* (New York: Harcourt Brace, 1992): "The actor is often like a starving man who attempts to cram whole handfuls of food into his mouth instead of taking bite-size morsels, which he can readily chew and swallow."

The actor must have a process he can use to analyze the many small components of the character, so that, when he has finished the process, he comprehends and appreciates the composition in fine details, both the external and internal realities. A process I have developed with actors on both the university and professional level enables the actor to tune into the external and internal aspects of both himself and the character. I call this method or process Essence Theory.

In Chapter 4, I dealt with the basic elements of Essence Theory as they apply to the individual actor. Briefly, by Essence Theory, I mean that the actor works to find the core of something. To do this, he also works to discover and develop the organic connection of the mind, spirit, and body that is basic to any individual. The ultimate goal, beyond that of providing a process of characterization, is to develop within the actor a capability to discover and to use onstage, the movement that comes from within, movement that is organic to the character, not simply layered or pasted on.

In this second phase of training I use essence study to help actors develop characterization, using physical, energy, internal-external, animal, rhythm, and emotional through-line studies to explore the total composite of the character. Once actors have done this, they are ready to work on the development of the scene, using energy, conflict, animal, intention, and emotional through-line studies of the scene.

The Essence Theory allows actors to flesh out three-dimensional characters they will know intimately. Working with the various essence studies helps the actor to reinforce what it is like to have an organic and true connection to a character, through thoughts, emotions, and actions. Each essence study is crucial, each builds upon the one before. All are like building blocks in bringing the character and the scene to life.

The *physicalization* of a character involves many different aspects of a character's movement: way of walking, posture, and mannerisms. Working in these elementary areas an actor is actually preparing the foundation for the scene study, since any movement requires the certain use of space, time, and energy. This is merely a more direct, less subtle manner of approaching the task of preparing movement within a scene. Some actors may not know where to start, which is typical of the problem actors face when confronted with a new script. This exercise only tends to highlight the problem. I inform actors, "Don't worry about it or think about it too hard. Read the play, make an educated guess, and experiment until you feel you have something you can work with." I caution them not to try to make any irrevocable decisions. "Don't try to be right the first time. This is not a test, just a task. Your decisions could change as we continue to work on this scene. I'll be very surprised if they don't. Just try it. This is only the first crude step in assembling the composite, the first pieces of the montage or puzzle that will shift as you find other pieces."

The Character's Walk. After you have read the script through a few times to familiarize yourself with the play and the character, do the following:

1. Get up and move around the room or take a walk. Think about what happens to the character, what she (or he) says and does. Try to put yourself in her shoes so that it is she who is doing the walking.
2. Have the character walk in different situations, and then choose the one most typical of her. For instance: Is your character nervous, or worried most of the time? Is she in a hurry, or slow, patient, methodical, meticulous? Plodding or light-footed? Awkward or sure-footed? Uncertain or agile and athletic? You will find something that most suits your character. When you do, remember it, hold onto it. It will be part of a longer presentation.

Posture. From finding the walk, some sense of the character's typical stance should evolve.

1. Try walking and stopping in different situations. It should become clear after only a little experimentation what feels most comfortable for this developing character.

2. When you feel you have found the physical center of the character—that is, the *character's* natural alignment—hold onto it and remember it. This too will be part of the presentation.

Mannerisms. Once again try to find situations this character is likely to encounter.

1. Experiment now by walking, stopping, and walking again. Perform whatever you thing are the character's typical movements, and experiment with different gestures. How does this character sit or stand up? Does she scratch (what, where)? Does she have facial twitches, nervous hand movements, repetitive facial gestures of any kind?

2. Find two or three mannerisms that the character could use and repeat them in different sequences between walking, sitting, standing, leaning, and so forth, until they become reflexive to the movement pattern.

The Presentation. Now you will prepare a presentation of the character's walk, posture, and mannerisms.

1. Keep it a simple presentation of these three elements that lasts no more than a minute. The order of the presentation will be to do the essence study, then to do realistic movement within a simple situation. This presentation should reveal your character's typical physical presence.

2. Make it a *simple* situation. For instance, the character walks into her (or his) home, goes to a table looking for something, thinks a moment, takes off her jacket, sits down, and lights a cigarette. Or, waiting for a bus, the character deals with an umbrella, handbag, shopping bag, hat, and a bench.

3. You should not put any other person in the situation. Don't put in any dialogue. Also don't make it a performance about some traumatic occurrence such as the death of a loved one.

    Do not mime anything. If your character has an umbrella, have a real umbrella. If your character opens a door, have a door.

4. Once you have a firm grasp of the physical movements, prepare an essence study based on that literal study. The essence study should not be any elaborate or prolonged dissertation on the character's movement in varying states of joy and despair. It should be a simple, straightforward attempt to find the essence of the character's *typical* movement pattern. If successful, it should help to clarify the literal presentation.

5. Concentrate on the character's physical presence within an ordinary, everyday situation. Bring this concentration into the presentation. Don't make it a performance. The key is simplicity.

The presentation can be conducted in several ways, but the most useful is simply for an actor to present the essence study once. Before any discussion, the actor should then present the literal element of the study. It may be useful for the discussion if the actor presents either (or both) the literal or essence portion of the study again, not trying for an exact imitation of movements, but with the same general shape and feel. Then the rest of the group, without trying to guess the play or character, should discuss the presentation in terms of what kind of person they felt they saw. The presenting actor should not attempt to confirm, deny, explain, or defend the presentation. This is neither a game of charades nor a competition to see who is best at telling who a character is—there are no winners here. Discussion serves as a tool for the presenter to analyze the many elements present in this development and execution of character elements. Usually, this process is rewarding for all concerned.

This exercise exists simply to illustrate the physical image structure for your character through a careful intellectual reading of the text and some intuitive insight. It can be based on a specific scene or any imaginary situation. Don't worry about what the character does in relating to specific people or about your character's emotional life at this point. Keep it an external portrait. You may know or glimpse the inner life already, but don't try now to analyze it or concentrate on feeling it. Communicate the character's visible externals, and use whatever props you need. As the group discusses the presentation, their perceptions will tell you something about your choices.

EXPLORING CHARACTER THROUGH ESSENCE WORK

In physicalizing a character there are many questions not usually considered consciously by actors, although they profoundly influence character choices. For instance: How does this character perceive and use space, time, and energy? What are his (or her) principal emotions and how does he react to them physically?

When these and other elements of the character's inner world are explored, it will rapidly become obvious to the more serious actors that this material not only radically alters their understanding of the character's external reality, but that the physicalized exterior is hollow without a volume of what some might consider unessential knowledge.

A space study may not be necessary after the physicalized essence is done. But for those wishing to use it, the format is supplied.

Use of Space. This is a study of the character's use of space to be prepared in both literal and essence form. Neither should exceed one minute in length. Again, this is to be representative of the character's typical attitude and actions regarding space.

1. Consider these and similar issues: Is this character expansive in his movement or timid and small in his range of movement? Is he confident, yet contained, or does he try to be unobtrusive? How does your character use space?
2. Presentation will follow the format laid down in the preceding physicalization of a character: First present the essence , then the literal.
3. Discussion again will focus on the observers' perception of the character's use of space: What kind of person do the observers think the character is (based on the presentation)?

The presenter should not become defensive, explanatory, apologetic, or passive. This is not a tool for analyzing the difference between perception and achievement, but for understanding and making valuable character choices.

Energy Essence. This is, for most actors, an extremely valuable tool for character analysis. Its importance cannot be overemphasized, because the manner in which a character employs energy affects almost every other element of his behavior, and so provides a wealth of information not easily obtainable otherwise.

Keep in mind that, as in music, all elements relate to each other to some degree, so the tone of each additional study will have a kind of harmonic effect on the work preceding and following. Whereas we concentrate on one problem, our organic nature pushes us in the direction of harmonizing and amplifying the tones of each study; our inner nature finds resonances with our prior understanding of the melody being created (that is, the character we are forming).

Some actors in their rush to find something startlingly new about their character try to overlook what they feel is mundane or repetitive of some previously discovered truth. Such an inaccurate perception of the situation can be destructive. As with all things, a truth about a character can be approached from many different directions and still remain true. So just because the studies may seem to the actor too similar in content and configuration, this is no reason to abandon that approach. Rediscovery of a truth is rewarding in itself. It is the use of the tool that we are concerned with, not so much the result or the destination. Besides, if the character is to have organic reality, the component elements must have some harmony.

1. Prepare a presentation of the character's use of energy. Work this time only on the essence. Don't prepare any literal study to pair with the essence.
2. After the essence has been presented, the actor should be given an instruction: "Now let us see you _____ as your character would." The specific instruction to do this or that should be different from the one given the previous actor, so that actors must react spontaneously to the suggestions. Suggestions could be: "walk around the room"; "pick up that sweater and put it on"; "take off your shoes"; "comb your hair," and so on.

3. After this, the actor should do the essence again.
4. Discussion should focus on which primary energy qualities this character uses (see "Energy Qualities," page 127), and whether or not the essence was felt to be carried through to the literal movement. Also, is there evidence that the character's internal energy quality is at variance with his external image? Was the presentation organic?

Some actors have asked me to demonstrate what I want from them in the characterization sessions. I do not do this, because it encourages imitation. Also, the only real learning actors achieve is in their own discoveries. I will at times supply very brief examples of how some theory might work. Here is one based on energy:

> If you use Chief Bromden from *One Flew Over the Cuckoo's Nest*, the energy essence could be ponderous and tentative—probably sustained, meticulously controlled small movements set into a simple repetitive pattern, interrupted with sudden un-jerky pauses would typify the Chief. Then in the realistic portrait you would probably want to use the broom the Chief is always carrying. From a position of watchful stillness, move to the broom, pick it up and sweep with it, stop, watch, put it down, and watch again—this is the sequence you might use.

The essence or abstracted portrait helps free the body so it can move into the center of the character's physical orientation, and will ease the character's follow-through. The realistic portrait is thus based on the organic essence study.

Animal Essence (Internal and External). Nearly every acting teacher has used and recommended the approach to characterization through animal studies. Many directors have even structured a set of characterizations on the analogy of a zoo, so that the actors conceive their parts through specific animals. The problem in acting always involves the leap from oneself to that of another character, and animals prove to be excellent bridges.

In these applications we use animal images to move into the individual nature of a person. Note, however, that the animal quality within an character usually takes different movement styles from those of the literally observed animal. Even in *The Hairy Ape*, by Eugene O'Neill, the actor in the title role, typically played by an apelike hulk of a man, would not literally imitate an ape's movements. This would be ridiculous and trite. But the use of the animal image can be beneficial and has a strong relationship to the use of energy.

While there are people who look or who act like a certain animal, perhaps their own pets, there are few who look *and* act just like an animal. We say a person behaves like a sloth, a snake, even a magpie, but very likely he bears no physical resemblance to that animal. Once in a while a very graceful, lithe, independent individual comes along, and we have a perfect cat. More often, we must conceive of people, unlikely as it seems, in terms of combinations. He looks like a _____ (externally) but behaves just like a _____ (internally). So we have a strange breed of crossed strains, dog-toads, bear-bats, rooster-lions. In this section we will experiment with looking at characters in terms of these combined animals (unless your character is the perfect lizard, elephant, or _____).

1. Prepare a four-part presentation of your character. You will first show what animal he is externally, in his essence; then follow with a realistic version of his external movement. Then (here is where most characters demand a switch in animal models), do an abstracted version of his inner animal nature, and end with a realistic exhibit of the character's movement. Try to prepare smooth transitions between parts 1 and 2, and 2 and 3, and so forth, until you are not dropping the characterization momentarily.
2. Discussion should focus on the qualities of the various essences, what there was in the animal that seemed to fit the character externally or internally, whether the quality of the essence carried over into the realistic, and so on.
3. You can present the order as detailed above, or you can experiment. For example, you can do both external and internal essences of the animals and then move to the realistic presentation.

Time Essence. The last basic element essential to all movement is time, and it is the one that most brings out the intellectual in actors. This is not an intellectually based application, though it may be intellectually stimulating. The focus for actors at this time should be on the kinetic feeling the character's use of time promotes. By this time the actor should not have to be cautioned against overanalyzing or intellectualizing any exercise. She (or he) is, if she has applied herself seriously, becoming aware and gaining control of the organic reality of mind, spirit, and body. Inspiration springs from an unidentifiable source, not just the mind.

This is the technique that will yield the most fruit and needs to be further encouraged, especially at this point. The "mind" most people identify is the conscious mind. Actors are no exception to the rule; many bow down before the conscious process. But as artists-creators, they should know that the conscious process is only a small portion of the mind and learn to trust other levels on which they function to help them find answers.

In this case, the question is, "How does your character use time?" If we phrase the question in that manner, however, the actor will think. So rather than ask a question, I give an order: "Find the rhythm essence of your character." Now the actor is motivated to act, and actors are never so creative as when they actively commit themselves to pursuit. Therein lies the genius that the movement instructor seeks to arouse. If further instructions are necessary about how to proceed, I tell actors, "Don't think about meter, or tempo, or accent, or defining anything. Find a quiet space and do your own movement exploration. Trust your instincts and the work that has preceded this, and the essence will shape itself for you. When you find the rhythm, explore it in every part of the body, and find what feels most typical or natural for the character."

Actors should know from exploring their own rhythm that rhythmic pattern will vary depending on external and internal changes. What we are looking for here, however, is a *norm*.

1. Find the rhythm essence of your character.
2. Prepare a two-part study that will flow from the essence to the literal.
3. For this presentation, try to find a series of literal movements your character would probably do in the scene.
4. Prepare the presentation so that the essence flows into the literal, and the literal flows back into the essence. The entire study is constructed: essence, literal, essence.
5. Partners follow each other as before, with discussion happening after both partners in a scene have presented their studies.

Emotional Thread. Perhaps the most powerful of all the actor's tools in terms of understanding and performing the character is emotion. It is often a misunderstood and misused tool, but it can also be very effective. This application of emotion through essence work should help to clarify many things about the scene and the character.

1. For the purposes of this exercise, assume that there are at most three to five major emotions one character experiences in a scene. There may be many smaller, finer, more subtle emotions, but choose just the strongest, most vivid emotions the character seems to experience. Envision these emotions as beads or knots on the time line of the scene. They are the backbone of the character's reaction to episodes that occur as the scene progresses.
2. Once you have chosen the major emotions in the scene, tie them together in sequence in your mind so that they can come to mind without your consciously thinking "That was hate, now what's next? Disgust. Now here's disgust." Try to make them flow one into another naturally, so that there is some transition from one to another.
3. When you feel you understand how the mechanics operate, prepare an essence study of each individual emotion. When you have an acceptable essence for each one, use the transitions you have found to tie each emotion to the next so that they form one long, smoothly flowing essence study of the major emotions the character experiences in the scene.
4. Presentation will be executed as follows: Partners will go one after another. Each person does her (or his) entire essence study twice without pause for discussion, until both partners in a single scene have completed their presentation.

5. Discussion is open-ended in terms of topics group members can discuss, but as a general rule, two or three minutes at the most is all the time that need be spent for any scene.

Total Essence of Character. At this point the actor is ready to prepare the total internal-external composite of the character. This study allows the actor to flesh out a three-dimensional being. The purpose is to integrate the internal and external aspects of the character into one essence study. Included in the study are aspects of the character's walk, posture, use of space, energy, animal, rhythm, and emotion. Choices have been made and explored, and now the actors must trust that each of their steps have brought them closer to the character's core.

1. Lie down in a relaxed, neutral state. Clear your mind, spirit, and body of any clutter. Journey back in your mind to the essences already explored. Think of what you discovered about the character's energy, rhythm, external-internal animal, and emotional through-line. Pack your psyche with as many of the particulars of the character as possible. Trust in your choices and just let go.
2. Allow your spirit to connect with your mind, thoughts, and ideas. Let your body react physically and explore the essence and core feelings of the character. Leave yourself open to new discoveries. Trust the work you've done up to this point. The work is your computer (mind), the spirit has connected it, so now let your body physicalize it to find the organic connection.

As you can see, the progress of the applications is beginning to move in the direction of the actors working together. It is still premature for them to rehearse together, however, and discussion outside the classroom can be more destructive than constructive at this point. Although actors at this time are beginning to assemble the framework of the scene subliminally, the organic awareness they are developing can easily be disrupted by intellectual interference.

Now that they have answered basic questions about their characters (who, what, when, where, why) the actors are ready to explore the material in the scene with their partners.

Exploring Together: Movement in a Scene

All effort thus far has been directed toward this point in the process. This is when the fruit should begin to ripen for actor and instructor alike, when the discipline begins to become enjoyable, and the work becomes creation. Here is where the tools of improvisation, essence, and movement terminology merge with two actors skilled in the same school of thought in the same scene, and a shared experience of each other's independent development of character.

Actors are usually more than eager at this point to begin this next stage of applying accumulated technique and theory. They should also be ready to begin completion of their sense of their own organic reality. Dialogue will be interjected gradually as part of this process, and will, in a sense, be de-emphasized, so that the focus and development stays not on the words or ideas, but on the commitment to maintaining a sense of the scene as an organism's response to an evolving situation. Memorization of lines is destructive to this process, so I discourage it. In the end the lines will be there, complete and exact, but not from preconception, as is typical in the theater. The words, we hope, will come naturally from the situation—spontaneously and not premeditatively; the dialogue will spill out of the joint explorations as a result of an inner activity, not as an intellectually inspired desire to achieve a startlingly effective performance.

This is the goal. And to reach it, it is important to maintain the sense of natural forward momentum we've been trying to establish. In this book I have tried to provide clear delineations between significant portions of work, including this one. But in the training session the importance of this phase of work should not be highlighted. Actors tend to become self-conscious when one says, "What you are doing is significant," because they begin to over-intellectualize once again.

There is, in the material as I have designed it, an apparent flow, a steady adding-on, a progressive acquisition of skills. This is no less true for the applications. It is important for the instructor to know, however, the value and subtlety of this last portion of activity and to provide a sense of steady forward momentum, rather than to suggest quantum leaps in significance of effort.

Not much has changed, after all: Actors will work with each other only in controlled training sessions and not at all outside them until the very end; this is still a period of exploration and experimentation (something actors get precious little of in this high-pressure, judgment-oriented profession). The addition of the voice is, after all, only the natural, logical inclusion of what really amounts to another physical instrument, another part of the organic whole that is the actor. Interestingly, if one is working in a conservatory situation, where acting, voice, and movement are taught simultaneously and separately by qualified specialists, by the time the actor is asked to use the vocal instrument in the explorations, he or she should have gained sufficient command of the voice that the incorporation of the two will be an efficient and natural release rather than an effort.

We start this newest portion of work at its beginning: without words, without sound; with essence alone. Then we can build from there.

ENERGY ESSENCE OF THE SCENE

Go back to the script of the scene. This time you should find the energy essence of the scene.

1. Answer these questions first: How does your character use energy in the scene? Does this use of energy change? (It usually will several times.)
2. Prepare your essence of your character's use of energy in the scene only.

3. Presentation:
   a. Partners will follow one another. As soon as one partner finishes presenting his (or her) essence without comment, the other will perform while the first sits with the rest of the group.
   b. Then, before any comment, both partners should go onto the floor and lie down and relax. They are then guided through the rest of the exploration by the voice commands of the instructor:
   c. "Close your eyes. Relax. Clear yourself. Breathe deeply and empty your mind." (Pause) "Now bring your concentration onto your energy essence. Try to feel your body moving in the essence movement, but do not move." (Pause) "Fill yourself with the situation of the scene and try to let that affect the growing sensation of the energy essence." (Pause) "When you feel ready, begin to move with the essence." (Pause) "Start alone, but begin to react to the other person. Allow the other presence to alter your essence. Free yourselves from your planned series of movements. Be spontaneous. Don't plan it. Let it happen."
   d. When the actors have explored, but not exhausted, the possibilities (or themselves): "Follow through with what you are doing. Then let go of your action and relax back onto the floor. Don't just drop off. Finish what you're doing." (Pause) "Relax. Breathe deeply. Release all your tension. Clear yourself. Bring yourself back to a neutral state." (Pause) "Good. Sit up, and we'll talk about it."
   e. Discussion questions include the following: "How did you feel about the exploration?" "What did you find?" "Anyone from the group have a comment?"

The Problem of Indicating. It is important in these explorations of the scene to try to keep both actors in the essence work. At times one or the other or both will begin *indicating* (that is, they mime "I feel bad," or "Don't hurt me, pretty please?" or "Let's have fun"), and when this happens positive results are impossible. The work becomes shallow, hollow, undisciplined, uncentered, not organic, and no one can take it seriously. If it happens, strong measures are needed to point up the fact so that work on other scenes is not destroyed by this kind of errant application of effort.

It shouldn't happen frequently in energy essence work, but because of the increasingly subtle and fragile nature of the ensuing work, and the addition of voice and dialogue, there is an ever greater danger of this occurring. That is why early detection and treatment of the problem is necessary and helpful.

ANIMAL ESSENCE WITH THE SCENE

Refresh and review your internal and external animal essence studies. Bring them to the next session. In the presentation, proceed as follows:

1. Partners follow one another. As soon as Partner A finishes both internal and external essence studies, Partner B will present.

2. The instructor says: "Now both relax onto the floor and clear yourselves. Relax. Breathe easily in and out. Clear yourself. Listen to the whole explanation of what I want you to do before you begin. Choose one of your animal essences, it doesn't matter which one, and concentrate on filling yourself with the feeling it brings to you. Fill yourself with the situation of the scene, and allow yourself to move (with the essence you are using) in that situation."

3. When you are ready, begin relating to the other person in essence.

4. If you feel comfortable and committed, you can allow yourself to use dialogue. Keep in the essence movement, and don't worry about the lines from the script.

5. Take your time, and don't begin until you're ready. Don't think about it. You're on your own now. Begin when you're ready.

At this point there are many different avenues that may be followed, and each depends on where the actors lead each other. This first time the dialogue may be stilted, or awkward, or halting. If they are really into the essence, however, it may be quite stirring and effective. Success should be warmly rewarded. Those failing should be warmly encouraged, and the source of the problem pinpointed if possible. It will be obvious to everyone where the exercise was effective and where it was not. Some scenes may be very verbose; in others, hardly a verbal interchange will occur. This is to be expected. Neither is more correct. But regardless of which path is taken, the exploration should end the same way.

6. Continuing, the instructor says: "Good. Follow through with what you are doing. Let go of dialogue. Go back into the essence alone. Take your time, don't just break off." (Pause) "Release your tension. Relax onto the floor." (Pause) "Clear yourself. Bring yourself back to a neutral state. Relax."

7. The discussion proceeds with these questions: "Sit up and let's talk about it." "How do you feel?" "What did you find?" "How did you respond to the addition of dialogue?"

It is normal for one or two scenes to have some seemingly difficult problem with the first addition of dialogue. Usually one or two scenes will seem to "click," but the majority of scenes will work sporadically so that no great experience is forthcoming. It is important for everyone to understand that some scenes and some individuals work better with a different focus of activity. A seeming failure here is not catastrophic unless we allow it to be. It is just as important at this point for the actors to understand that this effort can be rewarding regardless of success. Scenes that "succeed" this time may "fail" the next; others that "fail" now may "succeed" later.

It is also important to understand that the terms "success" and "failure" are not relevant to this work, and such concepts form a block to future effort. Even if the terms had some merit in this training, it would be over the long term—only at the end of the training period could such determinations be made. You could use the battle-war analogy: we won the battle but lost the war; or, we lost the battle but won the war; or, as in the case of the Romans, we lost *every* battle and won the war. "Victory" and "defeat" for the actor, like "success" and "failure," are true measures of no lasting reality.

Even that analogy is inaccurate, however, because there is no opponent and no losing involved. Each actor will gain (has already gained up to this point); it is only a matter of how much. No one can judge that because the effects of this training are quite likely to be more evident long after actor and instructor have parted company.

So, do not linger over success or failure, but reinforce the concept that this is a period of exploration and discovery, not a performance. Do not allow contemplation of it, but force the actors to rush headlong into the next project.

COUNTERPOINT, CONFLICT, YIN AND YANG

This next application requires actors to analyze the text of the scene in terms of the major conflict in the scene. All drama is based on conflict; without it drama does not exist. There are many different ways to conceptualize the problem. Here are several supporting images one can use to define it:

Counterpoint. As in the discussions and explorations of time, counterpoint represents a situation in which there are two contrasting sets of elements—in this case, two people with contrasting or opposing desires.

Conflict. Conflict is the clash of wills within a scene. In human relationships, will exerts an almost ever-present force. It is sometimes very weak or seemingly nonexistent, but it is a basic force that keeps human beings (perhaps all living things) alive. We use our will in even the most basic of voluntary functions, but nowhere is the application of will stronger than when a human being is faced with the obstacle of another contradictory and competing will. This is what makes for good drama—the clash of wills.

Yin and Yang. One of the primary principles in one of the oldest existing philosophies, Taoism, is that the universe is *one thing* composed of contradictory elements. No element can exist without its opposite also existing. This operates on many levels, but in no other discipline is the concept more readily applicable than here in scene work.

Simply then, if one character in the scene desires one outcome, the other character must desire a totally contradictory outcome. For this tool to be effective, of course, both characters' wills and efforts must be of great magnitude, and both must be extremely resourceful in their attempt to achieve the outcome they desire. This brings about conflict and provides counterpoint in the scene. This may not be true of every two-person scene in drama, but for any scene worthy of prolonged exploration the concept can be a formidable tool for unlocking the secrets within it.

With these three images to draw from, actor and instructor alike should very quickly see their usefulness. Actors should be given the problem several days before the presentation is to be made, so that there is sufficient time for each individual to clearly and succinctly state the major conflict of the scene and to prepare an essence study of it. Partners should not discuss it, because one strong-willed actor could force a viewpoint or concept for the scene and the problem on an unwilling and therefore uncommitted comrade. The major conflict should be simple enough to pinpoint, but different actors and different characters have seemingly different ways of verbally expressing or even conceiving the same problem.

Fortunately, the actors won't be spelling out the problem verbally, but relating it directly through the essence. Each essence will alter the other slightly, but neither partner is thus able to dictate terms; therefore, both are surprised and possibly more spontaneous in the resulting improvisation. Here is the way the instructor should guide the presentation:

1. Both partners lie on the floor and relax. Clear yourselves. Let go of all your tension. Breathe deeply.
2. Now, review the scene in your mind's eye, trying to visualize it in terms of the major conflict. Build your reaction to that conflict as though it were you who faced the problem. Let it touch you personally.
3. Let the feeling grow until you have to express your feeling in terms of the essence. Don't rush it or force it. Let it happen naturally.
4. When you begin, use the essence to express your emotion.
5. If you feel comfortable with it, use dialogue. Don't worry about lines. Improvise on the scene using the essence conflict as your focus.
6. Good. Follow through with what you are doing, and then let the tension drain from you. Let yourself relax onto the floor as the conflict drains away from you. Relax. Breathe deeply. Bring yourself back to a neutral state, letting go of all tension, all problems drain out of you onto the floor. Just relax.
7. Next, sit up easily, open your eyes. How do you feel? Let's talk about what you found. Does this help you with your character? The scene?

Please note that only the general shape of the instructor's verbal commands is listed here. Much depends on how the actors respond to what is specifically said. But it is obvious that this is a departure from the established technique in which one person presents, the other presents, then they explore together.

Although one could use that technique here, this shock treatment of both actors unaware of and unprepared for the shape of each other's essence is far more effective, and the results usually quite startling.

In a later application using this technique it is sometimes quite useful for actors to move from the essence to essence with dialogue and to dialogue with realistic movement without halting, pausing, or conscious deliberation.

For most movement training classes, this stage will be too soon to use the technique, but in advanced classes that are especially tuned-in I may suggest it during their exploration. Even when the suggestion is not verbalized, however, the movement may tend to become more natural because of the nature of the problem, so the transition into realistic movement is far easier than it sounds. It is so natural a process that some partners try to make the transition too quickly, and it sometimes takes a gentle reminder to stay with the essence movement.

Note to the Instructor. This exploration can be handled in two ways: in the manner presented, or in a more advanced situation whereby the actor can first explore the character's inner conflict with the scene, then the conflict between the two characters. If done the second way, each actor should present the essence of the inner conflict first, followed by the scene's external conflict between the characters.

MAJOR INTENTIONS OF THE SCENE

Intention is another concept frequently used in the craft of acting to help focus efforts in rehearsal and performance. Its definition and use is fairly standard in today's theater, but it never hurts to spell out the precise use of any term to a group of people expected to understand and use it in the same way. Briefly, intention connotes a particular type of application of will. In the theatrical context, an intention is a conscious design by one person to achieve a desired reaction in another person. It can most succinctly be defined by a statement declaring your intention toward another person: "I want to . . .

> . . . impress her."
> . . . make him feel guilty."
> . . . hurt him."
> . . . make her feel sorry for me."
> . . . entice her."
> . . . make him proud of me."
> . . . confuse him."
> . . . make her feel ridiculous."

These are subtextual statements, which must be supplied by the actor, that help to focus an entire series of lines. This is sometimes referred to as a "beat," a concise way of describing a small passage of dialogue that centers on one small, clearly defined element of contention within a scene.

Of course, you cannot play an entire scene with one intention. Usually there are between four and six major intentions, and the actor needs to spell this out. That is what this application is designed to facilitate.

One word of caution: Some actors confuse "intention" with "objective." Objective is an entirely different concept that refers to the ultimate goal of the character in the scene. For instance, a young man may have the objective: "To make my mother admit and repent her sins," but in the attempt to achieve that goal, he may have several different intentions: "I want to shock her . . . embarrass her . . . make her feel disgust with herself," and so on. (This in fact happens in Act III, Scene 4 of Shakespeare's *Hamlet.*

Now that we know how the term is being used in this context, let's find a way to translate the intellectual description into a meaningful organic context. This is not too difficult to do because the method of translation is the essence study.

1. Prepare an essence study, independently of your partner, of the major intentions of your character in the scene you're working on.
2. Do not be concerned about what the other character is doing. Concentrate only on finding and preparing an essence study of the four or five major intentions of your character. (You may have less or more, but this is unlikely if the scene is well written.)
3. Don't discuss this with your partner. There is no need for any kind of prior agreement about "who does what to whom at which time for which reason." That's what you will discover in the exploration of the scene.

When the actors have had time to sort these things out for themselves, the presentation will take on a slightly different shape.

4. Presentation:
   a. Partners again will follow one another, but after each presentation there will be a brief pause to discuss each actor's study. The essence should be clear enough so that the rest of the group can identify each intention. Of course, no one can expect the group to express their interpretation in the same verbatim manner as the person presenting the essence, but some synonymous approximation for each intention is possible. If this were not so, no meaningful joint exploration could take place. If the group is unable to identify the changes in even a rough approximation, it is evident that the presenter has not adequately specified the intentions. If this is true, he (or she) does not know what his character intends, so how can he fulfill that intention? This forces actors to make a choice, and provides a means of detecting whether or not they have. The

question of whether it is the "right" choice or whether it is appropriate for the character is not important at this point. What is important is that the actor make a strong choice and find and commit himself to the essence.

   b. After both actors partnering in a scene have presented their intention study, they should do an exploration together.

   c. The joint exploration will begin with both actors using the essence studies as a starting point, and then, when they are ready, they should make the transition into dialogue with essence movement, and then into realistic movement with dialogue.

Discussion afterward can involve any area of special interest aroused by the process, but observation should be noted about whether or not the organic movement of the essence carried through to the realistic level and the dialogue. Often actors will begin to indicate, leaving behind most of their internal organic sense of commitment, and begin to pretend and perform. This is the antithesis of the concept we are working for, and if I perceive this happening in the joint exploration, I will usually stop it soon after and begin the discussion earlier than I would normally, trying to gently, but pointedly, highlight the destructiveness of this tendency for the actors involved.

It can provide an extremely valuable learning experience if I am forced to do this, because then we have an immediate example I can use to illustrate the question: "Can you see the difference between when they were committed to and concentrated on organic movement, and when they came out of it and started indicating?" No one ever fails to see the difference, so obvious is the contrast to both observer and participant.

The fascinating thing about the process is that (in spite of the fact that actors have not been instructed to "memorize the lines") in explorations in which the organic commitment stays constant throughout, actors will be stunned by their almost flawless verbatim execution. It would take too long to explain why I think this happens, but the fact that it does is enough to make believers of some residual skeptics I have found in some of my sessions at this point in the training. It is not magic or supernatural in any sense. Rather, I believe it is the most natural occurrence given the type and intensity of analysis actors have used on the script.

EMOTIONAL THREAD WITHIN THE SCENE

Since the emotional thread has already been covered in this chapter, and for the actor it will have been relatively recently, actors should have a good grasp of the concept and perhaps even the essence study in their kinetic memories. All that is necessary now is to ask them to review and renew, if necessary, the essence of emotional thread.

The same procedure for presentation as has just been initiated should be used, or one of the previous methods explained may be returned to, depending on the actors' needs and abilities. The procedure described in the previous step is by far the most effective, however, and should be used, if possible. Less elaborate explanations to each pair will be necessary.

The group will be informed about the format to be used and the following instructions should be all that is necessary.

1. Lie down. Relax. Clear yourself.
2. Fill yourself with the essence study and the feeling of the scene. Begin only when you're ready. Take your time. Don't force anything, just try to hold onto the truth of the scene. Begin when you're ready.

The same discussion technique can be used, and depending on the nature of the group and the scenes presented, a wide variety of object lessons, conclusions, and illustrations can be made. This is the time when teaching a movement training class is a joyfully creative experience, because most individuals will have by this time broken through the more mundane and fundamental barriers of faulty conceptualizing, physical blocks, defensiveness, and so forth. They are a solid group of awakening craftspeople, challenging themselves, each other, and their instructor with the strength of their discoveries and creative energies. Most individuals are growing confident of their new sense of organic unity, and it may be difficult to keep the forward momentum as steady as it needs to be to ensure that everyone moves forward together.

The next step is, after all, only the next logical step on the developmental ladder.

WORKING TOGETHER OUTSIDE THE CLASS

Depending on how much time is remaining to the class, there are a variety of ways in which to proceed. Probably the most valuable is to use the following technique to further develop the sense of realistic organic movement in a scene:

1. Review and refurbish your _____ essence study. (Any of the essence studies could work for this; the most effective, however, may be emotion, counterpoint, intention, energy, or animal essences. Actors should choose the one they feel will best aid them in solving problems they have encountered with the scene.)
2. Meet outside of class time with your partner and, using the essence study, do your own exploration of the scene.
3. Prepare a realistic version of the scene using the universal elements you found in the exploration.
4. Bring it to the class and present first the exploration; then do the realistic versions. (Set up the realistic set before you start the presentation. Make

sure you have placed any prop and all furniture you need for the action in the scene. That way you can move right from the essence into the realistic without a break. This allows you to keep the organic connection established from the essence when you move into the scene. Don't mime anything. This will break the organic connection.)

5. Discussion will center on the ability to carry over the organic and universal elements from the essence to the realistic, as well as your perception of the discoveries you made in working this way.

Although this particular format could be used alternately with each essence study, there may not be enough class time for more than one or two of them.

Analyzing Applications

Application of any theory should lend itself to analysis. This is no less true of the theory of organic movement through use of essence work. How does one analyze it? What terms do you use?

Generally, the same tools of analysis are used in this case that are used in any theatrical or experimental presentation: Based on what we can see and hear, are we convinced of the sincerity, commitment, and reality of the people involved? Were they organically involved, and not just "play-acting"? Did they involve me in the problem or the situation? Did I understand generally the nature of the situation or problem? Was it appropriate to the nature of the scene or characters? Did they find or experience anything worthwhile?

The last question can only be answered by the people actually involved in the presentation. The other questions can be answered by either observer or presenter in many cases. Not everyone will agree in every case about the correctness of the choices, but anyone can readily see the degree of commitment, concentration, and focus present in an essence application. If there were a great focus and concentration and a high level of commitment to the exploration of the problem, comprehension and appreciation of the universal elements within the presentation should be a simple matter.

To help illustrate this, the following short series of photographs highlight two such explorations from two scenes being developed by actors from one of my movement for actors courses at the University of Connecticut (1994 spring semester). The two scenes were evolved over the course of the entire fifteen-week semester. Therefore they have, I think, qualities that can be analyzed. Although it is a difficult assignment to capture the "essence of an essence" in just a few still photographs, it is the best method available in book format because of the length of the exploration.

All four sets of photographs are arranged in the proper chronological order and were taken while the exploration unfolded so that none were "posed" shots. Two sets of photographs correspond to animal essence explorations (one exploration using animal essences from each scene), one set corresponds to an Emotional essence exploration, and one to an Intention essence exploration.

TRUE WEST BY SAM SHEPARD
Lee: Rob Harrison (gray sweat pants)
Austin: Brian Coughlin (navy shorts)

Note: To simplify matters, rather than using both actors' names and the characters' names, I will simply refer to the characters.

ANIMAL ESSENCE EXPLORATION I
In this series of photographs (Figs. 5-1 to 5-9), we see the concentration and fine focus necessary to any theatrical mode. These actors are awake and alert to the minutest changes in each other's actions. Their minds are actively involved in problem solving. While their movements are not literal, they are relating to each other on an abstract, or essence, plane.

It is obvious that their movements are not intended or shaped to be realistic in form. They are neither imitations of animal movements, nor miming movements indicating any intellectualized message. These actors are obviously engaged in an entirely different kind of activity. The movement does seem to flow from the center, and it appears to have a certain amount of follow-through.

If any negative criticism could be leveled at this scene, it is perhaps that the movement does not seem to be specific enough in terms of the character's intentions toward each other. But then that was not the focus of this exploration. The focus was internal-external animal essences as they shaped the scene. What were they?

Lee:
External animal—Kodiak bear
Internal animal—Lone wolf

Austin:
External animal—Ferret
Internal animal—Puppy/deer

As one would expect, given these choices, Lee begins as the aggressor and continues to dominate his weaker adversary. Austin's internal puppy reflects his instinctive need to be cared for. The essence of their relationship (parent/child vs. caretaker/patient) is apparent in this series of photographs. If other choices were made by both actors and this result did not occur, the choices would have to be wrong, because this is what happens in the script. But for these actors, these choices were good ones, as we can see from their use of them in this exploration.

Compare this result with the same scene explored with the use of Intention.

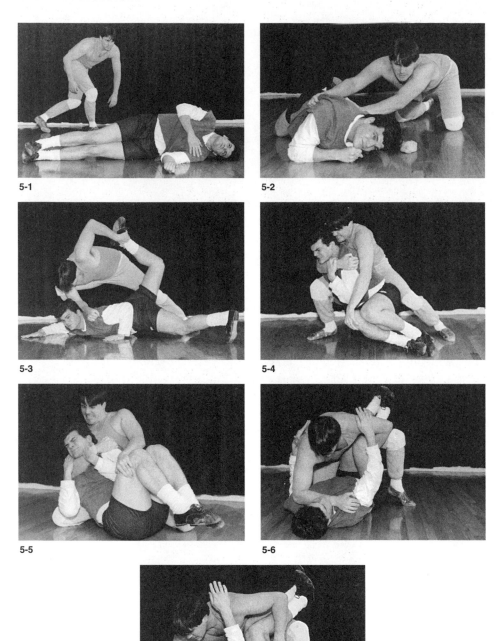

5-1

5-2

5-3

5-4

5-5

5-6

5-7

5-8   5-9

INTENTION ESSENCE EXPLORATION I

In this series of photographs (Figs. 5-10 to 5-22), we quickly see that both characters are relating far more specifically to each other. The focus, commitment, and concentration are just as strong as they were in the previous exploration of the same scene, but the movements are now very different, even though the quality of the movement stays very much the same.

The same relationship between the two characters is translated into action without dialogue from an entirely different direction. Lee is still dominant, even though Austin becomes more aggressive and even playful. He runs through a range of different tactics attempting to please, to taunt, to serve, and to pacify his older brother. In response, Lee continues to intimidate and control Austin as he attempts to get what he wants.

Notice that while there is physical contact, neither actor intends any hurt to the other, whereas the characters may (and in this case, *do*), intend harm, though perhaps only mentally, to each other. This is the First Law of Improvisation:

> "Thou shalt not cause, or intend to cause, physical harm to another actor, regardless of provocation."

In this way, we can ensure a maximum degree of safety for all participants, regardless of the apparent violence intended by one character to another.

This is another way in which this work performs a valuable service. One character may intend to crush another and because of the restraint of both the First Law of Improvisation and the requirement not to be literal in expression, the actor has two forms of conditioning *against* what may be a regrettable loss of control under less structured circumstances.

At any rate, although this series of photos may appear to show a violent struggle, what it really reveals, upon closer examination, is two characters locked in a battle of wills, which two actors (who are cooperating in a very professional manner) are striving to explore and express through nonliteral or essence movement. This is no attempt at illusion. It is not a game. Neither actor is attempting to "win" anything. They are working together to find the truth of the scene.

In this case, the exploration seems to have yielded even more fruit because although the general shape of the scene has remained the same as before, the new focus has provided for more active choices to be made. Also, the same physical relationship that was discovered in the animal essence has been retained in a slightly altered form, thus adding to the richness of this exploration.

5-10

5-11

5-12

5-13

5-14

5-15

5-16

5-17

5-18

5-19

5-20

5-21

5-22

EMOTIONAL ESSENCE EXPLORATION I

In the series of photographs (Figs. 5-23 to 5-33) two things are immediately obvious. First, this exploration is far more active and "violent" than the last one. Second, the general shape so closely resembles the other's that one could tell they belong together even if there were no descriptive passage to explain that fact.

Lee is dominated by envy: He is envious of his younger brother's model life—having a wife, children, high-paying job, and nice home. Lee is a drifter without stability or social respect. In contrast, Austin's emotions are more childlike. He responds to Lee's volatile nature with denial, fear, and dependence. His primal urge is to seek the approval of his brother. The photos capture the paradox of Austin's nature. He goes from being loving and caring to desperately hopeless.

Perhaps the only negative comment one might make is that both these explorations look more like a wrestling match than an application of basic character elements to a scene. If that observation is true, the actors will have largely wasted their energy in this effort, only to engage in a test of one actor's physical prowess as opposed to another's.

In defense of this particular case, however, I can testify to the high professional awareness and commitment of both actors, and because of the nature of the movement (as opposed to these still pictures, which may suggest quite the contrary) I saw that this was not the case. The actors involved cooperated with each other in a "violent-appearing contest" while exploring the emotional realities of their characters in the scene.

5-23

5-24

5-25

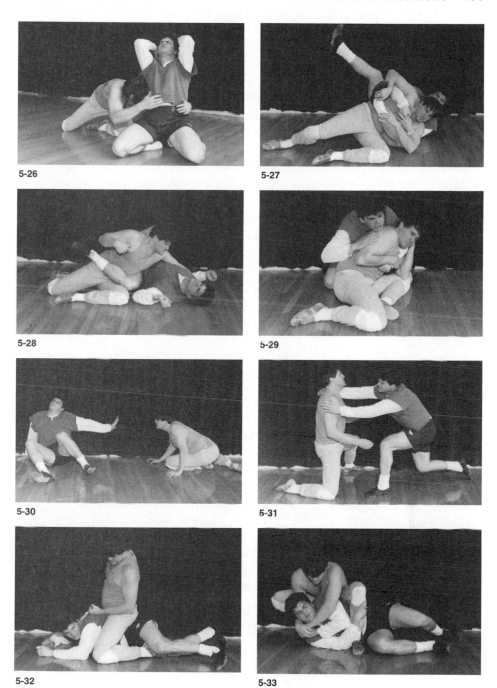

5-26

5-27

5-28

5-29

5-30

5-31

5-32

5-33

AGNES OF GOD BY JOHN PIELMEIER
Mother Miriam Ruth: Deidra Johnson (dark shorts)
Dr. Martha Livingston: Angela Parks (dark leotard and tights)

ANIMAL ESSENCE EXPLORATION II
In this series of photographs (Figs. 5-34 to 5-40), it is even easier to see the effects of the animal images. Even without knowing the actors' choices, one can almost pinpoint the type of animals and the actors' attitudes toward them. It is easier here to see how these choices relate to the scene and how the characters relate to each other. The choices are strong and specific, and the actions reflect an entirely different dynamic that is appropriate to the scene.

There is a lack of physical violence in the literal scene, but an emotional firestorm evolves. The focus is on the seemingly mundane problem of internal-external animal essences. What were they?

Mother Miriam Ruth:
External animal—eagle
Internal animal—puppy

Dr. Livingston:
External animal—cat
Internal animal—kitten

Analysis here is even simpler than in the last scene's animal essence exploration. Here, given the choices that the actors made, it is easy to recognize two strong-willed women battling for high status. The strength of Mother Miriam Ruth's eagle is an even match for Dr. Livingston's predatory and protective cat. They instinctively engage each other on the same spatial level.

While it is obvious, however, the movements seem to have follow-through and flow from an organic base. The essence appears to have served these actors very well.

5-34

5-35

5-36

5-37

5-38

5-39

5-40

INTENTION ESSENCE EXPLORATION II

In the next series of photographs (Figs. 5-41 to 5-48), the characters relate more specifically to each other. Their focus, commitment, and concentration are just as strong as in their previous exploration of the scene. Mother Miriam Ruth's protective instinct becomes her major intention. We see her concealing the truth from Dr. Livingston. In response, the doctor pursues the truth by catching the Mother Superior off-guard. She is aggressive in her pursuit, although by the end of the scene there is a reconciliation between the two and a recognition of themselves in each other.

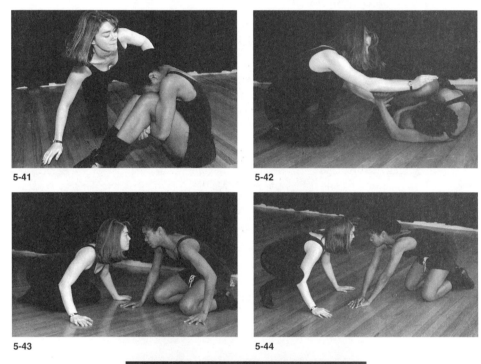

5-41

5-42

5-43

5-44

5-45

5-46

5-47

5-48

EMOTIONAL ESSENCE EXPLORATION II

This final series of photographs (Figs. 5-49 to 5-56) demonstrates the intensity and clarity of the character's emotions. Each is passionate in their commitment to these emotions. The doctor's anger dominates the Mother Superior's fear. Both experience frustration at their inability to communicate. Ironically, this brings them closer together. The scene resolves with their reconciliation, as is apparent in the final photograph.

What else can we say about this exploration? Commitment, focus, concentration are all present and used to good purpose. The actors are obviously organically involved, and if one weren't aware of the basic nature of this battle of wills and involved in or engaged by it, that fact would say more about the observer than about the presentation.

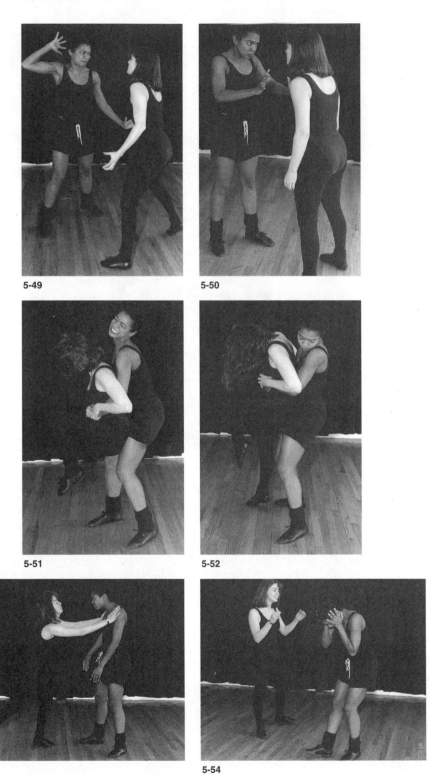

5-49

5-50

5-51

5-52

5-53

5-54

5-55   5-56

DISCUSSION

Now compare the general shape of one scene to the next, one study to the next. There are some universal qualities common to all well-written two-person scenes in drama (discounting, of course, the well-written scenes describing the happy fortune of two people in total harmony with each other). In each series of photographs, note the escalating nature of the confrontation leading naturally toward a climax. This also demands, in most cases, a winner. Note how the aggressor or dominant role seems to change through the course of the scenes. Sometimes the dominance will shift back and forth several times, but if it never shifts there seems to be far less dramatic potential.

One can use all these methods of analysis (and many more) to understand, evaluate, or dissect these explorations. The purpose of the entire training process should be the guide, however, in all discussion: to develop within each actor the ability to find and maintain organic movement in every character by helping him or her to develop the mind-spirit-body connection, thus reducing the gap between impulse and action practically to invisibility, and providing the actor with rehearsal and performance tools to achieve his or her purpose.

I have made several omissions in the program during the period of applications, but I make note of them here because they are fairly important.

First, there is the matter of the musical-cues tape. I generally use (and recommend use of) at least three tapes during this period. These tapes work best in this phase when the actors are instructed to react to the tape in essence (and, of course, nonverbally) as their character would. This can be done using one area of essence work to focus the exploration (emotions, intentions, energy, and so forth), or the instruction could be worded in such a way as to leave the exploration open-ended in terms of focus. Either way, by responding as their characters would respond, actors often make unusual and valuable discoveries about their characters, while at the same time gaining a new perspective on the work as a whole. This can be a very valuable experience.

Another valuable tool I have not yet mentioned is the class project. Although I have had groups that did not have the necessary creative energy or initiative to pursue this area of study, in those that did I found it rewarding in many ways. I have indexed some of the more valuable projects in the Appendix. Here, I will only say that in the more useful and exciting projects, actors have prepared (in and outside of class time) for up to six months, applying independently the principles learned in my (and my team instructors') sessions, to achieve some highly inspiring creative results that were worthy of production.

Concluding Remarks. Although each area of study provides its own rewards to various actors at various times, the period of study that seems to be the most rewarding is toward the end of the applications. This is probably because the results of all the long effort become more and more obvious. Because of the new physical fitness and kinesthetic awareness, actors are so much better prepared to follow their creative impulses that they are no longer inhibited by their misconceptions about their bodies' capabilities. They have a firm grasp of a reliable set of tools that they know how to use to answer more questions about their characters than they knew how to ask before. The gap between impulse and action is nearly nonexistent because of their awareness and command of the organic unity of mind, spirit, and body (thought, emotion, action). They now know, from first-hand experience, that what the body does has shape and substance in the mind and spirit and that no matter how the mind functions, the body naturally functions in like manner—automatically, spontaneously, naturally mirroring or relaxing the inner reality of the mind. They know it from their own experience. They've seen how it functions in others.

They trust this knowledge, and because they trust and understand it, they can begin to command it to serve them. When an instructor can see this happen, it is an incredibly rewarding experience. When an actor feels his or her own command, it is also quite a reward for the amount of hard work it required, and it reinforces the actor's self-confidence. But we must keep in mind that it is prolonged, hard work. It is the long periods of struggle followed by sudden awareness of progress and the many small breakthroughs that provide the platform for this success—if we can call it success.

As I have said before, "success" and "failure" have no lasting value in this context. But if they do, their measure is, at best, defined in relativistic terms—that is, "He has improved a great deal in this and that respect," or "She has grown incredibly from that first day when. . . ." If there is any external means of measuring the worth of this or any training, it is in this relative way: "How much has this aided this person to be more effective in the craft of acting?"

Although this determination can only be made over the long haul, the work in applications provides valuable assistance to actors in coalescing the accumulated material from all of the sessions into a single, cohesive, organic body of dynamic and interactive craft, something they can then develop individually, at their own pace, throughout their creative careers.

6 *Movement Training in Practice*

The movement training described in this book has served me well in the classroom and as part of the rehearsal process, both as a director and as a movement consultant. You may find my comments useful in helping you to understand how this work may help your own, but it may be more helpful, however, if you see how former students (now practicing professionals) describe their use of the theory. They have all taught the theory, as well as used it in their various artistic endeavors.

Laura Sheehan (M.A., Trinity College, 1995) is a teacher of movement at the University of Connecticut. Additionally, she is a founding member, producer, and performer of Hartford's Capital Classics Theater Company. She describes how she uses this work in her classroom.

David Hodge (M.F.A., Penn State, 1977) is a writer and professional actor. He comments on his use of the theory as an actor. Keith Grant (M.F.A., Yale University, 1981) is a professional actor, director, and choreographer. He is on the faculty of Cornell University. He shares his experience of using the theory in a professional setting as an actor.

The descriptions you will find here are not meant to be a definitive last word on how you should use or interpret the work, but are instead intended to describe ways the material has been applied by professionals other than myself in their academic and professional endeavors. I hope you will find their contributions to this text illuminating and provocative.

From a Teaching Perspective: Laura Sheehan

As theater artists, we know full well the elusive nature of acting. There is no easy formula, no structured path to success. Each actor must find his (or her) own way towards organic truth.

Actors, then, face numerous and continual challenges: how to achieve the organic connection between actor and character; how to remain physically active and alive, even in moments of stillness; how to exist in the immediacy of the moment; and how to merge impulse with instinct to make active, honest choices. The questions are infinite, the challenges monumentous.

Yet, as audience members we easily recognize great acting. We marvel at the seemingly effortless merging of actor with character, the mystical transcendence from one reality into another, and the conviction of this organic reality. While this greatness is easy enough to identify, it is difficult to define. How do we, as actors, directors, and teachers begin to analyze and recreate this magic?

In an ideal situation, every actor would be under the guide of a sensitive director who leads him towards clear and well-grounded choices. Unfortunately, the real world of theater falls short of this ideal. Directors confront challenges beyond the scope of the actor and cannot always serve as exclusive coach and guide. Every actor, then, needs to develop his own theory or technique, his own means of attaining the organic connection, reaching the point where mind, spirit, and body work as one and where the circumstances of the character and the words of the playwright flow unobstructed through the actor's being.

Jean Sabatine's essence theory of movement is just that—a practical technique designed to teach the actor to open his mind, spirit, and body, in order to fill himself with the particulars of a character, and to react instinctively.

As an artist scratching out a living in the theater, I've utilized Professor Sabatine's theory in different capacities—as an actor, student, director, and teacher. It remains the cornerstone of my work. For the last few years, I've had the privilege of teaching Movement for the Actor at the University of Connecticut. I speak to you from that perspective. As a teacher, I've witnessed, over and over, the magic of student actors discovering and experiencing the organic connection for the first time. I can honestly say that every single student who applies him- or herself to the work reaches this point of organic unity. Let us remember, though, that this is no miracle prescription for greatness, but is, instead, a working theory, often exhaustive in its abstraction, but ultimately always rewarding.

It has been emphasized throughout the text that Professor Sabatine's theory is an acting (not dancing) technique. Although a significant portion of the curriculum is devoted to physical conditioning, it constitutes only a third of the overall work. Consequently, the course should not be taught as a dance class, and you need not be a dancer to benefit from it. I've trained actors of all shapes and sizes, with varying degrees of physical flexibility. Every actor should work at his own pace and establish his own goals, with the ultimate goal being the achievement of truthful, full body expression. As part of this approach, then, one must stretch and strengthen the physical, along with the emotional and intellectual, instruments.

Having witnessed the repeated "success" of this work, I've given a lot of thought as to why. My assessment is that this theory picks up where most others leave off. Because the terminology of the essence theory is rooted in the method approach to acting, most actors are already familiar with its basic premise and vocabulary. What is unique, though, is Professor Sabatine's ability to work beyond our intellectual understanding of these terms. Through essence, the words become a visceral part of the actor's physiology. Placing fear in your gut creates greater believability and dimension than simply recalling fear intellectually.

Additionally, there is an inherent sense of familiarity in this work. Often after an exploration, a student will comment, "I can't explain why, but this just feels right." This is because Professor Sabatine speaks to the actor's deepest instinct. Her explorations tap into what we intuitively know we need to explore, even when we are unable to articulate it. The voice of a great director lives within this text, guiding the actor to ask and answer questions about the character and situation. Explorations of emotion, intention, energy, gesture, and so on, move us away from vague generalizations, towards specific, well-developed choices.

Too often, actors fail to tap into their own creative strength. This theory reminds us that we are our own greatest resource. The inclusion of innovative forms of expression such as journal writing, meditation, and balancing the chakras contributes to development of the spirit in conjunction with the mind and body. The result is a well-rounded, multidimensional character intact with personality.

Although I've had the luxury of working directly with Professor Sabatine, I am convinced that any instructor, actor, or director could do as well by following the structure of this text. The exercises, explorations, and applications can be taught verbatim, although one should feel free to improvise and adapt according to the needs of the group. Once the theory is learned, the actor has at hand an invaluable tool. In a professional setting, an actor can utilize the theory in part or wholly as a total approach to characterization or as a means to explore a complicated moment within a scene. Indeed, the flexibility of this theory is one of its greatest attributes.

In order to solve specific acting problems, I occasionally use the theory in conjunction with other established techniques. Quite often, students tend to fully explore the moments within the scene, but negate the crucial moment before the start of the scene. Consequently, the entrance is not as organic or honest as the rest of the work. Uta Hagen eloquently and effectively deals with this issue with her "three entrances" exercise. She offers a three-step technique requiring the actor to consider: What did I just do? What am I doing right now? What is the first thing I want? (see *Respect for Acting*, New York: Macmillan, 1973.) Certainly, her method forces the actor to make specific choices. The danger, however, is that many actors make only intellectual decisions. By taking this exercise one step further and exploring the answers in abstracted essence, the actor moves away from potentially literal and stereotypical decisions towards a fully connected, active entrance.

Anyone who teaches this technique will be rewarded by the magnitude of growth in their training sessions. There comes a point when actors lose themselves in the work and become, for the first time, truly organic. They forget the outside world exists, living only in the moment and setting of their scene. Often, they seem amazed at their ability to do so. Comments such as, "I've never felt so connected," or "I wasn't aware of the rest of the class" are common. As an instructor I cannot fully describe the thrill of this accomplishment. I relish the magic this theory has brought to my classroom.

Notes from an Actor's Journal: David Hodge

We have probably all heard the question, "How did you remember all of those words?!" spoken in awe at one time or another. As theater professionals we grimace at the naïveté and simply smile. We know that the words are easy— someone else had to write them. It's bringing them to life that is hard. And it is in the area of bringing those words to life that this theory shines.

Essence theory is a valuable tool I've grown quite fond of, like my car: Not only is it pretty to look at, I can get in it, drive across town and pick up the groceries. Essence work has not only brought home the bacon for me but saved it on more than one occasion. I don't always need essence theory, but the inspiration is always there to take me where I need to go.

AUDITIONS

Auditions are everyone's nightmare. You have thirty seconds to two minutes to prove you are worth a second look. Essence theory makes that easy, and I've used it in practically every form of theater.

Once I went to an audition for a commercial. The director was looking for a jogger who was wearing a Walkman, listening to a Redskins game, and reacting to a touchdown. I did the essence study of a 200-lb. kernel of popping corn (complete with sound effects) and landed the job. That's how I got my Screen Actors Guild card!

Once I landed a role in an industrial film by internally focusing on the essence of a frying strip of bacon. I was reading for the lead role in a film dedicated to training railroad personnel about the difficulties and uncertainties of the life they would be leading. The controlled anger of the frying strip of bacon, and the spitting, subtle rage it inspired in me gave me one week's work which was worth a month and a half of Equity LORT A wages at the time.

Auditions are a good place for essence work, especially if no one else knows you're using it. It makes you appear different (which is good) and, at times, inspired (which is even better!). Focusing on essence rather than trying to guess "what does he or she want?" gives you freedom to be natural and elastic. If you have the wrong essence they will tell you and ask for another. They will even suggest them to you (even if they don't know what essences are)! "Could you try that again, only less angry this time?" "Sure thing!" you say as you turn down the heat on the bacon and give the fatty strip a sense of humor (which I did).

But it is in the more demanding theatrical experiences where you are asked to be realistic madmen, murderers, lovers, artists, and plain damn people who have to live wonderfully impossible portions of very difficult lives, that essence work is truly a godsend.

PLAYING IAGO

Consider Iago, in Shakespeare's *Othello*. How do you bring this spiteful, mean little bastard to life? It is so easy to hate him. It is difficult to avoid doing a caricature of a renaissance Snidely Whiplash!

So you do his animal essences, and you find perhaps what I found—a crippled hyena in the inside, and a scuttling, clever wolverine on the outside. You do an emotional essence study and find profound insecurity compounded by raging fear, which causes immense explosions of self-protecting, other-annihilating hatred coupled with anger. You find boundless greed mated with envy and egocentric pride riding the back of self-amusement. And you might find, as I did, cycles of escalating fear, dread, hate, relief, spite, hate, fear, spite, hate . . . followed by joy, pride, and hysterical amusement when Iago successfully manipulates Othello and so has won another round.

When you do those Essences, you may begin to feel the utterly ugly, loathsome creatures you have to become in order to say the words and perform the actions onstage as Iago. You may even feel sorry for him (though you know he would hate and despise you for it), even if no one else will.

PLAYING SCAPINO

You can use the theory for a more pleasant purpose, with just as certain positive results, as I did with Scapino. *Scapino!* (The Frank Dunlop/Jim Dale version of Molière's *Les Fourberies de Scapin*) is a unique script. Molière's original script and characters were modeled on the Commedia dell' Arte. Dunlop and Dale tried (I believe successfully) to remain true to the major intentions of Molière and to the fun-loving spirit of the Commedia he copied. They updated the characters and dialogue to include all the local color and contemporary references that were such a part of the Commedia, while keeping the sense or suggestion of improvisation so essential to the form.

To help me in my task I eventually used every resource I possess, including endurance. Of course, I used standard script and character analysis. The following is an excerpt from my journal for this production:

The action revolves around Scapino. He is the innovator. As the play
progresses he assumes a more and more active role in the occurrences. His
performance has the quality of an ever-increasing metronome that reaches
its climax in the bag scene. Just as important, however, and also ruled by
the metronome effect, is the personal rapport Scapino has with the
audience. By the end of the first act, each audience member must feel a
close friendship with Scapino. By the end of the play, the entire audience
must be his unalterable ally. Laughter isn't enough for him (me); he (I)
must be magnetic, innocently worldly, intelligent, witty, benign, wise,
childlike, and generally lovable.

Scapino is on top of every situation. He is cool. He is an operator. If
there is a "No!" to any question, he can change it to a "Yes!" He refuses to
accept any fact as unalterable, because it is probably a fabrication of the
mind of a man. And most men are weak. To change the fact, therefore, all
he has to do is to change the man's mind.

This intellectualization was part of the external portion of my work on
Scapino! More important than this external understanding was knowledge I
gained from the essence studies we were all assigned.

Sunday, September 19

My essence studies have been quite rewarding. I have done all the
assigned essences. My (Scapino's) physical essence is a controlled self-
amused cockiness. . . . A civilized, controlled, vibrating zest for life hums
cheerily along his entire frame (and through each movement) in exquisite
harmony with itself. All his parts (physical, emotional, and intellectual)
are honed with immaculate precision into an interlocking network of
joyous unity.

My energy essence was actually a furthering of the physical theme. As
Scapino approaches life in his erect, self-assured, physical manner, an entire
continent of stored energy fills him with a vast potential for action, but
action as directed by his mind. Every action is controlled by his mind. He
controls the amount and direction and kind of energy used for a certain
activity. It is metered, measured, and ordered. But he is not a creature of
the mind alone: he depends a great deal on his instinct and inspiration to
guide his mind. These open patterns of thought reveal courses of possible
action spontaneously and inexplicably. He can afford to be cocky with this
kind of creative power backing him up.

He loves to place himself in positions that present great challenge, and
as all such situations present him with great potential for amusement,
they provide him with the most enjoyable contact with the world. He is
the Bobby Fischer of the game of life.

My exterior animal is an affectionate, wide-eyed, innocent, and guileless giraffe. Very controlled, very premeditated movement, constrained by his physical dissimilarity, almost aloof, but compassionate and understanding. He is not lonely, but he is alone.

My interior animal is an otter. Joyous, charming, fearlessly affable, agile, and quick-witted, he is everyone's friend. (And yet, because no one can keep up with this indefatigable character, he can never form a total bond with anyone. And as women tend to slow one down, he avoids "entanglements," although he has sex often in the same happy spirit as anything else he gets into.) He is sleek, smooth, strong, and in his own disarming, charming, harmless way, aggressive. Without fear or peer, he is king of the world which he need not own. Not only is ownership pedestrian and beneath him, it would also bore him witless and he knows it!

Monday, September 20

The performance of these studies before the entire cast (which Jean Sabatine as Movement Director required of all the cast), revealed in better detail, and more fully than any discussion could, each character's comedic potential. Also apparent was the true nature of characters' relationships and theatrical purpose.

Through occasional group improvisations based on these essence studies, the cast reestablished contact with the self-evident truth that the comedy in *Scapino!* is dependent, in large measure, on the contrasting character types and their skillful interaction. Although I always had believed that comedy is essentially a relationship (which is humorous), I had never had such a practical demonstration of that fact before this.

In this character, as indeed in most, once I found the proper animals I was off and running. But there are times when something truly special is needed. And when you find one of those characters, essences are there to help.

PLAYING TEDDY

The most elaborate and successful use to which I have put my movement training was in playing Teddy, in Mark Medoff's *When You Comin' Back, Red Ryder?* I did this show while I was still a student of Professor Sabatine's in the M.F.A. Acting Program at Penn State, and was fortunate to have her as movement consultant to the production. Since my graduation so long ago, I have often wished for that luxury again. Sadly, in professional life that is all too rare. I began, of course, with script and character analysis, did a complete series of essence studies, and still the fellow eluded me.

Finally, I decided on a movement tape for Teddy. I respond well to music and felt that it was bound to reveal something to me. No one else could make a tape for me, and since I had the proper equipment and had made several before for Professor Sabatine's movement course, I set out to find "Teddy music." Once I had accumulated some music, I tried to mindlessly throw myself into the project. When I was finished, I had a tape almost thirty minutes long composed of selections by over a dozen different artists.

I waited two days before I even thought about it again, and attempted to carry on with other rehearsal work. I believe that my subconscious was busy digesting the experience of the single three-hour taping session (for my work became somehow translucently different), but I avoided conscious deliberation of it.

Finally, I set up my tape recorder and speakers in a dance studio and did an easy physical warm-up and relaxation exercise. When I felt free from tension, I turned on the tape.

When the music was over, I lay down in a pool of sweat, utterly free of tension, my mind filled with images and memories I could have only formed in a dream state. The juxtaposition of types of music (such as the soul-rending "Lowland Lullaby" from Yusef Lateef's album *The Gentle Giant,* and the vicious "Non-Stop Home" from the Weather Report album *Mysterious Traveller*) opened up the organic connection in me that had eluded me until then.

March 12

At one point in the tape there was a piece of music ("One of These Days" from Pink Floyd's album *Meddle*) that inspired me to run in a huge circle around the perimeter of the room. At first it was just running for the sake of running, because it felt good. Then it suddenly seemed as though I were pursuing something. As I ran that thing changed into different images I had desired in my youth: a catcher's mitt, a watch, to play third base, to make the winning touchdown, to have people cheer for me. The progression led me farther into that part of myself that is insecure, and as that happened the images became more abstract: to be loved by everyone, to be respected by everyone, to be intelligent, to be wise, to transcend wanting. But the farther I ran and the harder I tried, the farther out of reach those things seemed. And as I realized that, the fear seemed to creep up on me from behind—as though the treadmill, as fast as I was running, was carrying me faster still in the opposite direction—toward failure, degradation, humiliation. Images came to mind, and it seemed I had to run faster to escape from each one. Soon, I realized I was running from fear more than desire, but I couldn't stop. I had to keep going but with each loop around the room I felt more tired, and with the fatigue came a profound hopelessness—an awareness of the futility of my action, finally the stupidity of my efforts came to me like a blinding light and stopped me dead in my tracks. As I stood there gasping for air, and watching my

sweat fall onto the floor, Yusef Lateef's "Lowland Lullaby" came on
again, and I saw all my own private hopes and dreams as a kind of three-
dimensional structure. The dimensions consisted of simultaneous sensations
of emotion, abstract ideas, and physical imagery. They stood briefly outlined
against a desolate background that made no sense until it rushed in upon
me (in the unreal timelessness of a dream where occurrences are both
extremely fast and slow). The background was all the sights and sounds,
odors, thoughts, and feelings of which I am ashamed and afraid. And as
they came at me the beautiful tower of dreams turned to ash and collapsed
in upon itself.

I writhed as if in a massive seizure, convulsed in upon myself, crying
out, and in that lost and desperate moment found all the anger at myself
and, still in pain, cried in rage—straightening and lifting, my arms flailed at
the air for a few moments until all my energy was gone and I was empty. I
sagged into myself, onto my knees and cried as I remembered scene after
scene from my past that moved me to tears.

The next moment, when the next violent piece of music began, the
juxtaposition of the selections stopped me from crying, sobering me almost
like the drunk who's been slapped in the face by his outraged wife, and I
straightened proudly—defensively—looking around to see if anyone had
seen me. (Through this entire process I never lost track of the awareness that
I was doing an exercise. It was as though someone had given me permission
to probe my psyche as though it belonged to someone else. In a sense it
did. I knew that there were memories that wouldn't fit the tape, and that
the tape was not engineered to reveal me, but Teddy—or at least the Teddy
within me. I was allowing the tape to restructure my experience to show me
the reaction this new structure would have on me. In this way, while reacting
honestly, I never "freaked out" or even worried about that possibility. I was
empathizing, as though I had direct mind-contact with a friend in pain. I
was safe, Teddy was in trouble.)

The reality of professional theater is profoundly different from the academic.
The academic should provide a great range of educational experiences as
preparation for your life beyond its borders. In the academic environment, you
should have the luxury of developing slowly the skills, talents, and knowledge
you need to mature as an actor and as a human being.

As a professional you are expected to be complete, and to be capable of
producing the goods when you walk on the set or on the stage. Directors and
producers don't care how you achieve this. Time is money, and they cannot
afford to wait for you to "mature" or "develop." So in professional life you
must prepare before you rehearse, and you need tools that help you to work
alone, for that is where you do the greatest bulk of your work.

The movement theory you find elucidated in this text can help in both academic and professional realities. It has helped me as a student, teacher, and actor. It is, if nothing else, a ready tool which I can use to achieve a dependable result quickly and efficiently. I have used it at times as the primary vehicle in my artistic process. And I have found it to be illuminating and inspirational. What more can we ask of a theory , or of educational opportunity?

An Acting Experience: Keith Grant

My association with Professor Jean Sabatine began twenty years ago when I enrolled in her graduate movement course at the Pennsylvania State University. The movement training I received prior to working with Professor Sabatine paled in comparison to her cohesive approach to the building of a physical characterization: the process of developing a character's alignment, movement through space, gesture, overall body language, and so on. The concepts and techniques I gleaned from my initial contact with Professor Sabatine's theories in 1984 and the subsequent work I have done with her has proven invaluable to me not only as a performer, but as a director, choreographer, and teacher as well. The clarity with which she presented her movement curriculum stood in sharp contrast to the movement theories espoused in the other professional acting programs I attended afterward.

I am currently a member of the performance faculty at Cornell University and have also maintained challenging and diverse professional acting and directing careers. Since my initial introduction to Jean Sabatine's movement training for the stage and screen, I have assiduously employed her theories. They have enabled me to develop into a "young character actor" whose range includes roles as varied as Ariel in *The Tempest* (at the Ashland Shakespeare Festival), Don Pedro in *Much Ado About Nothing* (at Indiana Repertory Theatre), and Bono in *Fences* (at the Connecticut Repertory Theatre).

I will use my aforementioned work on the character Bono in August Wilson's African-American drama *Fences* to discuss the manner in which I have employed Professor Sabatine's movement theories. At every juncture of the production's rehearsal and performance process, her curriculum proved invaluable. The preliminary explorations of the character's internal and external energy essences, his use of space and time, and the character's use of social/emotional gestures were all aspects of the curriculum that I utilized as I began working on Bono.

The movement techniques elucidated in this text enabled me to feel confident that I could create a credible physical characterization for Bono in spite of the fact that Mr. Wilson describes Bono as a fifty-three-year-old man. In stark contrast to this description of the character by the playwright, I was a very fit and very white-collar thirty-nine-year-old actor/instructor. Consequently, the physical choices I made for the character would be critical to convincing an audience that I was indeed over fifteen years older and considerably less physically agile. My middle-class white-collar manner and demeanor needed to be drastically adjusted in order to transform myself physically and emotionally into Bono, with whom I had very little in common. Bono was born to parents who were impoverished turn-of-the-century sharecroppers struggling to survive in the American South. He is poorly educated and is employed as an underpaid garbage man in pre-1960's Pittsburgh.

In order to tap into the emotional core of the character, I began by exploring Professor Sabatine's energy essence theory. Once I felt that I had a clear understanding of the director's vision for the production, and my character's contribution to his concept, I immediately began to think about and physically explore Bono's internal and external energies. After exploring the six qualities of energy (swing, suspend-collapse, percussive, vibratory, and sustained), I found that the movement studies based on suspend-collapse felt right (physically and emotionally) for the character both internally and externally.

The energy balance I discovered between Bono's internal and external energy essences validated choices I discovered about him after a deeper examination of Mr. Wilson's text, and the preliminary working sessions with the director and the other cast members. Like his balanced internal and external energies, Bono is also an emotionally balanced man who is in control of his rage. Bono's only confrontational scene with Troy (Act II, scene 2) is not resolved with a physical battle or verbal tirades, but rather through a compromise and a symbolic challenge. He manipulates Troy into agreeing to build a fence because Rose (Troy's wife) "loves you all and wants to hold onto you." Moreover, Bono is constantly playing intentions that humor or calm Troy and the other characters. Like his complementing internal and external energies, Bono is the play's source for moderation, balance, and the voice of reason.

Every decision I made when executing the director's blocking was influenced by the aforementioned decision to incorporate suspend-collapse into my physical characterization. The manner in which Bono gesticulated, stood, sat, and moved through the space was done in a suspend-and-collapsed manner. Likewise, the character's alignment was laterally dropped to the right side of his spinal column. His appendages were lifted and dropped in a bobbling manner as he walked. His gestures were often energized initially in an almost percussive energy, only to be released shortly thereafter in a collapsed fashion.

As the rehearsal period progressed and the director's stage patterns became established, I began to focus on Bono's movement through the performance space. It is important to note that the character's use of space was limited by several factors:

1. The scenic requirements noted in the text, which states that the action of the play takes place in a cramped front yard.
2. Bono's advancing age.
3. The fact that three-quarters of his scenes occur when he was returning home via Troy's house, after a grueling eight-hour working day.
4. He is often under the influence of alcohol, so his physical agility is often impaired.

Bono's movement in the space is therefore confined to choices that could be executed within these limitations. His advancing age and the limited acting area are the reasons why he never explored the levels in the space beyond his blocking, which required him to simply sit or stand on the porch in a manner befitting his age and physical state of being. Insofar as his movement across the stage floor is concerned, he always took the shortest path to his destinations, creating extended angular patterns through the space. Finally, the range of his gestures was for the most part restrained, primarily because of his advancing age, intoxication, and fatigue.

The fourth noteworthy element of space I explored was design. I selected an asymmetrical silhouette for Bono's stationary and locomotive physical movement. This choice was motivated by my earlier decision to explore suspend-collapse for his external energy. The nature of the external energy I developed (head and arms dropped to the right side of the torso) created an asymmetrical design; it was therefore impossible to select a symmetrically configured silhouette for Bono once the suspend-collapse choice was made for his external energy essence and incorporated into the character's alignment.

The final technique found in Professor Sabatine's text that I employed concerned the abstraction of the character's gestures. As I stated earlier, the physical characterization I created was diametrically opposed to my personal manner of standing, walking, or gesturing. I was particularly interested in finding emotionally connected gestures for Bono that were not at all like the conventional, functional, social, or emotional gestures I use in my daily life. I began by responding (emotionally and physically) as honestly as I could during the daily rehearsals conducted by the director. I would later work alone finding abstractions for the selected gestures I recalled from the previous day's rehearsal. I then attempted to incorporate elements of these abstractions, developing privately the work I was doing in rehearsals.

As a direct result of my essence gesture explorations, I was able to find Bono-like ways for the character to gesticulate and physically express his subtextual emotional states. For example, normally I would congratulate a friend by wrapping my arms about her or his torso, and giving a hug. My gesture abstractions revealed another more appropriate option. I moved the impulse (to hug) into my hands and proceeded to aggressively grab Troy's left hand with my right hand

and vigorously slap the two clasped hands with my right hand. This choice was far more appropriate for the relationship between Troy and Bono who were acutely protective not only of their personal space but of their emotional vulnerabilities as well. A gregarious hug between these two shielded (emotional and physically) men would have been out of place.

In my final scene with Troy, in which the two men are estranged, Bono carries his hat, and throughout the entire scene I chose to constantly move the hat I was carrying in a circular pattern with extreme agitation. Like the movement of the hat, my internal monologue was churning with the emotional tension prompted by my discomfort with the situation. Finally, I was also able to discover unconventional ways to communicate nonverbally my reactions to Troy's elaborate stories and monologues, delivered while my character Bono was onstage listening. Physicalizations that expressed support for Troy's sentiments were not limited to the predictable nodding of the head but were expanded to include nodding of the entire torso. I discovered pounding my feet on the floor became a substitution for approvingly clapping my hands together.

After abstracting and adapting a number of the gestures I found spontaneously in rehearsal, I was able to lock into a consistent pattern or style for the gesturing choices that would follow. The deeper I explored the aforementioned abstractions, the more emotionally connected my gesturing became. The gestures executed by my arms, hands, and fingers were all amazingly particular to Bono and in no way like the ones I habitually use in my personal life.

Before I encountered Professor Sabatine and her movement text, I was often forced to make physical choices for the characters I portrayed without the assistance of a clearly defined technique. The focus and clarity that her approach has brought to my work on the stage has been remarkable. When I am cast in a role that is challenging physically, vocally, and emotionally, I now have tangible goals for rehearsals that will not only transform me physically but vocally and emotionally as well.

The curriculum has also given me specific physicalizations and concepts that I can explore and think about before I make each and every one of my entrances onto the stage as the character. When I am in the wings of the theater preparing to begin the play, I first concentrate on Bono's external energy by reaching upwards and dropping my body to one side a number of times in a suspending and collapsing fashion; next I establish Bono's walk (his rhythms as they are affected by the suspend-collapse energy) and finally I move to the offstage quick-change mirror and note the asymmetrical silhouette the previous exercises have created in my otherwise symmetrically aligned and somewhat rigid stance. These external exercises begin to affect me internally, and I then turn my attention to his internal energy essence, my first dramatic action and finally his inner monologue.

The time I spend developing my physical characterization in rehearsals and in the wings before a performance is no longer a catch-as-catch-can pastiche of unrelated exercises, but rather a highly developed technique that serves to support and enhance the acting and vocal choices I have made. Like the vocal and physical technique classical dancers and singers have employed for centuries, this series of exercises and concepts enables me to prepare myself before every rehearsal and performance.

Conclusion

It has been our aim to provide three different perspectives on how the essence theory can be utilized in both the academic and professional arenas. By illustrating the individuality of the theory, and how it should be viewed in terms of its "success," we hope to reiterate that each artist must establish personal success points to mark individual progress. Each artist, then, adapts the theory according to his or her needs, while remaining faithful to its core philosophy and structure. The discoveries and developments of this work, as chronicled in this chapter, are as individual as the artists themselves, and must be approached as such.

Epilogue

The obvious focus of this book is the communication of what I feel to be important theories and training methods to instructors, and future instructors, of movement. A second and perhaps more important focus is the attempt to awaken in the theater profession as a whole (especially actors, directors, students, instructors, and related specialists) the need for a better understanding and appreciation of good movement training for actors.

My hope, beyond these two considerations, is that all theater specialists and generalists who read this book will be able to use some of the exercises, explorations, applications, and the principles behind them in their own work. Specialists should find that they can easily incorporate them into their own frame of reference and adapt the principles to special problems encountered in production. Generalists should find the useful unifying principles so necessary to them. Instructors in all performing disciplines (especially acting teachers) should find value in many areas of the book. This, at least, is my hope.

What I know to be true is that this method and these theories have worked for me and for my students. I know that the mind-spirit-body connection is the organic reality of human existence and that awareness and control of this reality are essential for an actor to achieve simultaneous thought, emotion, and action. And I know that each person must take responsibility for building a personal discipline and system of thought. Thus, I also know and desire that each person will take what is useful and make it uniquely his or her own.

Thousands of years ago, the Greeks lived by the espoused belief that the mind, spirit, and body must be developed equally to achieve a balance in the being. Their theater at its height was a dynamic example of and tribute to that principle. It is perhaps ironic that I find myself in a position of defending this principle in today's flourishing theatrical age. Perhaps the terminology or the manner of training, or even the application of the theory, is new, but the truth about the human condition has not changed.

If it is true that the mind, the spirit, and the body are mutually affecting parts of a single organic entity, can we, as theater artists, afford to ignore that fact, regardless of our specialization? And can we, as responsible professionals, content ourselves with our own awareness of this important fact without caring about the communication of our awareness and its uses to new or developing talents not yet so aware? Obviously, we cannot do either and continue to believe that we are sincere in our desire to perfect our art form.

Here, then, is one small part of my continuing effort to communicate my hard-won understanding of this most important reality. Here is the use to which I have put this fact. And here is my hope that at least some of you will find this work beneficial to your own.

Appendixes

Appendix 1
One Year's Work in Syllabus Format

Let us assume we are dealing with a college classroom situation in which each class is one-and-a-half hours in length; each week there are three class sessions (say, Monday, Wednesday, and Friday); and in this semester system there are fifteen weeks to the term. This means that the movement course will cover either one semester (half a school year) or two semesters (a full school year).

The ideal course for serious, professionally oriented students would be to study a full year. This is the only way all the material can be thoroughly presented and dealt with by the actor. Also, students need at least one year to maximize the potential of the work. In an introductory course with general college or even general drama students, a survey of the material provided in a single semester can be surprisingly effective and stimulating. Selectivity then becomes the key to constructing the course design. Let's concentrate on the ideal, however, because this allows us to examine the design in greater detail and, even for beginning students, is the *most* effective way to proceed.

Generally, in the first semester, I direct almost all the theory and effort toward the actor. In the second semester, the focus changes to characterization and then, finally, to scene work. The reasons for this deserve brief discussion:

1. The actor must always start with himself (or herself).
   a. The actor's only permanent tools are his body, voice, emotions, spirit, experience, intelligence, sensitivity, and creativity.
   b. The actor's tools must be disciplined, organized, and conditioned before he is ready to employ them meaningfully.
   c. It is important for the actor to understand, in a very immediate and personal sense, how these principles operate before he can hope to apply them to characterization.
2. Before the relationship of one character to another can be understood, each actor must understand his relationship to the character.
   a. An actor must first understand the character before he can hope to understand how the character relates to another and why.
   b. By applying the personalization tools first to the character, the actor draws on personal experience to build a past for the character so that the character's present has justification.
   c. Through the accumulated understanding of (and empathy with) the character, the actor builds a solid foundation for the scene work.
3. Work on a scene should never be imposed from preconceptions unsupported by practical understandings of the character's makeup and motivations.

a. Scenes are complicated interactions and can easily lead to an intellectual morass.

b. Once both actors in a scene are in command of their characters, the scene can naturally evolve from the dynamic interaction of the three-dimensional persons commanded by the actors.

c. Characters with an organic reality are essential to this kind of scene work, so unless an actor has first been trained to understand and work organically, scene work can be an exercise in futility.

Here, then, is the general outline of one year's work in this basic, organically oriented movement class. Keep in mind that it is only a model, and in practice it is very flexible. Also remember that while time frames within the sequence of sections may be altered (depending on the needs and capacities of the class), the general design is the one I have found most suited to the task at hand, and any significant decision to change the order of progression from one sequence to the next should first be carefully considered.

Movement Training for Actors (First Semester)

OBJECTIVE

My objective is to establish the organic connection: In the physical training of the actor is the integration of the mind, spirit, and body—the whole organism in harmony with itself so that it is ready for interaction. This is the natural organic connection.

I start by bringing the actor to a neutral state, ridding him of personal mannerisms. If an actor were to stick to a particular movement pattern, he would become incapable of portraying any other character, and he would be type-casting himself. He would limit himself, rather than expand his range, by not being able to experience and empathize with all physical movements, attitudes, and emotions.

Effective training of the actor can only begin when he is open to new ideas and can free the mind, spirit, and body of harmful physical and emotional problems.

Goal One. Help the actor to find the proper balance of tension and relaxation to bring the body to a ready state. The actor must find the proper balance between these two elements. This enables the flow of energy to go in and out of the body, rather than getting blocked inside—to feel alive, which most of all enables the actor to react. Even when just standing on-stage, an actor should be full of inner life (internal energy).

One of the main problems is excessive tension that cuts off the flow of energy, limiting physical movement as well as expression (inner life). The actor needs to work to find the proper balance of tension and relaxation to keep the mind, spirit, and body ready for action.

Goal Two. Help the actor to establish proper breathing habits in relationship to his movement. Improper breathing patterns increase unnecessary tension and decrease the mind's, spirit's, and body's ability to act and react freely to internal and external stimuli.

The work spent harmonizing breathing with movement patterns complements the efforts expended in voice and speech classes, and aids in establishing the positive flow of energy for both speech and movement.

Goal Three. Assist the actor in finding and maintaining his own natural alignment, and in developing an awareness of the related concept of *center.* An actor who can control his body attitude so that he can sense and maintain his natural alignment is well on the way to mastering the ability to center himself physically and emotionally. This is also helpful in eliminating radically personal mannerisms and many unnecessary tensions, which impede proper breathing habits and efficient flow of energy.

Goal Four. A carefully arranged series of physical exercises and explorations helps to reveal the natural interactive relationship of the mind, spirit, and body. An actor solely dependent on his intellect closes himself off to his natural organic reality, whereas one totally focused on his body is less capable of making intelligent choices.

SYLLABUS: FIRST SEMESTER

I. Daily Class Structure
   A. Tension/relaxation
   B. Exercises/technique
   C. Explorations
   D. Applications
   E. Discussion
II. Course Content
   A. Explore basic concepts in movement
      1. Explore basic concepts of space, time, energy
      2. Explore parameters of human movement—that is, body explorations
      3. Explore body/spirit/mind relationship—that is, internal/external
      4. Explore individual/world relationship through movement
   B. Subjects covered
      1. Alignment—internal (chakras)/external (physiology)
      2. Proper breathing techniques
      3. Body explorations

    4. Walking/posture (what this tells us about individuals)

    5. Space (what it is/how to use it [direction, levels, range, design, focus])

    6. Gesture (social/functional)

    7. Essence theory of movement/abstraction theory

    8. Energy (percussive, sustained, swinging, vibratory, suspend, collapse)

    9. Action verbs

    10. Fragment (follow through)

    11. Time (tempo, duration, rhythm pattern, accent, counterpoint)

    12. Animal essences (internal/external)

    13. Emotional through-line

    14. Total essence of self

  C. Projects (involving outside class time)

    1. Two walk studies (actor's own and another's)

    2. Two gesture studies (functional and social)

    3. Haiku abstraction

    4. Actors' energy study of themselves

    5. Action verb essence study

    6. Line essence study

    7. Animal essence study

    8. Emotional essence of self (emotional through-line)

    9. Total essence of self

    10. Two papers on:

      a. movement of character in a play

      b. your growth/progress

    11. Final project using essence theory (a poem, song, work of art, music, etc.)

    12. One class project on any area covered

III. Course Breakdown

  A. First and second weeks

    1. Tension/relaxation

    2. Alignment—internal (chakras)/external (physiology)

    3. Breathing techniques

    4. Teaching exercises

    5. Body exploration

  B. Third week (class routine)

    1. Shortened period of:

      a. tension/relaxation

      b. alignment and breath

      c. breathing

      d. exercises

    2. Body explorations
    3. Walks
C. Fourth and fifth weeks
    1. Establish class routine
    2. Space chapter
    3. First movement tape
    4. Folk dances
D. Sixth week
    1. Class routine
    2. Essence theory
    3. Gestures
        a. social
        b. functional
E. Seventh week
    1. Class routine
    2. Haiku essence (essence of meaning)
    3. Energy study
    4. First paper due
F. Eighth week
    1. Class routine
    2. Energy essence
    3. Action verbs
    4. Energy tape
G. Ninth and tenth weeks
    1. Class routine
    2. Action verb study
    3. Line essence
    4. Line essence study
H. Eleventh week
    1. Class routine
    2. Animal essence
    3. Animal essence study
I. Twelfth and thirteenth weeks
    1. Class routine
    2. Time (tempo, duration, rhythm pattern, accent, counterpoint)
    3. Exploration of above elements
    4. Time tape
    5. Rhythm essence
    6. Second paper due
J. Fourteenth week
    1. Class routine
    2. Emotional essence of self

K. Fifteenth week
   1. Total essence of self
   2. Presentation of final project (actor's choice)
   3. Presentation of class project (as it stands)
   4. Discussion of relation of past to future work

Movement Training for Actors (Second Semester)

OBJECTIVE

This semester focuses on physicalization of a character and movement in a scene. The objective is to reinforce and extend the organic connection to include characterization. The actor as a human being has a natural organic connection, so any character she (or he) will be asked to play will also have a mind-spirit-body relationship organic to her. This phase of study focuses on assisting the actor to find, through her now sensitive instrument, the organic reality of the character.

Goal One. Maintain and further develop all the positive elements the actor has learned in the preceding semester (that is, proper tension/relaxation, breathing, alignment, and so on).

Goal Two. Establish the understanding that manipulation of internal (memory, emotions, attitudes, and so on) and external (bodily positions, altering center, alignment movements, and so on) elements aids in the creation of a new sense of self—that is, characterization.

Goal Three. Develop and control specific characterizations through the manipulation of the elements previously covered, using sophisticated extensions of techniques already learned.

SYLLABUS: SECOND SEMESTER

I. Daily Class Structure
   A. Warm-up exercises
   B. Explorations
   C. Applications
   D. Discussion
II. Course Content
   A. Reviews the major elements covered in last semester's work
      1. Basic elements of movement
         a. space
         b. time
         c. energy
      2. Elements of tension/relaxation/alignment

      3. Essence theory
        a. line
        b. action verb
        c. gesture
B. Physicalization of a character (inner/outer) through essence work. (Actors will select a scene from a contemporary play, choosing characters that are close to themselves in age.)
    1. Walk
    2. Posture center
    3. Mannerisms
    4. Moods/emotions
    5. Interest
    6. Wants/needs
    7. Other (who-what-where-why)
C. Understanding inner and outer being
    1. Use of space
    2. Energy
    3. Rhythm essence (internal conflicts)
    4. Animal studies (inner/outer essence of character)
    5. Emotional makeup of the character
    6. Total essence of character (external/internal)
D. Movement in the scene
    1. Energy essence of the scene
    2. Counterpoint (yin-yang) of scene
    3. Animal essences together with scene
    4. Major intention of the scene
    5. Emotional thread
    6. Line essence work extended
    7. Free choice of essence to work into the scene
D. Additional work
    1. Movement tapes
    2. Projects
    3. Other problems we find during our work

Appendix 2
Sample Class Structures

Because of the changing nature of the material, the makeup of classroom activity and breakdown of class time into various activities will change according to need. For instance, my first classes are usually devoted mainly to teaching exercises and working on alignment, breathing techniques, and relaxation/tension problems.

Later classes, while using these techniques in an approximately thirty-minute warm-up, will be devoted to body or movement explorations, while even later classes will be broken down into perhaps three separate portions of warm-up, exploration, and application or presentation. Some classes will involve a single warm-up, and the rest of the time will be devoted to students working together (under my supervision, if not guidance) on the class project (see Appendix 3).

I have outlined two sample class structures: one from the first semester and one from the second semester. Notice that the outline of the first semester class involves an exploration of energy and a presentation of haiku essence studies introduced and assigned from a previous class. This is a useful tool to demonstrate similarities between seemingly unrelated topics and provides the sensation and awareness of organic growth for students. Please notice also the increased number and sophistication of exercises in the second semester. Arm patterns are added by this time, as well as the more difficult balancing exercises.

Finally, the basic difference between the two classes is that, although both involve the concept of energy, the first semester class deals with energy as it affects and applies to the actor, and in the second semester those same concepts are used by the actor in relationship to the character.

Sample Class Structure: First Semester

Remember, we are using a one-and-a-half-hour class period as the model. This is a session seven weeks into the fifteen-week term. The class will be divided roughly into thirds.

CLASS STRUCTURE

I. Exercises and warm-up session (25 to 35 minutes)
II. Explorations (20 to 30 minutes)
III. Presentation (20 to 30 minutes)
IV. Discussion (5 to 10 minutes)

I. Exercises: The usual sequence for developmental warm-up on a typical day:

A. Basics
1. Relaxation
2. Breathing and spine work
3. Posture alignment
4. Spine studies

B. Isolations: Head, shoulders, rib cage, pelvis

C. General exercises
1. Stretch and swing
2. Stretch to side
3. Pliés (demi- and grand)
4. Side stretches
5. Leg extensions
6. Parallel pliés
7. Brushes
8. Eight-count stretch

D. Floor exercises
1. Head and spine
2. Up over the back, shoulder stand press (yoga plow)
3. Sequential sitting up
4. Knee into chest
5. Pushups (men, 15; women, 10)
6. Flex and extend
7. Second position flex and stretch
8. Pulse, pulse and up

E. Ending the warm-up
1. Foot flexibility
2. Jumps
3. Frustration jumps
4. Balancing of chakras
5. Breath rhythm

II. Explorations of energy: In the warm-up, lead into this exploration by focusing on energy qualities in the individual exercises; pliés, for example, can be executed with an awareness of the sustained energy quality they require.

A. Energy and pure movement
B. Energy and gesture

III. Presentation: Haiku studies

IV. Discussion: Relate haikus to energy

Sample Class Structure: Second Semester

Again, we are using a one-and-a-half hour-class period. This perhaps begins seven weeks into a fifteen-week term. The class is divided into thirds:

CLASS STRUCTURE

I. Exercises (30 minutes)
II. Exploration (20 minutes)
III. Application and Discussion (40 minutes)

I. Exercises
  A. Spine Studies
    1. Breathing in
    2. Swing and up
  B. Isolations
    1. Head rotation
    2. Head percussive
    3. Rib cage
    4. Pelvis (sustained circling)
    5. Percussive pelvic
    6. Shoulder roll
  C. General exercises
    1. Stretch and swing
    2. Stretch to side
    3. Plié sequence
    4. Side stretches
    5. Leg extensions
    6. Brushes
    7. Eight-count stretch
    8. Stretch, side flat, side, back
    9. Layouts
  D. Floor exercises
    1. Up over the back
    2. Constructive rest
    3. Up over each other's back sequential sitting up
    4. Pushups (men, 25 to 30; women, 15) head and spine
    5. Leg up and stretch
    6. Knees into chest
    7. Flex and extend
    8. Second position flex and stretch
    9. Breathe on hands and knees

    10. Stretch, sit, push through, and sit

    11. Sit, push, sit, roll

    12. Arch and A

    13. Pulse, pulse and up

  E. Ending the warm-up

    1. Foot flexibility

    2. Jumps

    3. Frustration jumps

    4. Breath rhythm

II. Explorations: Explore the concept of the character's energy in terms of the internal versus external qualities that may be present. For instance: Does this character wish to be perceived as being one thing by those around her (e.g., as having a swinging quality—cool, calm, easygoing) but in reality being something far different internally (having a vibratory quality—nervous, unsure, insecure)? Does your character think he or she is one thing (e.g., having a sustained quality—even-tempered, meticulous, disciplined) but in reality is something totally different (having a percussive quality—domineering, dogmatic, compulsive)? This is another way of discovering hidden facets to your character, or reaffirming previous discoveries, whether or not they validate this concept of the character being different inwardly from the way she or he appears, or attempts to appear, outwardly. Many people are exactly what they seem and/or are what they want us to think they are.

III. Presentation and Discussion: The major portion of this class is set aside for presentation and discussion of each person's energy essence of a character. Depending on class size and the discussion that evolves from ensuing presentations, a second day of presentations may be necessary. This is typical of the problem of setting a firm line for the second semester classes.

Appendix 3
Projects

There are many ways to apply a given program of instruction, but one of the most valuable is in the context of the classroom. A student can use the techniques described there either independently, in an actual production, or in some other collaborative effort outside the classroom. In each of these approaches, however, there are obvious drawbacks. Independent application provides no external validation of the work. In actual productions, actors may be bombarded with processes, approaches, techniques, and personnel that have no connection to the methods they are trying to work with. Consequently, actors may have difficulty discerning the value and relationship of the various concepts they are forced to accommodate. In other less formal structures (say, a group of friends exploring a given work together), no one can be certain of an accurate communication of the theory, and so any results tend to be problematical. However, in a classroom of students all concentrating on the same problem from the same types of experiential development, using the same conceptual tools and being assisted or guided by an impartial and committed observer (the instructor), process, progress, and discovery can be observed and participated in by all.

Thus, the class project is a valuable tool for developing understanding and appreciation of the theories and methods being discovered in class. It is rather like a laboratory experiment in which each class member can experiment in a controlled environment so that the results are immediately verifiable. More importantly, it provides a supportive atmosphere of trust and respect not always found when an actor tries to experiment with tools unfamiliar to his fellows in a production. The class project gives license to the actors to use the tools they are acquiring in the classroom without fear of ridicule from others. Since ridicule, or the threat of it, tends to stifle and invalidate any test the actor may wish to conduct, this is a very important and valuable tool for the movement instructor.

Not all my classes have had the interest or energy to develop a project, and so I do not always require one. But when a group of students *have* applied themselves to a project they are interested in, sometimes the results have been stunning.

The prime consideration, then, is that the class as a whole be interested in working on a project. Once that has been decided, the next step is to find a focus or material for a project. This may be the most difficult step to take, and many of my classes have stumbled at this point. To help with this, I may make suggestions, depending on the interests and composition of the class.

The possibilities are enormous, and I list here only a few of the types of projects proposed or executed by classes in the past.

Types of Projects

THE MUSEUM
Students as a group go to a selected museum and try through an essence study (vocalized and silent) to find the form and essence of the museum and its contents.

THE POEM
Students may break into two groups and, either with two poems or with the same poem independently, endeavor to express the core or essence of the poem through sound and movement. An individual, selected individuals, or the entire group may read parts or all of the poem before, after, or as the movement occurs. The focus is to attempt to encapsulate and express in sound and movement the reality of the poem.

THE MESSAGE
A class may choose to deal with some topic or message. One class dealt with the concept of the childish, innocent, commercialized Saturday morning television fare of the late 1950s, as contrasted with the chilling, frequent nuclear-war air-raid drills of the same era. It ended with the entire group huddled in a circle producing an unending wail of the air-raid siren in unison, trailing off until only one, then none, of the unmoving participants was vocalizing the sound, very similar to a child's wail.

THE CONCERT
Students attend a concert and, perhaps using a recording of some of the music played there, attempt to capture the sights and sounds, emotions, and so on, of the audience and the musicians, from arrival at the theater to the intermissions and the final departures after the performance. Space, time, energy, animal essences (for people, instruments, or orchestrations), and other elements could provide quite a rewarding exercise.

THE HAPPENING
This could be anything from a party to a funeral; from a circus to a battle; from a college football game (complete with half-time) to a night in a delivery room; and so forth. Any meeting of people can provide excellent material requiring the creative application of theory.

THE SCRIPT
This is the broadest category, and the one most frequently used. It is also the most time-consuming and, perhaps, the most ambitious. Sources for scripts are limited only by library facilities, time, and interest. There is Reader's Theater, Experimental Theater, Classical Theater, Children's Theater, and so on. There are

Radio Dramas, Film Scripts, Television Dramas and Theater (that is, *Playhouse 90,* and so on). The focus in each of these, insofar as the project is concerned, is generally the same as in any project: to attempt to encapsulate and express, in sound and movement, the reality of the work being considered, using the techniques being learned in the classroom.

A Brief List

Some of the following projects have been used in my classrooms, and work on them was done in special in-class lab sessions; outside class; in conjunction with speech and acting teachers; with only a respected class member as director; or, most of the time, with a combination of directors and much independent initiative. The point is that each class will pursue whatever they will produce in a manner totally unique to them, and the instructor's responsibility is to provide as little control, guidance, and discipline, and as much support and class time, as possible. The rest is up to the class.

THE POEM

These volumes of poetry offer some excellent selections for projects. :

1. *Transformations* by Anne Sexton (Boston: Houghton Mifflin, 1972)
2. *All My Pretty Ones* by Anne Sexton (Boston: Houghton Mifflin, 1961)
3. *Leaves of Grass* by Walt Whitman (there are many editions of this American classic)
4. *Knots* by R. D. Laing (New York: Pantheon Books, 1970)

THE SCRIPT

As this list suggests, I tend to favor less formal theatrical genres in connection with the class project. Although any script can be analyzed and explored using the tools described in this book (particularly essence work), works more of the environmental-theater and experimental mold tend to guide actors away from the sometimes stultifying assumptions about how a certain type of play should be presented, interpreted, and performed. Also, since most students have not seen a production of one of these, preconceptions about character, message, and method are simply avoided.

1. *The Serpent* by Jean-Claude van Itallie (New York: Atheneum, 1969)
2. *Alice In Wonderland: The Forming of a Company and the Making of a Play* (New York: Merlin House/E. P. Dutton, Inc., 1973)
3. *Terminal: A Collective Work Created by the Open Theater Ensemble* (co-directed by Joseph Chaikin and Roberta Sklar), in *Scripts,* Volume 1, no. 1 (New York: New York Shakespeare Festival, November, 1971). *Terminal* is also the title of one of the many fine pieces included in this

unfortunately short-lived series of scripts. Some of the scripts that appeared in the series, such as *The Basic Training of Pavlo Hummel* by David Rabe and *The Rock Garden* by Sam Shepard, can be found in other publications, but other scripts suitable for class projects contained in these publications are not so easily accessible.

4. *Collision Course: 17 Brief Plays,* compiled by Edward Parone, (New York: Random House, 1968)

A Final Word

The class project can be an excellent tool for uniting the three primary disciplines of actor training: acting, voice, and movement. In a conservatory situation in which the students in one class are also receiving instruction from teachers collaborating in the complementary disciplines, students may receive special advisory assistance from those teachers (based, of course, on the discretion of the movement teachers and the convenience of the other teachers' time and desire). Where such a collaboration of specialists exists, the results can be extremely fruitful. Even when this is not the case, however, the class project can help actors cement their understanding, awaken creativity, inspire new growth, and fuse the separate disciplines into a single cohesive and creative tool.

Appendix 4
A Music Reference to Exercises

Generally, warm-up sessions are more interesting and energizing when done to music, provided that the exercises are known so thoroughly that the music is not a distraction. Music should serve rather to focus and punctuate the work. Since constant music can also serve as a distraction, careful selection of musical pieces to coordinate with selected series of exercises is the best avenue of approach.

The best type of music to use has a definite 4/4 beat and provides a relatively easy reference point for the majority of the students; it is familiar or performed by musicians appreciated by the students. I often ask students to bring in music they find suitable for the warm-up. This provides a relaxing atmosphere and establishes the comforting feeling that "This is something I can relate to," which in turn subliminally translates to the feeling "I can do this," and "I want to do this."

Music that is not currently popular can foster competitiveness. If students begin to vie with one another over whether a movement from Mozart unknown to most of them is "elitist," much has been lost compared to the relatively minor gain of having the tempo and count established for you.

When choosing music, one should always use common sense and personal taste as a guide. Also, although music is a useful tool, it should not become a crutch. Counting verbally or using a hand drum may be a useful alternative method. Common sense should also be employed in finding the optimum tempo for each exercise. Listen to the music, try the exercise in half-time, normal 4/4, and, if appropriate, in double-time. Use the tempo of that selection which feels right. If none of the three seems good for that exercise, don't use it. I have seen injuries result from attempting to force an exercise to fit a piece of music not suited to it. It is fairly easy to find music in a wide range of tempos that can work to aid the performance of the exercise, so it is not necessary to use inappropriate music.

The following list pairs exercises that can benefit from music with suggested recordings by the Beatles. Since any guide to the latest popular music would be obsolete before it could get to the presses, I adopt the Beatles' songs as standards of recorded popular music. I rarely use them in my classes anymore, but to help one establish the optimum tempo, they are a most reliable reference point, for their place in twentieth-century music appears to be set for the foreseeable future. Moreover, copies of their recordings should be easy to secure even in small communities for a long time to come—unlike some of less historically significant contemporary recording groups.

Exercises marked with an asterisk (*) can also be used in conjunction with all the songs in the following list:

- Honey Pie
- Everybody's Got Something to Hide 'Cept for Me and My Monkey
- Birthday
- Blackbird
- While My Guitar Gently Weeps
- The Word
- Wait
- Kansas City
- You Won't See Me
- Baby You Can Drive My Car
- I Want to Tell You
- Love You Too
- Yellow Submarine
- Taxman
- What You're Doing
- Getting Better
- When I'm Sixty-Four
- Sgt. Pepper's Lonely Hearts Club Band
- Penny Lane
- Baby You're a Rich Man
- Your Mother Should Know

BREATHING IN
- Get Back
- Maxwell's Silver Hammer
- Don't Pass Me By
- I Should Have Known Better
- Ballad of John and Yoko
- Honey Don't
- Rock and Roll Music

SWING AND UP
- Lady Madonna
- Get Back
- Maxwell's Silver Hammer
- Glass Onion
- Back in the USSR
- Eleanor Rigby
- Good Day Sunshine
- Flying

HEAD ROTATION *

- Ballad of John and Yoko
- Get Back
- Maxwell's Silver Hammer
- Ob-La-Di, Ob-La-Da
- Flying

RIB CAGE (PELVIS) *

- Old Brown Shoe
- Get Back
- Maxwell's Silver Hammer
- Glass Onion
- Birthday
- Honey Don't
- Eleanor Rigby

SHOULDER ROLL *

- Old Brown Shoe
- Don't Pass Me By
- Maxwell's Silver Hammer
- Savoy Truffle
- Why Don't We Do It in the Road
- Honey Don't
- Eleanor Rigby
- Everybody's Trying to be My Baby
- Magical Mystery Tour

STRETCH AND SWING—STRETCH TO SIDE *

- Get Back
- Maxwell's Silver Hammer
- Lady Madonna
- Eleanor Rigby
- Good Day Sunshine

PLIÉ SEQUENCE PARALLEL—CLASSICAL *

- Lady Madonna
- Paperback Writer
- Here Comes the Sun
- Dear Prudence
- Back in the USSR
- Eleanor Rigby
- Good Day Sunshine

SIDE STRETCHES *

- Two of Us
- Maxwell's Silver Hammer
- Eleanor Rigby
- Good Day Sunshine
- Savoy Truffle

LEG EXTENSIONS *

- Everybody's Trying to Be My Baby
- Two of Us
- One After 909
- Polythene Pam
- Dear Prudence
- Ob-La-Di, Ob-La-Da
- Savoy Truffle
- Don't Pass Me By

BRUSHES *

- What You're Doing
- I Should Have Known Better
- Good Day Sunshine
- Rain
- Two of Us
- Get Back
- Maxwell's Silver Hammer
- Back in the USSR
- Glass Onion
- A Little Help from My Friends
- Flying

EIGHT-COUNT STRETCH *

- Two of Us
- Maxwell's Silver Hammer
- Here Comes the Sun
- Back in the USSR
- Ob-La-Di, Ob-La-Da
- Don't Pass Me By
- Savoy Truffle
- Honey Don't
- Eleanor Rigby
- Good Day Sunshine
- Rock and Roll Music

STRETCH SIDE, FLAT, SIDE, BACK *

- Maxwell's Silver Hammer
- Back in the USSR
- Savoy Truffle
- Ob-La-Di, Ob-La-Da
- Eleanor Rigby
- Good Day Sunshine
- Lovely Rita
- Flying

LAYOUTS

- Rain
- Get Back
- Back in the USSR
- Helter Skelter
- Cry Baby Cry
- Honey Don't
- Taxman
- Run for Your Life
- When I'm Sixty-Four

SEQUENTIAL SITTING UP, HEAD AND SPINE, LEG UP AND STRETCH *

- I Should Have Known Better
- Two of Us
- Here Comes the Sun
- Helter Skelter
- Back in the USSR
- Dear Prudence
- Glass Onion
- When I'm Sixty-Four
- Honey Don't
- Eleanor Rigby
- Rock and Roll Music
- Ob-La-Di, Ob-La-Da
- Honey Pie
- Magical Mystery Tour

KNEES TO CHEST *

- Hey Jude
- Maxwell's Silver Hammer
- Here Comes the Sun
- Honey Pie
- Honey Don't

FLEX EXTEND *
- One After 909
- For You Blue
- Maxwell's Silver Hammer
- Rock and Roll Music
- Magical Mystery Tour
- Flying

BREATHE IN ON HANDS AND KNEES *
- Old Brown Shoe
- For You Blue
- Back in the USSR
- Honey Don't
- Rock and Roll Music
- Magical Mystery Tour
- Don't Pass Me By
- Honey Pie

STRETCH, SIT, PUSH THROUGH, AND SIT
- Get Back
- Glass Onion
- Little Piggies
- Blackbird
- Don't Pass Me By
- Honey Pie

SIT, PUSH, SIT, ROLL
- Blackbird
- Two of Us
- Honey Pie
- Don't Pass Me By
- She Said She Said
- Lovely Rita

ARCH AND A
- Mean Mr. Mustard
- Back in the USSR
- Little Piggies
- Octopus' Garden
- Don't Pass Me By
- Lovely Rita

PULSE AND UP
- Glass Onion
- Honey Pie
- For You Blue
- You Won't See Me
- Kansas City

FOOT SERIES *
- I Should Have Known Better
- Rain
- Maxwell's Silver Hammer
- Yellow Submarine

JUMPS
- Mean Mr. Mustard
- Little Piggies
- Why Don't We Do It in the Road (1/2 time)
- Glass Onion
- Everybody's Got Something to Hide 'Cept for Me and My Monkey
- Blackbird
- Lady Madonna
- Rain
- Flying
- The Word
- Kansas City
- Fixing a Hole

Bibliography

Adler, Stella. *The Technique of Acting.* New York: Bantam Books, 1988.

Ardrey, Robert. *The Territorial Imperative.* New York: Atheneum, 1966.

Artaud, Antonin. *The Theatre and Its Double.* Translated by Mary Caroline Richards. New York: Grove Press, 1958.

Barker, Clive. *Theatre Games.* New York: Drama Book Specialists, 1977.

Benedetti, Robert L. *The Actor at Work.* Englewood Cliffs, N. J.: Prentice-Hall, Inc., 1976.

_____. *Seeming, Being, and Becoming.* New York: Drama Book Specialists, 1976.

Bentley, Eric. *In Search of Theater.* New York: Vintage Books, 1957.

Berry, Cicely. *The Actor and His Text.* New York: Charles Scribner's Sons, 1987.

Birdwhistell, Ray L. *Kinesics and Context.* Philadelphia: University of Pennsylvania Press, 1970.

_____."Background to Kinesics." *ETC: A Review of General Semantics,* XII; No. 2 (Autumn 1955), 10–18.

Chekhov, Michael. *To the Actor: On the Technique of Acting.* New York: Harper & Row, 1953.

Chopra, Deepak, MD. *Ageless Body, Timeless Mind.* New York: Harmony Books, 1993.

Cole, Toby. *Acting: A Handbook of the Stanislavsky Method.* New York: Crown, 1960.

Darwin, Charles. *The Expression of the Emotions in Man and Animals.* Chicago: University of Chicago Press, 1965.

Dyer, Wayne W. *Real Magic: Creating Miracles in Everyday Life.* New York: Harper Collins, 1992.

Fast, Julius. *Body Language*. New York: M. Evans & Lippincott, 1970.

Feinstein, Alice, ed. *Training the Body to Cure Itself.* Emmaus, Penna.: Rodale Press, 1992.

Grotowski, Jerzy. *Towards a Poor Theatre*. New York: Simon and Schuster, 1968.

Gunther, Bernard. *Sense Relaxation Below Your Mind.* New York: Collier Books, 1968.

Hagen, Uta, and Haskel, Frankel. *Respect for Acting*. New York: Macmillan, 1973.

Hall, Edward T. *The Hidden Dimension*. New York: Doubleday, 1966.

Henderson, Harold G. *An Introduction to Haiku*. New York: Anchor, 1958.

Hodge, David G. "On Acting the Role of Scapino in *Scapino!*." A Monograph in Theater Arts for Master of Fine Arts Degree in Acting. Pennsylvania State University, August 1977.

Johar, Harish. *Chakras: Energy Center of Transformation*. Vermont: Destiny Books, 1987.

Johnson, Albert, and Johnson, Bertha. *Drama for Classroom and Stage*. New York: A. S. Barnes & Co., 1969.

Johnstone, Keith. *Impro: Improvisation and the Theater*. New York: Routledge Press, 1979.

Karagulla, Shafica, M.D., and Kunz, Dora Van Gelder. *The Chakras and the Human Energy Fields*. Wheaton, Illinois: Theosophical Publishing House, 1989.

Laban, Rudolf. *Modern Educational Dance,* 2nd ed., revised by Lisa Ullmann. New York: Praeger, 1968.

_____. *The Mastery of Movement*. 2nd ed., revised and enlarged by Lisa Ullmann. New York: Drama Book Specialists, 1967.

Langer, Suzanne K. *Feeling and Form.* New York: Charles Scribner's Sons, 1953.

Leadbeater, C.W. *The Chakras,* Wheaton, Illinois: Theosophical Publishing House, 1927.

Lichtenberg, Georg Christoph. *A Reasonable Rebel.* Translated from the German by Bernard Smith. London: Ruskin House, 1960.

_____. *The Lichtenberg Reader.* Translated, edited, and introduced by Franz H. Mautner and Henry Hatfield. Boston: Beacon Press, 1959.

Linklater, Kristin. *Freeing the Natural Voice.* New York: Drama Book Publishers, 1976.

_____. *Freeing Shakespeare's Voice.* New York: Theatre Communications Group, 1992.

MacLaine, Shirley. *Going Within.* New York: Bantam Books, 1989.

McGaw, Charles. *Acting Is Believing.* New York: Holt, Rinehart & Winston, 1966.

Moore, Sonia. *The Stanislavski System.* New York: Viking, 1965.

Oxenford, Lyn. *Design for Movement: A Textbook on Stage Movement.* New York: Theatre Arts Books, 1952.

Peale, Norman Vincent. *The Power of Positive Thinking.* New York: Fawcett Crest, 1952.

Robbins, Anthony. *Unlimited Power.* New York: Fawcett Columbine, 1986.

Schutz, William C. *Joy: Expanding Human Awareness.* New York: Grove Press, 1967.

Seidelman, Arthur A. "Movement and the Actor," *After Dark,* 13, no. 8 (December 1970), 40–41.

Spolin, Viola. *Improvisation for the Theatre.* Evanston, Illinois: Northwestern University Press, 1963.

Stanislavski, Constantin. *An Actor Prepares.* Translated by Elizabeth Reynolds Hapgood. New York: Theatre Arts Books, 1959.

_____. *Building a Character.* Translated by Elizabeth Reynolds Hapgood. New York: Theatre Arts Books, 1949.

_____. *Stanislavski Produces* Othello. Translated by Dr. Helen Novack. New York: Theatre Arts Books, 1963.

Strasberg, Lee. *A Dream of Passion.* Boston: Little, Brown, 1987.

Thomas, Jameson, PhD. *The 7 Steps to Personal Power.* Deerfield Beach, Florida: Health Communications, Inc., 1992.

The Wellness Encyclopedia. Compiled by the editors of the University of California, Berkeley, "Wellness Letter." Boston: Houghton Mifflin Co., 1991.

Wellwarth, George E. *The Theatre of Protest and Paradox.* New York: New York University Press, 1964.

White, Edwin, and Narguerite Battye. *Acting and Stage Movement.* New York: Arc Books, 1965.

White, Timothy P., Ph.D. *The Wellness Guide to Lifelong Fitness.* New York: Rebus, 1993.

Zora, John W. *The Essential Delsarte.* Metuchen, N.J.: Scarecrow Press, 1968.

Index